Interpreting the Church

Through Press and Radio

Interpreting the Church
Through Press
And Radio

ROLAND E. WOLSELEY

MUHLENBERG PRESS • PHILADELPHIA

Printed in U. S. A.

UB712

TO BERNICE

A Born Editor

Preface

The idea of this book was born when more and more persons active in many different types of religious journalism and church publicity asked the author for a little assistance in helping solve some of their problems. Some were editors of denominational publications. Others were ministers, church secretaries, or other persons responsible for parish publications and local church radio programs. Most frequent requests came from church people with all degrees of responsibility, in many different denominations or in nondenominational religious work, who must do news and feature writing for both the religious and the secular press.

Although numerous church publicity books have been published in the past half century, all are centered in the secular newspaper and other old and tried media. The fact that the church—whatever the denomination—has the opportunity to effect its interpretation also through magazines, wire services, syndicates, radio, television, and other powerful media has hardly been recognized.

The existing books, although many are outdated, have been of great usefulness to theological students, new staff members of churches and synagogues, and denominational board secretaries responsible for publicizing their institutions. But they have provided little help for the editor of the denominational weekly newspaper or magazine, or of the nondenominational religious periodical, or for the minister who realizes that buying or being given space in his local newspapers is only one of all the channels for interpreting his church to the public. The churchman puzzled by the potentialities of television asks for aid toward an understanding of what may be done to use this medium. The author has tried to meet the basic needs of all types of churches and churchmen, albeit he knows this is impossible because of the great number of denominations and their varying terminology. For convenience, however, he has used *churchman* to designate religious workers of any sect or creed—for curate, priest, rector, preacher, pastor, minister, religious educator, church secretary, board secretary, bishop, or monsignor.

While in general the local church is kept in the foreground, since this is the area where help seems most needed, the principles enunciated and many of the techniques dealt with are valuable also to the larger organizations, such as mission boards, publishing houses, boards of education, and national and international committees.

Courses in religious journalism and church public relations or publicity are increasing in number. The work being done at Oklahoma Baptist University, Candler Seminary of Emory University, The Chicago Theological Seminary, The Southern Baptist Theological Seminary, Andover-Newton Theological School, and a score of other institutions helps produce more persons with information and some training in religious journalism. This educational effort, slight as it may be, deserves the encouragement of a book which may provide descriptions and explanations of techniques applicable to church interpretation.

Acknowledgements

The author has received the assistance and encouragement of numerous persons. His greatest debt is to the late Ernest Fremont Tittle, senior minister of the First Methodist Church of Evanston, Illinois, for thirty years. More than a quarter of a century ago Dr. Tittle first asked him to turn his small journalistic talents to the service of the church. Through the years Dr. Tittle himself supported the highest possible standards of interpretation in his own remarkable congregation, his local community, and indeed the whole world of religion in which he was a force.

Several other persons have been extraordinarily helpful:

Mrs. Marjorie Moore Armstrong, former managing editor of *The Commission;*

C. E. Bryant, director of public relations, Baylor University, and before that director of publicity for the Southern Baptist Convention;

Louis Minsky, executive director, Religious News Service;

Miss Lillian Block, assistant managing editor, Religious News Service;

Miss Jo-ann Price, religion editor, Milwaukee *Journal.*

Burke Walsh, assistant director, Press Department, National Catholic Welfare Conference.

Among the many other persons who have provided examples of materials and similar assistance the author particularly wishes to thank:

Dr. Clifton J. Allen, secretary, Division of Editorial Service, Sunday School Board, Southern Baptist Convention; The Rev. Cecil A. Baker, pastor, Tiptonville (Tennessee) Methodist Church; Prof. Floyd K. Baskette, associate professor of journalism, College of Journalism, University of Colorado; The Rev. W. E. Brashares, minister, First Methodist Church, Hartford, Wisconsin, and former official of the Wisconsin Conference public relations committee; Dr. Emory S. Bucke, editor of *Zions Herald;* Dean Laurence R. Campbell, School of Journalism, Florida State University; James J. Cavanagh, publisher, *The Church Bulletin;* the late Dr. William T. Ellis, president, The Ellis Service; The Rev. Walter C. Eyster, executive director, Wisconsin Conference Council, The Methodist Church; Dr. Harold E. Fey, managing editor, *The Christian Century;* Lillian Garber, secretary, Hebrew Theological College, Chicago; Frank J. Gilloon, president, Catholic Institute of the Press; The Rev. Myrus L. Knutson, pastor, Ascension Lutheran Church, Milwaukee, Wisconsin; Dr. William B. Lipphard, editor, *Missions,* and former president, Associated Church Press; James W. Low, department of promotion, the National Council of the Protestant Episcopal Church; Hubert J. Mertz, president, Fine Art Features; Dr. T. Otto Nall, editor, *The Christian Advocate* and former president, Associated Church Press; Rabbi Jacob M. Ott, The Anshe Emet Synagogue, Chicago; William C. Reilly, promotion director, *The Sign;* Louise M. Schultz, American Committee for the World Council of Churches; Dr. Ralph Stoody, director, Methodist Information; Prof. William F. Tanner, head, department of journalism, Oklahoma Baptist University; Robert Walker, editor, *Christian Life* magazine; director Christian Writers' Institute, and former secretary, Evangelical Press Association; Charles A. Wells, publisher, *Between the Lines;* the Rev. Fred S. Wintle, minister, Kirklin (Indiana) Methodist Church, and Sister Mary Madelena, B.V.M., of the faculty of Mundelein College, Chicago.

The following book and magazine publishers and broadcasting companies have kindly granted permission to quote from their publications or provided other materials for this book:

Abingdon-Cokesbury, Nashville, Tennessee; *Advertising Agency and Advertising and Selling*, New York; All-Church Press, Tulsa, Oklahoma; *The American Press*, New York; Appleton-Century-Crofts, New York; Bobbs-Merrill, Indianapolis, Indiana; *Broadcasting*, Washington, D. C.; *The Christian Advocate*, Chicago, *The Christian Century*, Chicago; *Christian Life*, Chicago; Columbia Broadcasting System, New York; *Editor & Publisher*, New York; Harper & Brothers, New York; Houghton Mifflin, Boston; Alfred A. Knopf, New York; Macmillan, New York; Pilgrim Press, Boston; Time, Inc., New York.

R. E. W.

Syracuse, New York

Contents

List of Illustrations

For Writers and Newspaper Men

O thou great source of truth and knowledge, we remember before thee all whose calling it is to gather and winnow the facts for informing the people. Inspire them with a determined love for honest work and a staunch hatred for the making of lies, lest the judgments of our nation be perverted and we be taught to call light darkness and darkness light. Since the sanity and wisdom of a nation are in their charge, may they count it shame to set the baser passions of men on fire for the sake of gain. May they never suffer themselves to be used in drugging the mind of the people with falsehood and prejudice.

Grant them boldness to turn the unwelcome light on those who love the darkness because their deeds are evil. Put into their hands the shining sword of truth, and make them worthy successors of the great champions of the people who held truth to be a holy thing by which nations live and for which men should die. Cause them to realize that they have a public function in the commonwealth, and that their country may be saved by their courage or undone by their cowardice and silence. Grant them the heart of manhood to cast their mighty influence with the forces that make the people strong and free, and if they suffer loss, may they rejoice in that as proof to their own souls that they have fought a good fight and have been servants of the higher law.

—Walter Rauschenbusch
in *Prayers of the Social Awakening*
(Boston: Pilgrim Press, 1910) pp.
79, 80. By permission.

CHAPTER I

What is to be Interpreted?

One of the journalists covering the World Council of Churches assembly in Amsterdam in 1948 included this sentence in his report: "This greatest church meeting since the Reformation could not even agree on a definition of the word 'church.'"

This situation would be nothing new to a denominational director of public relations, the members of a publicity committee in a local church, or the publicity chairman of a missions board in the United States. For the church in this country contains many elements. Within it are debating societies, charity groups, missionary organizations, music conservatories, radio stations, colleges and universities, seminaries, publications, and meeting places for the worship of God.

By being so many things at once the church makes the task of interpretation in some ways easier and in others more difficult. An active and dynamic institution is easier to interpret than an idle and lifeless one. But action and dynamism make enemies, for they mean taking a position. Interpreting an institution to its enemies is one of the more difficult psychological accomplishments.

The public is puzzled

But the public—especially the unchurched portion—which the interpreters wish to reach is puzzled. Citizens who

1

remain outside the organized church hear that the Roman Catholics and the Episcopalians do not consider Methodists, Presbyterians, and other Protestants as members of "the true church." They read that Southern Baptists have one concept of baptism and the Lutherans another. They note many varieties of Presbyterian and Methodist churches and not a small number of minute sects of whom one hears only when one of their members is poisoned by snakes or is arrested for resisting military service or public education. They observe that some churches condemn dancing as a sin and that others arrange for dances in their parish houses.

It is this inconsistent and uncorrelated body which is to be interpreted. All its segments need interpretation—international councils, national groups, world-wide denominations, regional jurisdictions, synods, big city and village churches, and the Double E Sunday School Class. They must be interpreted to themselves, to one another, and to the unaffiliated public watching or ignoring on the outside.

What is interpretation?

To interpret is to clarify, to explain, or to provide sufficient background to provide understanding of an idea, an action, or an institution or person. For centuries theologians have been explaining biblical meanings. Pastors, priests, and rabbis alike customarily interpret the great documents of Christianity and Judaism. English professors for years have interpreted the poems and stories and plays that have survived the ages. As modern writing has become more complex they have been needed, as well, to explain the work of James Joyce, Gertrude Stein, Henry Miller, and Kenneth Patchen. Fine arts lecturers likewise have been called upon to explain the work of Picasso and Honegger, Dali and John Alden Carpenter.

The church, which is just as divided on theory and action

as the arts, also is in need of explanation, clarification, and backgrounding. Any institution which is not regimented and standardized requires interpretation to a citizenry which is itself neither completely regimented nor wholly standardized in its thinking and reactions. The public should have the opportunity better to understand the church. The church constantly should be reminded that what it does, since it is in the sight of the public, can be misunderstood and misjudged.

Interpretation of the church has grown far beyond explaining the significance of a passage from Holy Writ. It has come to include many of the functions of public relations work, publicity counseling, and press agentry. *At its best* it is more than any of these; it must be more. It must not be on their level, for public relations and publicity advisers and press agents in secular life seek mainly to put the best face on the actions and policies of the institutions they represent. Interpretation today is telling the story of the church through all the accepted media of communication. But it also is telling the *whole* story, not merely that portion of the story that pleases the priests in the temples or the laymen in the pews. Under that definition, it is soon realized, there exists too little genuine interpretation of the church to the world. But this lack does not mean that such interpretation is not needed or cannot be provided.

The church must employ means of interpretation that are as worthy as the ends in view. At times the professional public relations expert, accustomed to using sly methods which the business world sometimes does not question or laughs off because such devices are frequently used in its circles, resorts to policies which cheapen the church and further confuse the public. The honest interpreter not only uses methods which are churchly but also explains the bad with the good. He does not pose as the advance agent for an institution that believes it can do no wrong. He is realistic. He admits shortcomings. He wants his interpretations to help the church set its house in order. He does not want interpretation to serve as a cover-up for institutional failures and for political chicanery within religious circles.

Above all, he knows that for the church to succeed in its goals it must have the confidence of the public, inasmuch as a trusting public is an understanding public. It is an informed, enlightened, knowledgeful public.

The church, as it is, cannot be understood of itself. Sometimes its message can be gained through its action. But it is too complex an organism, it has too many ramifications, subdivisions, and separated parts to be as readily understood as more coherent and cohesive institutions, such as public accounting or glass manufacturing.

Everything is a subject

Thus everything the church does, everything it stands for, and every part of it is a subject for interpretation. All this does not have to be interpreted in the same manner or always to the total public, inside as well as outside the church. How the interpretation shall be made and when it shall be presented and through which media are matters of judgment, knowledge, and experience which will complicate a policy of interpretation. Difficult as such judgments are to form and technical as such knowledge will be, they offer no difficulty so great as does a policy of refusal to acknowledge the need for interpretation or a failure to co-operate in interpretation.

The answer to the question, "What is to be interpreted?" becomes more clear when we realize that the public itself interprets everything pertaining to the church. It does not wait for the church to explain itself properly, fairly, and thoroughly. It jumps to conclusions, frequently unwarranted conclusions. Therefore the question might be put as, "What is being interpreted about the church?" Since everything already is being interpreted, often by inexpert, gossipy, and malicious interpreters, it is wise for the church, in all its reaches, to show concern that the intepretation be informed, reasonable, and complete.

What should not be interpreted?

Literally, of course, it is untrue that everything done by the church can or should be interpreted. If a sexton absconds with the Sunday offering the church should co-operate with the police and the press and radio in tracing the criminal and keeping the public informed. But what a minister learns during a private interview with a troubled parishioner need not be relayed to the world. The names of persons who borrow from a fund to aid the needy are not newsworthy. Nor, in seeking to interpret itself, should the church violate the laws against libel, sedition, obscenity, and gambling. A thorough-going program of interpretation will protect the church against itself. If the press is encouraged to cover the sermon (or an abstract is sent to the newspapers, radio stations, and wire services in advance) libelous utterances are less likely to be made. If the church knows that its raffle or bingo game news story might violate the postal regulations on lotteries its administration may question the activity to begin with.

Absolute freedom of the press or speech does not exist, even in the free United States. Nor should there be such freedom. Absolute freedom would be anarchy; it is undesirable because it would do greater harm than does the limited freedom now enjoyed. More freedom we might well have, but not total freedom. Without libel laws any medium of communication would be free to spread lies and to defame persons of good repute. Without the restraints against indecency and sedition, far from perfect as those laws now are, the common good would suffer greatly. The church must co-operate in these legal aims. It cannot, therefore, insist that all it does be publicized and interpreted.

But it must, within the legal framework, make available all possible information about itself so that the world knows the truth about it and not merely the rumors and talk of the byways. Then the critics of the church will know that the church is honest with itself, acknowledges its shortcomings, and is seeking to correct them. The total result of proper interpretation can be that the church will be better understood and that more of the people will be drawn into it. They will see the church realistically.

CHAPTER II

Organizing for Interpretation

Churchmen sometimes argue against planning the interpretation of the church. But the obstacles are not so much lack of faith in the workability of organization as lack of knowledge of how to organize and of money to pay for the work planned.

The Rev. Robert E. Luccock, minister of the Church of the Redeemer, New Haven, Connecticut, writing about his seminary studies, declared:

In the matter of effective public relations, a number-one concern of every church in the contemporary social setting, absolutely nothing was taught in seminary. I learned nothing about the ingredients of an effective program of finance. I was never taught anything about writing in a way to win assent ... All these paraphernalia of parish administration are no substitute for the basic training of theological thinking. But there is not a man going out from theological school into the parish ministry who does not run smack into these things in the first month of the first pastorate.[1]

The results of this lack of preparation are shown by a survey made by James D. Woolf, an advertising agency executive. Reporting on his results after writing one hundred ministers, whom he asked for new ideas in church advertising and publicity, he was discouraged. Twenty answered with keen interest; the other eighty either ignored him or

---

[1] "Seminary in Retrospect," *Christian Century* (April 26, 1950) p. 524.

said they had nothing to report. "I found on the whole," he wrote, "a shocking paucity of new ideas." One answered smugly:

> My church is not among those which use new approaches and novel promotion methods to stir the interest of young people in Sunday School and Church Services. The only method we employ is to teach them the glorious Gospel which tells them of God's love for them.[2]

The young minister in a small church, of course, is so busy with many more important and immediate duties that he puts aside to some less rushed moment (that seems never to come) the task of working out a public relations policy. The shepherd of a few thousand is more likely to have organized this phase of his work. But often the machine, probably a committee of five, with no orders, is old-fashioned, inexperienced, or has lost interest. Only in an occasional church and in a few overhead religious groups is there efficient and competent organization for interpretation.

Although their goals presumably are alike, the denominations in the United States have no interchurch public relations program. Only ten per cent of the more than two hundred denominations have organized their publicity activities so as to interpret the work of the denomination. This minority functions mainly for large religious bodies, such as the Roman Catholic and Methodist churches. Church agencies within denominations make some type of provision for interpretation of their work, but it varies widely and changes constantly in vigor and continuity.

The financial obstacles to adequate organization must be overcome as part of the general church program. But organizing the interpretation does not proceed with complete

---

[2] "Why Should Ministers Study Advertising?" *Advertising Agency* (formerly *Advertising and Selling*) (October, 1948) p. 38.

indifference to the economic feasibility of what is proposed. In the local church and on a denomination-wide basis, publicity efforts have been known to pay for themselves in direct revenue for their work or in stimulating the giving that eventually benefits those efforts.

The goal of interpretation

In planning to organize for interpretation of its work, the church naturally must understand the purpose of what it is attempting. This is no less true for a country church than it is for a nation-wide denomination. A single goal unites them all, at least in so far as they agree on the function of the church as an institution: to realize God's plan for men. Yet specific church groups tend to see these goals denominationally.

Harold Fey, managing editor of the *Christian Century*, in 1945 outlined to the Home Missions Council of North America his concept of the purpose of a program of public relations by the Protestant churches. It would oppose "clerical fascism and every form of totalitarianism," he said. He went on:

It will also seek to instruct all the people in the Christian basis of the social order. It will interpret the essential spiritual foundation of the community in places where new communities are forming and in regions where older communities are changing. It will attempt to show the larger significance of the church's place in the community by telling the story of what it is doing and why. It will tackle the problems of human welfare involved in immigration policies and the treatment of migrants as a Protestant equality. It will magnify the inestimable work of the Protestant community in working for racial justice and for equality of opportunity as an innate human right.

The Catholic Press Association of the United States the next year defined the function of the Catholic press in America by making the following statement in a booklet commemorating the thirty-fifth anniversary of the association's founding:

> The Catholic Press in America stands as the one reliable informant for a sick and troubled world. An effective dissemination of truthful news and a Christian interpretation of current events represent the first phase of a salvation of a civilization duped by atheism and indifference . . . .
>
> Catholic editors follow a policy established by Jesus Christ. Truth, morality and religion are their themes.[3]

Broadly, the goal of interpretation is to gain understanding of the church and its purposes. Although the details of the goal probably will vary as do the two statements quoted here, the organization to accomplish one or the other of the goals need not be so varied. It is too much to expect, of course, that structurally the organizations will differ as little as the ink and paper used in printing church publications. Printing machines are neither Presbyterian nor Greek Orthodox; local church committees on public relations, if they wish, can be practically as undenominational in their mechanical operations. They will be more or less democratic, depending upon the degree of democracy at work in the supervising institution. Power will rest with them if the church policy is to invest such committees with power. Who controls the machine and for what purpose will not alter the machine's major characteristics.

In a church the goal of the public relations plan or program must be to enable the institution itself to achieve its goal. Church aims vary. Theoretically they may be intended to "advance the work of the Lord"—to quote some of the pat language of the religious world—or to function as a social settlement in a neighborhood, or to support some

---

[3] *I Am the Catholic Press* (Catholic Press Association of the United States, 1946) p. 1.

dogma, or to spread a particular doctrine. It may be to serve as "a pulpit for the proclamation of the word of God," or, as Walter Rauschenbusch put it, "as an agency to create the Kingdom of God." Actually it sometimes is only a place where a minister can earn a living or a dependable source of economic support for some central ecclesiastical organization or a substitute for a country club. Rauschenbusch also said that the church "practically . . . came to regard itself as the Kingdom (of God)."

It is not necessary here to evaluate the goal of a particular church, although obviously an unchurchly goal will not help a public relations program. The goal must be worthy of the church at its best; the church, on the other hand, must be worthy of the goal. A church with an idealistic aim does not support that aim if it is given to policies that defeat that aim. For example, a church that stands for decent treatment of working people in a community must treat its own employees in the way that it expects business and industry to treat those who work for them.

Planning the program

To provide the best interpretation of its work, the church, or a subordinate body of the church, must use as many of the media of communication as it can. It is not enough to conceive of church public relations as the buying of advertising space or time, as printing a bulletin or parish paper, or as sending news stories to newspapers and radio stations. The church must do each of these, to be sure, but it can and should do still more, through planning.

All major church bodies in the United States have developed public relations plans through which they hope to achieve the church's goals and aims. But only the most efficient overhead groups and an occasional local church deal with problems of public relations in any but the usual

manner. And the customary fashion is to handle difficulties
as they arise, often ineptly and inconsistently. Consequently there is confusion over what policy shall be followed
on one problem or the other. In the local church, likely as
not, there is no committee, no elected or appointed special
official, or any other provision. The problems therefore must
be handled by the head of the church. Sometimes that
pastor, rabbi, or priest is competent to do so. Whether he
is or not, this burden should not be his. He should be able
to delegate it as he does such other matters of policy as
financing, proper use and care of the building, and training
of the choir.

Merely by existing all churches have public relations.
They may be good or bad, effective or inoffective, but they
are public relations. In a tiny community church little
needs to be done in the way of especially planned public
relations work; in a big city institution much must be done.
A program that can be adapted to the needs of any size
church is worth considering, but it is likely to be so general
as to be little more than a series of signposts. The word
program implies a planned, systematic approach. A plan or
program is needed if the church is to have improved public
relations. What that plan might be and how it can be
implemented are our main concerns.

The heart of any church public relations program is the
leader of that church: the pastor, priest, rabbi. This leader
should not do all the work but he can—and generally does—
establish the goal. He may not do so consciously. But he
does so by the standards he develops in the church program
through encouraging or discouraging activities and enun-
ciating viewpoints in his sermons and other public utterances. If the head of the church is a person of high principle
it usually results that the church, as a whole, follows his
lead and reflects the goals he has chosen for it. Much the

same situation surrounds denominational leaders, board secretaries, and other persons placed in positions of responsibility.

Knowingly or unknowingly, then, it is the church leader who develops the public relations plan. Usually it is unknowingly, for the concept of planned interpretation of the church to the public is relatively new in organizational work.

A four-part plan

Of what should a local church public relations plan consist? Here are four essential parts; these are presented as possibilities for action:

1. A *sociological and religious survey* of the community or other area served. This study can have many purposes. To aid in the task of interpreting the church it should learn: *a*) what position the church now occupies in the community; *b*) what function the church can have in the community; *c*)what relationship the church can have to other churches or co-operating religious or nonreligous groups. Such surveys have been made for years, in co-operation with other organizations. Thirteen churches in Waukegan, Illinois, for example, during 1949 conducted a religious census there, led by Prof. Samuel Kinchloe of the Chicago Church Federation's department of research and survey. A visitation evangelism program followed the study, which was carried on by 350 persons. Similar surveys have been made in urban and rural areas from time to time under the direction of Dr. Albert Z. Mann, formerly of Hamline University; Dr. William V. Dennis, formerly professor of rural sociology at Pennsylvania State College; Dr. Murray H. Leiffer, professor of sociology at Garrett Biblical Institute; Dr. Rockwell C. Smith, professor of rural sociology at Garrett, and by men from other seminaries and church groups in various denominations. Some lessons can be learned by examining

their findings, but there must be a local application if no study has been made in a particular community recently.

2. *A survey of the local church itself.* The objectives of such a survey are to find out if the church is doing all the work it can, internally; to determine if all personnel, both paid and volunteer, is being put to work advantageously; to learn if the needs of all members, by ages and interests, are being met; to discover overlapping of organization work and to detect the gaps in such work. Churches became conscious of these objectives during World War II, when the problem of meeting the needs of members in military service arose.

The board of education of a church, for example, was discussing the necessity for teachers, and the suggestion (made on the basis of experience in a church in another city) was offered that teachers might be found and, at the same time, parents of church-school children brought into closer relation to the church by the formation of mothers' and parents' groups.

At a subsequent meeting of the board, one member was asked to begin the organization of a mothers' circle, for mothers of children under six, to help with their problems in relation to the upbringing of their children and to relate them to the church school.

This committee of one obtained from the church office a list of eligible women. In co-operation with the minister she called a meeting of a half-dozen who might be potential leaders. The general idea was presented to this preparatory meeting and the group was made a sort of interim committee to put the idea into motion. Over the signature of the group a letter was sent to all prospective members outlining the plan and inviting them to a meeting. At this session, which included some music and light refreshments to give it a social aspect, the idea again was presented in full, and the larger group decided to form a permanent organization. A nominating committee was elected, to report at the next monthly gathering, and an interim program committee was named to prepare for that meeting. Programs were planned to deal not only with the religious nurture of the small child but also with other phases of his development and the preparation of the mother to aid him in his growth.

The organization of parents' groups closely related to church-school classes was handled somewhat less formally. The superintendent of the school and the pastor presented the general idea to the teaching staff, urging that committees of both fathers and mothers be used in all possible ways in carrying on the work of each class—week-time activities, checking on absentees, and calling on sick persons, among others.

3. *A program to meet the needs* so discovered and give the church its proper place in the community. This might mean establishing new organizations, reorganizing others, shifting personnel, and so on, all with the democratic consent of everyone concerned and after thorough understanding of the aims and purposes of the plan.

4. *Use of church publicity,* in its broadest sense. It would be intended to keep the public, both internal and external, informed of the work of the church. Such use of publicity would mean employing, in the best professional manner, the general newspaper and magazine, radio-television, parish paper or magazine, the Sunday bulletin, announcement boards, posters, letters, leaflets, special printed matter, spoken announcements, congregational meetings, billboards, telephone campaigns, dramatics, and motion pictures.

Many possibilities are mentioned in the list above; naturally no one church can use them all unless it is well-financed and staffed. Every church, however, can use certain of these tools. Even sending the sermon topic to the community weekly paper is an act of interpreting the church to the public.

The methods of carrying out the first three steps do not come directly into our province here. Guidance in them must be obtained from the conventional sources: boards of ministerial education, seminars and institutes at theological seminaries, and reading and study of the increasingly large literature on church programs and administration. Courses like "City Research and Survey," offered at the annual School for Urban Ministers at Candler Seminary, Emory University, are typical of what is available.

Techniques in church publicity, the fourth step, are dealt with in this volume. The general newspaper is the basis, technically, for the parish paper; the general magazine for the parish or other religious magazine. This is not to say that they need be imitations but simply that religious journalism applies the production methods developed by the commercial publications. Likewise posters and leaflets are an application of the principles of the graphic arts.

The publicity machine

How shall the publicity machine be set up and operated? Like public relations, publicity is internal and external. A church's program can be subdivided thus. Part of its publicity activity will be to deal with agencies outside; another part inside; some will overlap. A news release in the evening paper will be seen by members of the church, who will note similar information in the parish publication which arrived that morning.

Organization to carry out interpretative work will differ with churches according to their size, personnel, and financial resources. So few do everything possible—and still seemly for the church—to get publicity that one can generalize safely with the comment that almost any existing plan can be improved.

Two systems dominate: the individual and the committee. In moderate-sized churches, that is, between 500 and 1,000 members, the minister, his secretary, or some lay member will be responsible for what little publicity work is done, perchance sending the sermon topic to a few newspapers, preparing copy for a duplicated bulletin, and changing the lawn bulletin board lettering every Thursday or Sunday morning. In larger churches a committee sometimes does this and more elaborate work, when possible subdividing the responsibilities according to the skills and connections of the members.

If a church is aware of its total public relations program the interpretative duties may be in the hands of a subcommittee or an individual. If the head of the church decides to organize the public relations work he must remember the publicity needs. At the First Methodist Church of Evanston, Illinois, a large institution, for some years the public relations planning was the responsibility of what is known as the board of education. All major standing committees and organizations of the church had board representatives. It authorized certain publications and called upon particular individuals to produce them; these persons were the ones who usually have been responsible for the major types of publicity: paid advertising, newspaper editorial copy, printed matter, and radio (although the latter is not widely used at this particular church). In recent years the responsibility for the newspaper portion of the work has been placed in the hands of a press committee, responsible to the official governing body of the church.

A public relations committee should have a budget of its own, a minimum based on expenditures made over several years and taking into consideration economic changes, such as the greatly increased costs of production in recent years. The committee needs a budget, for it will have to pay for advertising space contracted with publications and radio stations, for special printing jobs, for duplicating, lettering, photography, and bulletin boards. If such costs are left to a general or office supplies budget the committee may find itself short-circuited by a careless administrator of some other department. Also, the committee should have official status, should itself be given a little publicity now and then, and should contain personnel suited to its function.

Despite its obviousness, this last suggestion seems rarely to occur to churchmen themselves. Even small churches have advertising agency employees, members of the staffs of publications, artists, printers, photographers, and sometimes professional publicity and public relations personnel. In forming a publicity committee a minister, priest, or rabbi can examine the occupations represented in his congregation and call together such laymen. If he does not know what these occupations are, there is a job for the committee on surveys. If the church is in a college or university community, young people invariably can be found who are willing to carry out some of the mechanical duties of interpretation: writing news stories, drawing posters. In many high schools as well as colleges there are advertising, photography, printing, and journalism classes that will be cooperative if the students can be shown that their work is valuable and helpful to the church; others, like choir members, will respond to an invitation to serve if they can gain practical experience from what they are asked to do.

Training the committee

It is useful to spend a little time, after the committee has been formed—or even with an existing committee if it has not been given much direction and guidance—to call a series of short meetings to be used in explaining the purposes and duties of the committee. Also, if possible, it is well to use such sessions to provide a small amount of professional training. A large church will need a small overhead publicity committee, one to decide policy and provide direction. Some journalistic member of this body might be asked to conduct a short "school" for those persons in the congregation who serve as publicity chairmen for organizations. Although this training plan will be superficial, for it cannot make accomplished news writers out of these chairmen, it does not need to be more than superficial. It will enable the larger committee to obtain better-prepared copy, will sharpen the understanding of the way the work is handled in general, and will improve the relationships between the committee on publicity and the organizational publicity chairmen.

Regular meetings should be held by the committee on publicity. The group should be large enough so that personnel constantly is being trained and prepared for larger responsibilities. A continuing group of persons, familiar with policies developed over the years, is essential.

Ideally, all news stories, copy for posters, direct mail letters and the like should clear through the publicity committee, whether for the whole church or an organization within it. Practically, however, this will not work for an institution of considerable size because the committee cannot be on duty constantly. Nor can its chairman be expected to devote the necessary time. Publicity ventures are too numerous to permit such close supervision by one person. An Art committee can pass on all paintings to be hung in the church or make other decisions of that type, but it can do its work easily with a bi-monthly session. The Use of the Church committee need meet only monthly or on special call for emergencies that arise in between, but probably the problems it confronts are only occasional or can be delayed until a meeting occurs. But if the church school is to function through the use of many pieces of printing and other interpretative media it cannot wait upon a publicity committee to approve its plans.

In practice, then, the average committee on publicity leaves to organizations and church groups the decisions on their interpretative materials and holds itself responsible for general policies and for the promotion of all-church activities. As a result there is considerable duplication, waste, competition, and confusion. Under the loose organization of the ordinary small church they are inescapable. Only if some staff member happens to have had wide experience in publicity work, using most of the media already mentioned, can there be any centralized supervision of the church's efforts.

One way to counteract such a situation is to give the officers and publicity chairmen of organizations within the church instructions and information about publicity techniques and to set standards which they are expected to meet. If the minister gives away watermelons on Sunday morning as an inducement to churchgoers he cannot complain if the young people sensationalize their publicity for their Sunday evening meetings. If the church's own interpretation of its work in general sets a high tone, the interpretations of its subordinate units are likely to be in that same tone.

Possibilities for work by a publicity committee are unlimited. Although some church publicity devices are costly (advertising, printed matter, and elaborate or frequent mailings, for example, can drain the budget rapidly unless controlled), many of them are not, and depend largely upon the expenditure of effort. If an event needs publicizing within the church, effective signs can be hand-drawn or a group of committee members can serve as minute men to announce events at meetings.

Finally, the most effective publicity committee is one which has something attractive to publicize. The most efficient committee in the nation could not gain favorable attention for a church that is inactive. Actually, although it is something of an over-simplification, publicity is a relatively small problem in a church that is teeming with useful deeds being accomplished. A mechanism is needed to guide the interpretation, but such a church nearly publicizes itself in the way wanted. Word-of-mouth publicity, one of the most effective of all types, does much of the interpretative work under such conditions. This is only another way of saying: an active church uses a publicity committee mostly as a traffic guide.

Practical methods

James D. Woolf, after making the survey referred to at the beginning of this chapter, wrote that he encountered such methods as these:

Bethany Presbyterian Church of Omaha, Nebraska, is in a building opposite an interracial school. Short talks and hymn singing are broadcast through a loud-speaker at noon recess; each day several hundred pupils stop to listen. In the same city, the First Presbyterian Church sends out red and blue mailing pieces to call young people to church parties.

The Church Federation of Dayton and Montgomery County, Ohio, arranged for a weekly rally called "The Best Saturday Night in Town." A downtown church, St. John's Evangelical and Reformed, was the scene. The federation took these promotional steps:

1. Gave a luncheon for the heads of newspapers and radio stations. The plan was explained at this meeting.

2. Invited the editors of labor union weeklies, neighborhood papers, papers for the Negro people, and other special editors, to a similar affair.

3. Issued a series of weekly news releases, with cuts and mats.

4. Bought advertising space in three daily newspapers.

5. Used radio announcements.

6. Employed outdoor posters.

7. Sent folders and leaflets to country schools, youth centers, Girl Reserve and Hi-Y clubs, churches, and other organizations.

8. The Tuesday before the first Saturday party gave a dinner for 300 community leaders, with speakers and a musical program. Invited were representatives of the Chamber of Commerce, social agencies, labor unions, and youth workers' groups.[4]

Typical organization schemes

Church agencies and local churches commonly use the familiar organization plans of business, clubs, industry, and associations of other types. Such plans have in common the attempted use of all media of communication and the disposition of personnel according to individual talent and the needs of the program.

All large denominations now have news bureaus or publicity offices. In a few instances several related denominations have joined forces to maintain a public relations office serving them all. The National Lutheran Council maintains a News Bureau in New York City which represents the interests of the eight churches which are members of the Council. Four of the thirteen Baptist groups in the United States are served by the Joint Conference Committee on Public Relations.

One of the first of such groups was the publicity department of the Seventh-Day Adventists. Among the larger and more widely known are the Department of Publicity of the National Council, Protestant Episcopal Church; Methodist Information, Methodist Church; Committee of Publication, Presbyterian Church in the U.S.; and the Baptist Press, Southern Baptist Convention.

Such organizations function externally as well as internally, sending releases to the church press as well as to the

---

[4] *Advertising Agency* (October, 1949) p. 122.

Organization Plan – Public Relations Work of the Southern Baptist Convention

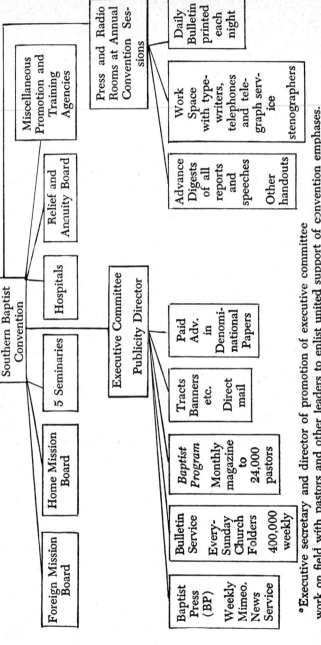

*Executive secretary and director of promotion of executive committee work on field with pastors and other leaders to enlist united support of convention emphases.

Organization Plan

Press Department of the National Catholic Welfare Conference

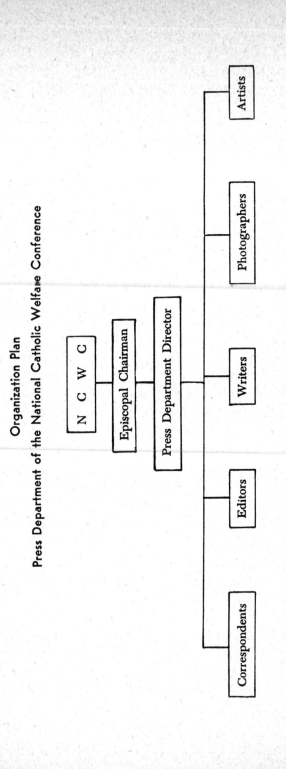

Organization of

The Commission on Public Information of the Methodist Church

(Known as METHODIST INFORMATION)

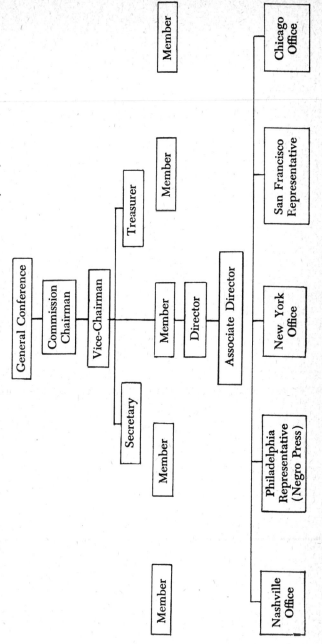

Organization Plan

Public Relations Work of the First Methodist Church, Evanston, Illinois

- Official Board
  - Finance Committee
    - Promotion Sub-Committee

- MINISTER
  - Board of Education
    - Special Publi-cations
  - Editorial Secretary
    - Parish Paper
    - General Public-ity
    - Bulletin and other Printing
  - Press Committee
  - Press Chairmen of Church Organizations

secular. The Roman Catholic Church, however, keeps these functions clearly separate. Thus far it has emphasized the internal public relations work, through the National Catholic Welfare Conference. In 1949, however, this thirty-year-old organization was altered so that it would be equipped to do both internal and external public relations work.

The Press Department of NCWC during those years had the "function of promoting, developing and assisting the Catholic Press of the United States." Through its News Service, the department sent out approximately 50,000 words weekly, reporting Catholic news throughout the world. About 400 church papers and magazines published in the United States and daily papers in Latin America subscribed, but secular papers within the United States were refused as clients so as to protect the exclusive material sent to the diocesan press.

Auxiliary to the NCWC News Service are the Catholic Feature Service, Catholic News Picture Service, a Washington letter, and other materials.

In 1949, however, the need for external organization was realized and the Bureau of Information of the National Catholic Welfare Conference, also in Washington, was reorganized. This group, it was explained by the organization committee, will "send out publicity releases . . . and . . . answer questions by secular papers regarding Catholics."

Interdenominational groups in the United States in some instances have had public relations offices or departments. The Missions Public Relations Office in New York served the Home Missions Council of North America, the Foreign Missions Conference of North America, and the United Council of Church Women. In Chicago has been the International Council of Religious Education, with its publicity office. Since the merger of eight interdenominational agencies in 1950, these offices are now united in a central department of public relations of The National Council of Churches.

In 1940, a public relations office was established in New York by the Federal Council of Churches of Christ in America. Its director, Donald C. Bolles, was for twenty-five years on the Associated Press staff and also has had experience in religious public relations, having served as public relations consultant for the Federal Council's Commission on a Just and Durable Peace. Mr. Bolles is now director of the Department of Public Relations of the National Council of Churches.

Diagrams of the schemes of organization of several of the denominational or local church groups that have given careful attention to the interpretation of their work to their own constituents or to the public at large are to be found in this chapter. They look different, but fundamentally are much the same. Each has at its head an experienced journalist who also has had religious training and is familiar with public relations techniques. With modifications, smaller or similar groups can follow these patterns.

An overhead group at work

An example of a functioning church public relations organization is the external group known as the Wisconsin Conference Public Relations Committee of the Methodist Church.

This committee has done effective work in an area which ordinarily is difficult to organize for public relations purposes. Single local churches often can maintain public relations programs because their territories are small enough to cover thoroughly. Entire denominations can carry on such activities, also, because they can be organized to do so, have the money to finance such an organization, and possess the administrative personnel that is likely to include persons of experience and talent in the world of communications. Regional groups, such as a diocese, council, assembly, district, synod or conference, usually do little more than issue publications and devote a little time to church public relations at a pastors' school.

The Wisconsin Conference Committee grew out of just such a training school. The Rev. Walter C. Eyster, executive director of the conference council in Oshkosh, Wisconsin, invited Dr. Ralph Stoody, director of Methodist Information, to take part in a public relations workshop held in 1947. From that came a suggested program of public relations for the Wisconsin area of the denomination (See Appendix II). The following spring, at the hundred and second annual session of the conference, the program was approved and a conference committee appointed. It was made one of the standing committees and its organization and duties were outlined thus:

There shall be a Public Relations Committee to be composed of a chairman and one member from each district, to be nominated by the cabinet. Such committee shall be responsible for press releases, story coverage, and other aspects of Conference public relations covering the sessions of the Annual Conference and such newsworthy projects and events as occur between such sessions. It shall also be the duty of this committee to give leadership to the pastors and laymen of the Conference in securing and maintaining the best possible public relations through the use of the press and radio.[5]

The Rev. W. E. Brashares, minister of the First Methodist Church of Hartford, Wisconsin, reporting as secretary of the committee a year and a half after its formation, said that "the plan does work and obtains the hoped for results." Mr. Eyster, executive director of the conference council, added,

We work very closely with the bishop's office and the district superintendents and try to keep in close contact with the newspapers of

---

[5] *Year Book and Journal,* Wisconsin Annual Conference of The Methodist Church (1948) p. 180.

our conference as well as the radio stations. Also, we are constantly sending news and pictures to *The Christian Advocate*. We have been very successful in getting information from our annual conference sessions to the newspapers and radio.

More specifically, the minutes of a meeting of the committee, held in February, 1949, show the nature of the group's work. Another public relations workshop was planned; three projects for street signs were recommended; the religious news policies of the Milwaukee press were discussed; the increase in the amount of space on Wisconsin Conference activities in *The Christian Advocate*, the national weekly of the Methodist Church, was reported; plans were made to obtain time on radio stations for recorded religious programs; arrangements were made for an exhibit of church bulletins, papers, and promotional materials at the annual conference meeting; detailed plans were made for press and radio coverage of the annual conference, including such details as preparation of a press room, steps in obtaining biographical information on speakers, and means of getting copies of reports to be made.

Later the Rev. Mr. Broshares was "borrowed" by the Indiana Conference of his denomination to conduct similar work in that state.

At local church level

At the level of the local church the organizational plan is centered in the head of the church, although the pastor or priest may delegate the public relations function to a committee. Personnel naturally is small. The major duties are much the same but the varieties of material are not as great as with a large agency serving an entire denomination.

The plan used at the First Methodist Church of Evanston, Illinois, for the past two decades, is explained in the reproduction of its *Press Chairman's Manual* at the end of this book (see Appendix I). In this suburban Chicago church of 2,700 active members, who live in various parts of the Chicago area, the interpretation of the church is centered in one secretary with responsibility for editing the weekly four-page, letter-size newspaper, the Sunday bulletin, the weekly calendar, and any special publications required by order of official bodies. She also runs the machinery of providing copy for the publications issued in the geographical area and for the denominational publications.

The Rev. Fred S. Wintle, minister of the Methodist church of Kirklin, Indiana, a typical small-town church of the denomination, divided the program of interpretation of his church's work into two parts: internal and external, with greatest emphasis on the use of printed materials.

The outline of his plan reads thus:

I. *Internal Public Relations*
   A. Making and keeping friends
      1. In general
         a) Maintain quality standards in all elements of worship service, including sermon
         b) Teach congregation to be smiling and friendly
         c) Keep room temperature comfortable
         d) Encourage positive complimentary attitudes, not negative, criticizing ones
         e) Call on the sick
      2. Specifically
         a) Write courtesy letters: thank you notes, congratulations, conciliations, helpful information, greetings
         b) Appoint official greeters
         c) Give people specific jobs to do
         d) Promote co-operative group projects
         e) Appoint committees
   B. Publicity materials
      1. Routine program
         a) Bulletin
         b) Church newspaper

        c) Literature racks
        d) Propaganda leaflets and materials
        e) Bulletin board
  2. Special activities program
        a) Direct mail
        b) Announcements

II. *External Public Relations*
  A. Making and keeping friends
    1. In general
        a) Co-operate with the press
        b) Show dignity and integrity of church institution and leaders
        c) Maintain standards of personal courtesy and neat appearance
        d) Establish solid business and credit foundations
        e) Keep church building repaired and painted
        f) Visit new residents
    2. Specifically—promote and publicize activities of general interest
  B. Publicity materials
    1. Routine program
        a) Capitalize on uniqueness of the church
        b) Use an attractive outdoor sign
        c) Seek and prepare news copy for distribution to all channels
    2. Special activities program
        a) Make use of paid advertising through all channels
        b) Give school chapel talks and speeches in other organizations

An organizational scheme can be devised for any size church or church group that seeks to put its efforts at interpretation on a systematic basis. No one existing plan can be superimposed on a local or national situation and work perfectly. But if the person or committee responsible for the interpretative activity will acknowledge the value and importance of planning and will develop a suitable scheme adapted from those of other groups the work to be done will be less haphazard and uncharted.

Religious journalism's organizations

Religious journalists and publicists have formed associations through which they obtain technical assistance, discuss their common problems, and give concerted support to their special viewpoints. Such groups are a factor in interpretation of the church. They exist in the worlds of press and radio.

Among the most diligent denominations in maintaining such a specific group devoted to religious journalism is the Southern Baptist Convention. The Southern Baptist Press Association, whose membership is comprised of the editors of about twenty state newspapers and magazines, meets semi-annually. At one session it offers two days of round tables and discussions on professional problems. A much larger group, the Division of Editorial Service of the Sunday School Board, for many years has sponsored a week-long conference each August at its summer camp grounds in Ridgecrest, North Carolina. To this, writers and editors connected with the nearly one hundred magazines issued by the Board or by other bodies of the Convention are brought for short courses. In recent years the United Lutheran Church and the American Baptist Convention have held similar conferences.

The Roman Catholic Church likewise sponsors several journalistic organizations. Most widely known is the Catholic Press Association, founded in 1911 at Columbus, Ohio,

to bring together the nation's Catholic editors, publishers, and writers into a co-ordinated, aggressive society, to promote Catholic literature in all its fields, to encourage Catholic writers to increase the efficiency of the news service (National Catholic Welfare Conference News Service), to reduce through co-operation, cost of mechanical production, to secure general advertising.[6]

Another active Roman Catholic group is the Catholic

---

[6] *I Am the Catholic Press, op. cit.,* p. 12.

School Press Association, intended to assist editors and advisers of Catholic educational publications. A journalism teacher edits *The Catholic School Editor*, which attempts to improve publication standards.

Far larger than either of these is the Catholic Institute of the Press, at least by number of members. Founded in 1943, it is an organization of about 1,200 persons engaged in newspaper, magazine, radio, and public relations work in New York City. Its objects are to "unite all Catholics regularly employed" in such journalistic work, to foster fellowship, "to inculcate spiritual ideals that the members may become better Catholics and more worthy citizens," and "to support the work of the Catholic Hierarchy . . . ." Prominent Roman Catholic journalists have been its officers. The monthly lectures by leading churchmen or Catholic journalists are attended by about 300 persons and more than 1,000 members and guests appear for an annual communion breakfast. Separate yearly week-end retreats are held for men and women members. The Institute, according to the constitution,

> awards medals, prizes or other suitable recognition . . . to individuals or units contributing most to the advancement of Catholic thought and principles in a literary fashion . . . It shall be the duty of this (awards) committee to invite national competition for the awards . . . .

A former president, describing the Institute to Mrs. Marjorie Moore Armstrong, formerly managing editor of *The Commission*, explained:

> When I came to New York ten years ago I did not know a single fellow journalist of my faith; now at any time I want anything at N.B.C. or *Time* or the *Herald Tribune* all I have to do is pick up the telephone and call a C.I.P. member over there.[7]

In the Methodist Church are the Methodist Press Asso-

---

[7] From Mrs. Armstrong's unpublished thesis on religion in the newspaper.

ciation, similar to but less active than the Southern Baptist Press Association. But a somewhat different and energetic group maintained by this denomination is the Joint Committee on Public Relations for Methodist Educational Institutions, which is devoted to the "study and application of the public relations aspects and concepts" of the Methodist-affiliated institutions of higher learning in the United States, which in 1950-1951 numbered 126.

Three interdenominational Protestant groups are the Associated Church Press, the Evangelical Press Association, and the Christian Amateur Press Association. The first, founded in 1919, is an organization of editors and managers of approximately 100 publications, denominational as well as nondenominational and interdenominational. Members meet for three days annually in convention, reward church editors for distinguished performance, and sponsor Protestant Press Month. There have been several off-the-record interviews with the President of the United States; at times its officers are asked to act as spokesmen for the Protestant press in such matters as the discussion of postage rate increases.

Formed in 1948, the Evangelical Press Association is intended to serve what Religious News Service, in reporting the founding of the group in Chicago, called "conservative Protestant denominations." With the self-help objectives of similar associations of religious journalists, this one held its first national conference in 1949 and heard speeches on techniques by writers on religion and by executives of secular publications.

The Christian Amateur Press Association is described by its founders, Walter and Dorothy Coslet, as an interdenominational nonprofit religious association and has as its purpose, according to its constitution,

to promote and to encourage the production and enjoyment of

Christian literature, by giving Christian writers an opportunity to obtain training and actual experience in the writing and/or publishing of their own material, and to receive the reaction of their audience.

Three years after its founding in 1948, this group had about twenty-five members and was issuing *The CAPA Bulletin*.

The Christian Authors' Guild, a nonprofit, undenominational group directed by Mrs. Edith F. Osteyee of Media, Pennsylvania, is mainly a correspondence course in writing for religious publications, although persons who complete the work are made members of the Guild. This organization issues a monthly publication, *The Compass*, discussing problems of religious writers, offering market news and tips, and reporting on student accomplishments.

An international trade association of denominational church publishing houses, the Protestant Church-Owned Publishing Association, was formed in 1948 during the convention of the International Council of Religious Education. It was begun by thirty-eight members of the Publishers' Section of the Council. Its purpose is to "consider all matters of mutual interest affecting the official Protestant church-owned publishing houses." It devotes attention to trade relations and such legislative developments as postal regulations.

Another division of the Council is the Editors' Section, which meets as part of the Council's annual convention. Interdenominational and Protestant, it functions to unify persons active in religious journalism but gives special attention to the problems of issuing church school materials.

In 1949 religious journalists who serve the secular press as well as men and women on the staffs of various religious journals formed their own group. The Religious News Writers Association was founded at Buffalo "in recognition of the growing importance of religion in the news and to advance professional standards of religious journalism." The first officers represented large newspapers in Cleveland, Newark, Chicago, New York, and Washington, including a newsmagazine, a denominational monthly, and a denominational news bureau.

Lambda Lambda Lambda, a religious journalism fraternity, was organized in 1947 at Oklahoma Baptist University; this institution has been developing a religious journalism curriculum for its denomination. Tri-Lambda makes an annual award for "Distinguished Service in Journalism."

Besides these largely editorial-side groups are organizations intended to promote interdenominational co-operation in radio-television, motion picture, and public relations work. These include the Joint Religious Radio Committee, the National Religious Broadcasters, the Religious Radio Association, and the Protestant Radio Commission, each of which is mainly interested in radio presentation of religion but giving increasing thought to the possibilities in television programs for religion. The Protestant Film Commission has not only promoted the use of films by churches but also has stimulated the production of more religious motion pictures and has sought to set standards in the religious film world. The Film Commission and the Radio Commission are now merged in the National Council's Central Department of Broadcasting and Films.

Three publicity groups have been interdenominationally prominent: the Missions Public Relations Office, the National Religious Publicity Council, and the Public Relations Office of the Federal Council of Churches. Co-operation has existed between them and such groups as Methodist Information, the Department of Publicity of the Presbyterian Church in the U.S.A., and the National Lutheran Council News Bureau. In 1951 the Missions Public Relations Office, the Federal Council Public Relations Office, and **various** other interdenominational publicity departments were merged in the new Central Department of Public Relations of the National Council of the Churches of the U.S.A.

CHAPTER III

The Media

Assuming that the church organization is convinced of the need for interpretation of its work, that it has clarified its goals, and has set up a mechanism for providing such interpretation; it must decide these next questions: Through which media will it work to reach the public? How do those media function?

Which medium to use can better be determined after there is understanding of each medium and after deciding which can be most efficiently and economically employed in a given situation Therefore in this chapter we shall give primary attention to the organization of the major media of communication, with special reference to their use by the world of religion.

An examination of the manner in which the media are organized would seem valuable because church workers often complain that the press does not understand the church and journalists, in their turn, just as frequently say that the church does not understand the press, does not know how it works, and makes unreasonable demands, as a consequence.

Probably it would be salutary if every churchman should do for a short time what Irwin St. John Tucker, known familiarly as Friar Tuck, does all year round in Chicago. This priest at St. Stephen's Protestant Episcopal Church of that city works on one of the Chicago newspapers at the same time that he serves his parish. By the same token, it would be instructive, if feasible, for a church news reporter to work in a church office, make calls with a pastor, help on a finance campaign, make out conference reports, and perform some of the other duties of a local church. Unfortunately, such an exchange of pulpits, as it might be called, is not feasible. Both groups are much too busy. Yet, in the long run, they might save themselves work all around by such an arrangement.

The exchange would be easier for the churches than for the press and radio to arrange, for churches far outnumber newspapers, magazines, and radio stations. In the United States there are about 1,750 daily papers, 500 Sunday papers, 8,000 weeklies, 11,000 magazines of all types and approximately 3,000 radio and television stations, with radio divided between AM and FM in a ratio of three to one in favor of the older (AM) type. The specialized press, which includes religious, trade, technical, labor, art, and other special-interest publications, adds several thousand more to the total of newspapers, since the magazine-format publication is included in the 11,000 figure given for magazines. Thus the total number of outlets in print or over the air comes to around 30,000.

Newspapers and magazines are organized similarly. Each is built around a departmental system including at least six major divisions: business or administrative department, advertising department, editorial department, mechanical department, circulation department, and promotion department. Some publications add art, research, photography, or other subdivisions.

Functions of the departments

The general nature of the functions of these departments is evident from their names. The advertising department sells space in the publication, prepares some portion of the copy for these advertisements, and services the accounts. The space is sold to national or local advertisers. National advertisers buy mainly display, as differentiated from classified, space and do so through the publication's representative in a firm of such agents; local advertisers buy space directly from the publication's staff salesmen. Both local and national advertisers buy classified space, but such space is chiefly a local community commodity and characteristic of the newspaper's advertising content rather than of the magazines, although by no means a novelty in the magazine, particularly the trade journal.

More than editorials are turned out by the department bearing the name "editorial." It gathers and writes news, prepares other types of copy, handles manuscripts received from the wire services, syndicates, and other sources, sends out writers, obtains and takes pictures or other art work, processes manuscripts and the other kinds of copy, and sees the preparation of all material through to the finished stage.

The mechanical department takes the editorial and advertising copy, both manuscript and illustration, and translates it into type or engravings for printing in magazine or newspaper. This task involves setting type with the aid of different kinds of machines, making up pages into forms, stereotyping or electroplating them or otherwise making them ready to be printed directly, producing the engravings and other illustrations, printing the paper or magazine, folding it, binding it, and otherwise getting it ready for the circulation department to handle. Offset printing, an increasingly popular technique useful to small-circulation publications, is a partial variant on this procedure, which is known as the letterpress method of printing.

It is important for churchmen to realize that the mechanical department works on a dependable schedule just as does the editorial department. Both departments follow staggered deadlines. That is, any publication cannot set into type or any radio station cannot broadcast at one time all copy received. When the churchman does not comprehend the matter of production schedules he expects impossible performances from the media of communication.

Magazines and newspapers differ in their relationship to the mechanical department. General newspapers, both daily and weekly, as a rule own their own printing plants and equipment; in the rural field, in fact, the operation of the plant often is first, the printing of the newspaper second, for job printing may bring in more revenue than the paper. In the consumer or general magazine world, however, this is not the situation. Only a few magazine companies own their own equipment. Instead, magazines hire printing firms to do the work for them just as churchmen may engage a printer to produce stationery. A few big firms, such as McCall's and Curtis, own printing plants, but Time, Inc., publisher of several of the largest circulation magazines in the nation, has contracts with printers in various parts of the United States to print, simultaneously, copies of each issue. Such an arrangement has its implications in the matter of speed, of workmanship, and of ultimate control.

Magazine issues are prepared weeks and sometimes months in advance. All big magazines are being prepared about three issues at a time; portions of other issues are planned as much as six months and a year in advance. The editors order manuscripts and illustrations for any number of future issues, particularly covers and seasonal materials.

Copy for some pages is received from several days to two weeks early even in newspaper offices. Editorials, much of the society news, special pages such as those devoted to gardening, fashions, and cooking, are sent out to be set in type the day before publication. On efficient and business-

like publications literary and other feature pages are prepared as much as a week before the public sees them. Thus,
on an afternoon paper's schedule, the morning of the day
of publication is taken up mainly with the handling of fresh
copy—news and other material unavailable earlier. The
mechanical department receives these manuscripts on a
similar schedule, and readies them for advance or last minute
printing as possible or necessary.

Therefore a forty-eight-page daily paper may be two-
thirds completed five hours before it goes to press. Thirty
pages may be in type, locked up, the stereotype plates made
and on the presses, and only the front page, the back page,
and certain inside pages that are to hold last-minute information—such as sports and finance—must be handled in that
five-hour period. These pages, too, will be closed one or
two at a time, so that the plates can be cast at spaced intervals. The first page, or whichever is completed last, is known
as the "starter." Pages must be completed on schedule or
trains, busses, trucks, and planes that carry the copies will
be missed, readers will be annoyed and disappointed, and
advertisers will lose possible sales.

Editorial, mechanical, and advertising departments have
been likened to a three-legged stool. Remove any leg and
the stool will not stand. Remove any of the departments, or
interrupt its schedule, and the publication cannot be issued.
The mechanical department must have the co-operation of
the other two if it is to do its work; the advertising and
editorial departments can produce the most readable and
effective copy man has ever seen but if there is no mechanical department to convert the copy into newspapers and
magazines the world will never appreciate what has been
written and photographed, for it will not see it. That is why
printers' strikes were more effective before substitutes were
found for some of the mechanical processes, as demon-

strated by the long typographical union strike in Chicago in the late 1940's. Although the substitute (engraving the copy instead of having it set by automatic type-setting machines) left much to be desired, it enabled the Chicago general newspaper publishers to continue issuing several editions daily.

Sharing responsibilty for seeing that the public and the publication are united is the circulation department, which receives the finished product from the mechanical department. Readers obtain their copies by hand delivery, via trucks connecting with newsstands or distributing companies, or through shipments of bundles of magazines or papers on trains and other vehicles. The circulation department also must keep records, make collections, prepare addresses and correct labels, wrap publications, and meet transportation schedules.

Newer than the others is the promotion department, which serves all groups concerned. Its job is to propagandize the paper or periodical, to place advertisements about the publication in trade journals, to prepare copy for car cards, billboards, and the sides of trucks, to send out circulation or advertising sales letters or other direct-mail materials, to help the advertising department service the advertisers, to deal with the public in any way that will improve the public's reaction to and opinion of the publication. Only large publications can afford to make a separate department of this development in modern communications.

Business departments, where they exist separately, sometimes envelop the work of the advertising and promotion departments or those of the financial, accounting, or payroll, or all of these. Administration, naturally, is made up of the executives responsible for steering the press: the publisher, the owner, the editor-in-chief, the managing editor, the advertising manager, the circulation director, the superintendent of the mechanical department, and the like.

Each department has its own hierarchy, with a top manager or editor responsible to the owner or publisher. The organization chart of a newspaper or magazine is not unlike that of a religious denomination or of a steel company, in general appearance; the titles and duties are different but responsibility—at least theoretically—is subdivided.

Most publications simply planned

Such an elaborate breakdown describes, of course, only the largest publications. The majority of newspapers and magazines in the United States, it is fair to say, have simple organization plans. The country or community weekly, which outnumbers the general or city daily by about four to one, usually consists of one or two persons in the editorial department and maybe two or three to take care of the work of all other departments. Thus there is overlapping. That is, the editor may sell advertising space as he goes around town picking up personal news or the man in charge of advertising may collect news items as well as help run the printing press on Wednesday night.

Only about 100 magazines are large enough to have well-developed departments. Thousands of trade journals, house publications, science magazines, and others that deal with special interests, have staffs of from five to fifteen persons and leave much of the routine work to advertising agencies, promotion companies, printers, and distributors. As with the rural newspaper, the ordinary magazine expects its staff members to perform multiple and varied duties.

Sources of revenue

Whether the publication be newspaper or magazine, the main revenue source is its advertising, with circulation second, and sales of reprints, special publications, yearbooks, and manuals last. Once, circulation revenue was negligible; often it was a department that lost money, so far as direct revenue was concerned. But with the growth of circulations in the United States of both newspapers and magazines and the increase in per copy and subscription rates the press has come to expect from 30 to 50 per cent of its earnings from its circulation department. Some newspapers and magazines obtain even more: the *Reader's Digest,* the magazine with the largest circulation in the world, derives only circulation revenue from its United States editions and is a financially successful and wealthy publication. Before World War II the ratio on general news papers was 70 per cent of the income from advertising and 30 per cent from circulation; on consumer magazines advertising revenue accounted for 40 or 50 per cent of income. In the postwar years the ratio is closer to 60-40 for newspapers, with advertising first, and 50-50 on general magazines. Trade magazines, such as *Steel, Power, Boys' Outfitter,* and *Office Appliances* have a quickly attained saturation point in circulation and depend upon advertising, therefore, for as much as 70 or 80 per cent of their income. The larger the magazine the greater the cost of production and the greater, therefore, the need for advertising and circulation revenue.

Churchmen enthusiastic about the power of print often do not know that a magazine can have too much advertising, if the rate at which the space is sold is too low to offset the cost of production. Nor do they realize that a publication can have too much circulation, if the cost of production per copy is so great that it cannot be offset by direct revenue. *Life,* for example, sold advertising space during its first year on a basis of 350,000 circulation, but that picture magazine was more popular at once than its publishers, Time, Inc., had anticipated. The firm is said to have lost about one

million dollars during that first year because it cost so much
to produce the magazine in proportion to the returns from
advertising and circulation. *American Boy,* a magazine
which undoubtly was childhood reading for many of today's
middle-aged churchmen, died when it had 300,000 circulation. It had lost so much advertising to radio that its owners
could not continue to send so costly a magazine to such a
large number of subscribers. *Sports Illustrated, Science Illustrated,* the newspapers *PM* and the New York *Star* and many
other magazines and newspapers that ceased publication in
the late 1940's did so for similar reasons. There were no
notable cessations of religious publications because few
magazines and papers of religion are expensively produced
and few of them are involved in big advertising contracts
the removal of which would cut away the necessary, strong
financial support.

An example of the opposite situation in the religious field
is the Methodist devotional bi-monthly and the most widely
circulated religious publication in the United States, *The
Upper Room.* For many years it has been sold for five cents
a copy and has not carried advertising. But it is essentially
an inexpensive publication to produce and its distribution
system is ready-made, being mainly the ministers, churches,
and church schools of the denomination. Thus it has achieved
the surprising circulation of more than three million copies
per issue and has been able to add high profits to its publisher's accounts.

The circulation department brings in money by the direct
sale method. Newspapers and magazines differ, however,
in the way this selling is accomplished. Being local publications, newspapers do little business by mail, making their
sales by home delivery and from newsstands. Home delivery
can mean running a truck into country areas and poking the
paper into tin cylinders mounted in front of farm houses. It

also may be a "little merchant" tossing the paper on the front porch of a house in an urban center. Popular national magazines do a heavy business on newsstands and an even larger one through the mail. Consumer as well as specialized magazines both depend upon the mail for delivery. This is especially true of the approximately 2,000 trade publications and the additional thousands of other specialized periodicals, including the religious magazines and newspapers. The dependence upon the mail system accounted for the opposition of religious publishers and editors, in 1951, to the proposed increase in second-class mailing rates. Had increases, as originally requested by the postmaster general been placed in effect, scores of religious publications would have had to cease operations or find subsidies to offset the high cost of mailing.

Advertising, too, is a direct money-maker. But the rest of the departmental family is a money-spending group. The others, strictly speaking, do make money for a publishing firm, but their method is indirect. Few publications, after all, are bought for their advertising alone, although in specialized publications the advertising actually amounts to "newsvertising." Yet the nonadvertising content is the chief reason for being, especially in religious publications, whose motive is promotional and propagandistic rather than revenue-earning. The enterpreneurs of the press, whether they be religious bodies or commercial groups with the main motive of dollar profits, never can allow themselves to forget that, if they are to keep solvent, the advertising and circulation departments must be so organized that they bring in money at the least expense and the editorial and other departments must function at their best and also at the least expense. Such a balance is difficult to strike and to maintain, but it must be achieved and held under the American system of free use of the press.

Radio organization

Radio organization in most respects is entirely different from that of the publication world. Confining ourselves still to the United States, it must be noted that radio, like all other types of communications media, is privately owned and operated, whereas in many other parts of the world it is state-owned. An important (and misunderstood) exception is Great Britain, where radio is only indirectly government controlled. The British Broadcasting Corporation is not a government department, but an autonomous public corporation, on a nonprofit basis, and operates under a royal charter subject to renewal by Parliament every decade.

Although United States radio is completely private and there are no franchises, it is under some government control from which the rest of the communications industry is free. Radio sets are not taxed and there is no government subsidy but stations must hold licenses issued by the Federal Communications Commission. These licenses are granted for three-year terms. Newspapers and magazines need not be licensed to operate. The Commission is empowered, among other things, to describe the nature of the services that each station may perform, to ascribe frequencies for individual stations and classes of stations, to determine the power and the call letters, and to study new uses of radio.

Just as there is a similar organizational pattern for newspapers and magazines, regardless of size, so there is for radio stations. Generally there are four departments: management, engineering, programming, and sales. Roughly these might be compared with the newspapers' and magazines' departments thus: management corresponds to administrative; engineering to mechanical; programming to editorial and advertising; sales to advertising, promotion, and circulation. Likewise, depending upon size, the personnel may be large and divide all the functions one by one, or small and overlap on the duties within departments. (See Chapter V.)

Of special value to church people and others who wish to make use of radio as well as printed journalism is the knowledge that radio stations fall into three groups: the nonaffiliated commerical, those with network affiliations, and religious and educational stations. There are organizational differences between these types.

Nonaffiliated stations (all of them AM stations) generally cover small listening areas and include about one fourth of those of the United States. Although they do not belong to major networks, namely National Broadcasting Company, Mutual Broadcasting System, Columbia Broadcasting System, and American Broadcasting Company, they may belong to state groups of stations. These might be called local stations. They, therefore, are the stations the city priest, minister, or other religious leader can turn to for co-operation with somewhat more expectation of getting it than from the network affiliated stations, the second group. The latter differ from the others chiefly in their power and the size of the area they serve. About two-thirds of the stations of the United States fall into this classification, with the Mutual Broadcasting System the largest in 1951. Organizational differences are at the point of responsibility for handling communications to and from the network and a different plan of programming. An affiliated station clearly has less time for local programs. It may accept the network programs only or to within six hours of its total broadcasting time. The time it devotes to local programs will in part be with the hope of finding a popular one that may develop into a network feature, thus giving the sales department an unusual opportunity.

The third group—religious and educational stations—is of direct interest here. But they are few in number and in the

hands of specific bodies or individuals that do not provide
an outlet to the local church unless that church happens to
be of the same denomination and in the city where the station
is operated.

About thirty stations of this type were in operation in
1949; they were propaganda agencies for their owners, as
is to be expected, but a few sold commerical time. Two of
the better known in the list are WWL, New Orleans, owned
by the Jesuits of Loyola University, and WMBI, operated
by Moody Bible Institute, Chicago. Others were in Los
Angeles and Pasadena, California; Denver, Colorado; Boone,
Iowa; Lapeer, Michigan; St. Louis, Missouri; Zarephath,
New Jersey; Brooklyn, New York; Richmond, Virginia;
Seattle, Washington; and Appleton and Green Bay, Wisconsin. Some are owned by a local church, or a religious
leader, but most of them are run by religious groups, generally a denomination, or a subdivision thereof. Religious
broadcasting was affected in a way not finally known as
this book went to press in 1951 when a hearing examiner
of the Federal Communications Commission recommended
that the Committee refuse to grant a license sought by a
church. Granting of the application by the Reorganized
Church of Jesus Christ of Latter-Day Saints was ruled a
violation of the First Amendment to the Constitution, which
guarantees church-state separation. The Supreme Court
decisions in the Everson and McCollum cases were cited. If
the Commission wished, it could outlaw all religious radio
stations; some interpreters of the ruling believed it can be
used to show that religious broadcasts on any radio station
violate the Constitution.

The organization of radio networks and of publication
chains or groups is complex; understanding it would not aid
most churchmen in their use of radio as an interpretative
tool. The effect of such joint ownership and operation is

standardization of content, which is both a disadvantage and an advantage to local groups seeking co-operation from networks and chains. The organizational plan is not unlike that of an individual unit, but it operates horizontally instead of vertically only. There are internal benefits to network organization of radio stations or group organization of newspapers and magazines which must not be overlooked, such as lower costs and wider distribution for advertising.

Philosophy of press and radio

Economic necessity explains, for the most part, the objectionable features of the press and radio as communications institutions. If press and radio must achieve and maintain financial solvency, as all unsubsidized institutions must in our economy, they must be permitted to print or broadcast what will enable them to be solvent. Their owners, under such a system, must be trusted to avoid disseminating what is harmful to the public as a whole, subject to legal restraints which experience has found imperative. The owners of press and radio usually stop short at distributing in print or over the airwaves conventionally vicious materials. In the opinions of some critics they should eliminate many more.

Joy Elmer Morgan, editor of the *Journal of the National Education Association,* told the members of the NEA at their 1949 convention in Boston, for example, that "in most cases" comic books, movies, radio, and television are guilty of "commercial exploitation and violation of the child mind." He said that these media of communication "are filling children's minds with the trivial and the unreal. In most cases the primary motive is not the perfection of child life but the making of money."

Other critics have added to Dr. Morgan's list certain comic strips, particular types of news pictures, radio soap operas, and biased news accounts. Churchmen are natu-

rally sympathetic with the educator's viewpoint in such a
situation and understand the problem the journalist is facing. To remain solvent the press and radio must give the
public what it wants or at least what they think the public
wants. If they give the public what it wants, as they see it,
they may not be able to find space or time to give it what
they may, in their best moments, want it to have despite
public desire or what church people think it should have for
its own good.

Considering the long record of public indifference to
publications and radio stations that have sought to give the
public something better than is ordinarily wanted, who can
be harshly critical of the journalist who strikes a middle
road or compromises?

A clear example is provided by examination of the taste
of individual citizens. Groups of ministers, when asked to
indicate the nature of their periodical reading, have shown
their selections to be little different from those of men and
women in less intellectualized walks of life. To a minimum
of professional publications, such as magazines for pastors,
denominational weeklies, and devotional literature, are
added the usual mass circulation periodicals and a rarely
mentioned periodical of controversy, public affairs, or literature. Church people are ready to admit that the *Atlantic
Monthly, Harper's, Religion in Life, Tomorrow, Christian
Century, Yale Review,* and others are excellent journals, but
rarely give evidence of subscribing to them or reading them
in libraries. Sometimes they are critical of the local press,
often justifiably, but they do not as frequently take the pains
to read the *Christian Science Monitor,* the New York *Times,*
or the New York *Herald Tribune.* In New York and Chicago,
in the 1940's, newspapers that sought to improve such social
conditions as inadequate housing, racial discrimination, and
black marketing failed from lack of public support.

The religious press

If the general public, including the church people, cannot or will not support enthusiastically the highest type of secular newspaper or magazine, it may be that the money, time, and energy of at least the religious-minded are devoted to the religious press. In some denominations this describes the situation, but for the nation as a whole it does not. With a few notable exceptions, the religious press is characterized by small circulations, need for financial subsidy, and expenditure of excessive energy to gain and hold reading attention. The reasons for this will be considered at length later in the discussion.

The religious press is a member of what sometimes is called the specialized press. It consists of newspapers and magazines published by or for persons of religious interests. Their number is not certain, the uncertainty occurring because of difficulty of classification. The Sunday bulletin or leaflet showing the order of service, announcements for the week, and other such information, is a publication in the sense that any issue of a press is a publication. As many as 100,000 of these may be printed or otherwise regularly reproduced in the United States. The parish paper is a religious publication in a truer sense. About 30,000 are issued weekly and monthly. Most denominations have one or more internal publications that can be likened to industrial house publications. From 1,400 to 1,500 such publications exist. Since the external religious newspaper and magazine are the most complex of all, their organization needs most attention here. (Their production is closely like that of any secular publication of similar format; consideration of that aspect can be left to volumes on the techniques of the secular press.) The church bulletin and parish paper as a rule are the work of one or two individuals only, and have the simplest of organization. But they vary sharply from secular periodicals and therefore will be given special attention in later chapters.

The largest religious journals are organized precisely as are other big publications. *The Christian Science Monitor,* in so far as it is to be considered a religious journal, operates much like any other newspaper, technically speaking; its standards are far higher but that is another matter. The *Monitor* is published by a church to exert influence and as a model of good journalism. *The Christian Herald,* one of the most popular and largest magazines of religion, is in many ways like any other big periodical. Two essential differences exist: one is that the average religious publication has a smaller personnel and a less well-defined operating plan than the general or consumer publication and the other that group ownership and operation are much more common in religious journalism. (It is not unusual for a denomination to finance, edit, print, and distribute a whole set of publications serving various interests in the constituency.) The significance of these organizational distinctions is that the first makes for poorer workmanship and the second for better workmanship but greater standardization and denominational censorship and control. The religious publication differs from the secular in these ways also: 1. It can obtain support on a basis of group loyalty but not an intense readership. 2. Its circulation department need not consider newsstand sales too seriously. 3. Bulk distribution through Sunday schools and other groups is available. 4. Mail circulation, that is to say, direct mailing to individual subscribers, is at a minimum.

Church publishers, to a surprisingly large extent, own their own printing plants, so that the organization of the mechanical department is more complex than in the case of many secular papers and magazines.

Other media

Newspapers, magazines, and radio stations are the leading media available for ready interpretation of the church but they are by no means all. Wire services, syndicates, advertising agencies, motion picture companies, television stations, and public relations offices are channels also. Each is organized more or less departmentally, as is business in general. Wire services, using the Associated Press as an example, gather and process news and features and send copy by telegraph, radio, mail, and messenger to members or subscribers. Newspapers, magazines, and radio stations are their chief customers. Branch offices, known as bureaus, cover the world. Religious information is part of the total knowledge communicated, but usually only a small part.

Syndicates, which have assumed increasing importance in church interpretation, likewise serve press and radio with copy of many kinds, but usually emphasize features, editorials, pictures, special columns, and other largely non-news types of material. (See Chapter VI.) They work through central offices chiefly, but some maintain bureaus or branches.

Advertising agencies are set up to prepare and place paid advertising. They buy space in newspapers and magazines, on billboards and car cards, purchase time on the air, or space on a television screen, or see to the preparation of special printed pieces, or motion picture films, and arrange special events. (See Chapter XV.)

Public relations offices, variously known as publicity offices, press agents, and public relations counsels, are advisers in the use of the various other media. They will undertake to produce the material needed, and work with press, radio, and advertising agencies to accomplish the goal of interpretation.

The answer to the question posed at the outset of this

chapter—Which medium shall the church use?—cannot be answered by naming any one of the media. Churchmen should make use of as many as their organizations can afford and have found, after fair trial, to be effective. No one medium can accomplish all that is desired. Some are inherently more effective than others. Believers in the virtues of visual education, for example, are certain that great use of audio-visual aids is imperative. They are right. But some persons whom the churches wish to reach can be reached only via the printed word, for they live in communities so small and undeveloped that motion pictures and wire recording machines are expensive luxuries. The choice of media, therefore, depends upon the amount of money available for interpretation through print and radio, the personnel available for carrying out the plans, and the capacity to respond of the people who are to be reached, or, as the business world puts it, "the nature of the market."

Church groups need an exchange of information on the use of media in given situations. Newspaper and magazine publishers and radio station owners spend fortunes on the making of reader-interest and market surveys, to determine the nature of the audience and the effectiveness of the medium. A few students of religious journalism and publicity have examined the results of such surveys and noted the low position of religious information. Similar surveys of the church press and radio are needed before churchmen can do much more than guess at the relative merits of the several media.

CHAPTER IV

Religion in the General Press

The official board was in session. It was the week after Easter. The size of the new budget was under consideration, although the old budget had not yet been entirely raised. As sometimes happens at board meetings in churches, the discussion shifted to attendance and from there to news of church events.

"I should like to know," one board member said severely, "why the *Morning Telegram* did not have an announcement of the Easter service, either last Saturday or Sunday."

When no one answered, the inquirer went on to make a motion. It was that the lay leader of the church go to the newspaper office and "give them a piece of his mind."

The secretary of the official board quickly advised against such action. That *would* bring about lack of co-operation, he observed.

"Did the office notify the *Morning Telegram* of our Easter services?" he asked the minister.

The reply was that the paper had not been so advised. The minister added that about a year before, when the *Telegram* had omitted some other story, he had written a letter of complaint. "I think relations have been strained ever since," he observed.

"I think the *Telegram* has a grudge against our church," another board member said. But still another, this one a man more active in civic life than the first, said that he knew the staff members of the paper and that he doubted anyone of importance at the office had a feeling of spite or resentment against the church, this one or any other. And a woman member of the board, charged with publicizing the women's group, pointed out that her organization's activities were covered well and regularly by the *Morning Telegram*.

This scene from a board meeting in a medium-sized city church is not exaggerated. Its like can be found at many sessions of religious folk. The attitudes revealed are not restricted to church people. Any group which has relationships with the press and does not understand how newspapers and magazines function is quick to reach the conclusion that someone on the publication's staff is prejudiced, is playing favorites, or is nursing a grudge. With slight changes, it is possible to hear similar talk at labor union meetings, gatherings of educators, and club women's sessions.

Churchmen, despite these difficulties, must learn to get along with the general press, just as the press must learn to get along with the church. As shown elsewhere in this book, public interest in religious content of the press is relatively low. The newspaper and the magazine print little religious news and almost no religious views. In many communities they could omit such copy altogether and there would be complaint only from the most zealous. And since zealots are in the minority and the press survives by meeting the needs of majorities, it is the church which depends more upon the press than the press does upon the church.

Consequently it is important for the church to understand the place of religion in the general press, which is one of the most important media through which to interpret the church, for it reaches individuals not already touched by the more specialized instruments. Citizens who do not read religious papers and magazines are likely to be among the many millions who read newspapers and magazines of a general nature.

By the general press is meant any of the approximately 1,750 daily newspapers, the 8,000 country weeklies, and the 100 general or consumer magazines. Typical of dailies is the Los Angeles *Times,* Scranton *Times,* Hartford *Times,* or New York *Times.* Sample weeklies are the Ritzville (Washington) *Journal-Times* or the Reedsburg (Wisconsin) *Times-Press.* Representative consumer magazines are the *American, Better Homes and Gardens,* or *McCall's.* Trade journals, house publications, religious weeklies, and other specialized publications are omitted here.

Newspapers, whatever their frequency of issue, treat material about church and religion differently than do magazines. Weeklies and dailies alike print religious news, explanatory articles, editorial comment, cartoons, and departmental material, although the quantity, in proportion to the total available reading matter space, is small.

In the field of religion, magazines commonly publish little more than a special article now and then and an occasional editorial or special column. Because it goes stale quickly, religious news has little place in the general magazine, which is prepared months before publication. Interpretations of the news appear, it is true. Occasionally they may deal with the church. News magazines, which are few in number, have weekly departments on religion and in this are the exception among magazines.

The traditional attitudes

Traditionally newspaper and magazine publishers have avoided religious controversies for fear of alienating too many readers or of bringing down upon themselves objections from the organized churches. Since all denominations are guilty of attempting to exert pressure upon the press,

no attempt to point a finger at any one group will be made
here in citing examples.

In the section on "Pressure Groups Attempts on the
Press" in their book, *The Newspaper and Society*, Professors
George L. Bird of Syracuse University and Frederic E. Merwin of Rutgers University pointed out that church groups
are included among those that work "through suppression
as well as through propaganda." They quoted evidence that
named a particular denomination. Later the authors themselves encountered such pressure at firsthand when their
book was released. They were waited upon by a member
of the denomination involved. He requested that they ex-
punge the allusions. That they refused to do.

Journalists as well as authors of books have been visited
at their offices by committees of churchmen or individual
clergymen bearing demands that they cease publishing certain types of religious material. During the years of the
Spanish Civil War, the proving ground, as it later developed,
for World War II, the managing editor of a small daily in
Illinois was visited one day by a churchman. The young
man objected to the wire service dispatches reporting the
conflict in Spain. The paper, he said, was giving government
troops too much space; it should publicize more widely and
prominently the activities of the insurgents, supporters of
General Franco. If the paper did not do so, he declared in a
threatening tone, the members of his church would boycott
it and notify the advertisers.

The journalist's attitude, as a consequence, becomes
cautious. Too busy to find out the full story of religious dis-
agreements, he inclines to stay out of trouble by printing
only the innocuous or the routine.

What, on the other hand, is the usual attitude of the
churchman toward the general publication beyond this
occasional venture into special pleading or lobbying? As a

rule he either is highly critical or complacent. A disinterested attitude is rare. The critical attitude is expressed in letters and visits of the type already described, but it is manifested in other ways as well. Objection is registered to liquor advertising, to the publication of comic strips, to various other types of content which the critic thinks waste the reader's time or the publisher's space or are of bad social effect.

The complacent churchman, at the other extreme, simply never thinks much about the social values in his general newspaper or the social effect of his secular magazine. He seems no more likely to do so than he is given to question the quality of the chlorine that went into the manufacture of the pulp upon which the paper is printed.

Typical of the criticial attitude are the words of the late William K. Anderson, editor of the Commission on Courses of Study of The Methodist Church. In his book, *Pastor and Church,* he wrote:

> We of the church often bemoan the efficient way in which the world is set up for the advertisement of sin as contrasted with the scanty publicity given to goodness and the agencies for its promotion . . . not much space in the daily press is given to religious news.[1]

The complacent view

An example of the complacent but not entirely thoughtless attitude appeared in *The Christian Advocate* in 1948. That widely circulated weekly published an article describing the policies of a daily in Philipsburg, Pennsylvania. It began by saying:

> That Methodism is workable seven days a week in business, as well as in personal and church life, is the conviction of the only woman editor and publisher of a daily newspaper in Pennsylvania.

---

[1] William K. Anderson, *Pastor and Church* (New York: Abingdon Press, 1942) pp. 292-3.

To prove it *The Daily Journal* at Philipsburg, Pa., conforms closely to the tenets of the Methodist Church.

The policies described as evidence that "Methodism is workable seven days a week in business" and that *The Daily Journal* "conforms closely to the tenets of the Methodist Church" are:

It prints almost no crime news. It uses at least 10 per cent of its reading matter space in a week's issues for church notices and news stories about the local churches. It does not use advertisements, pictures, and reading matter that "might be harmful to our young readers." This means that "no beer or liquor advertisements have ever appeared . . . nor have advertisements of Sunday sports or other forms of Sunday entertainment ever been allowed . . . ." Pictures of celebrities shown drinking are not published. "And the sports editor has strict orders not to write any Sunday baseball or football games for the Monday columns . . . ."

Finally: "Few court cases are reported . . . About once every five years a case comes up . . . of such intense local interest it cannot be ignored."

Such conformity to the conventional tenets does not go far enough. These superficial policies are practically no test at all of the religious sincerity of newspapers. What standards might more nearly determine the religious earnestness of American editors and publishers than these? Here are some possibilities that might occur to the less complacent critic:

Does the paper, through its editorials, fight the forces of evil in the community? Does it expose political chicanery, police dishonesty and inefficiency, or other types of community mismanagement, if they exist in its territory (and in what area do they not appear)? Or does it wink at violations of the law committed by the influential people of the neighborhood? Or is it silent about all but the most trivial issues and instances of graft and corruption?

Does the paper print not only the church notices or news stories about the town's or city's churches, but also news of the co-operative store (which does not advertise), the minority political party meetings, and other such unpopular subjects? Does it go out of its way to see that minority groups of all sorts are given space, so that readers will know that there are dissatisfied or rebellious elements in the community? Does it print enough crime news and court reports to serve as a thorough record of community criminal action, so that possible new victims of criminals are warned and so that criminals are exposed to the spotlight of publicity? Does the paper seek to apply Christian principles by attacking and exposing racial discrimination, misrepresentation of individuals by name-callers and gossips, vigilante groups that take the law into their own hands, and religious bigotry and assigning of guilt by association?

There are other tests as well, but these are samples of what may have been overlooked, if it is granted that such standards have anything to do with religion. Certainly the tenets of the Methodist Church include more than refusal to print crime news, allowance of generous space for church news, ignoring Sunday sports, and refusing liquor or certain other kinds of obnoxious advertising. This is clear from an examination of the Discipline and of General Conference actions.

Another analysis

An editorial, based on a discussion of ways to get space in newspapers for a particular church, appeared in *The Christian Advocate* during the regime of Dan B. Brummitt as editor.

One of the committee members, the editorial reported, stood up among them and said:

'Men and brethren, and sisters also, when you find that the news-papers will not print the good news of your church's success and your pastor's eloquence and your people's faithfulness to their God, do not lament, and do not rail against the newspapers. Rather, be ye thankful.

'It is the newspapers' business to report the unusual. And the unusual is not good, but evil. The unusual is war and crime and disaster and conspicuous folly and glaring sin.'

The committee member went on to develop this, pointing out that

The faithfulness of your people to their religious vows has no chance in the papers against the unfaithfulness of a man to his marriage vows, or of a woman to her womanhood, or of a public servant to his oath.

Do not be fretful over all this. Be thankful. Think for a moment what a hell we should all be living in if goodness became news; if reporters were sent to the scene when the papers were tipped off that somebody was behaving decently . . .

That committee member had a sharp understanding of the realities of the press. He would not expect the impossible either in the general policies of the press or in the treatment of religious news.

The church editor

Midway between the church and the press stands, in some communities, the church editor. He or she is the press's middleman in its relations with the church, its expert, its buffer, its strainer of the news, its moderator of local rivalry. This editor has no control over the general policy of news treatment that disturbs the skeptical churchman. The person in charge of the church column or page of a newspaper, the church section of a newsmagazine, or the church copy for a radio station, is one of several specialized editors, who, when efficient and well-informed, are antidotes to improper handling of church news other than the church pages or sections.

The church editors employed by daily newspapers of the United States (there are almost five hundred in 1951) rarely are kept busy entirely with church news work. On small dailies they may cover clubs and schools as well or serve their turns on a copy desk. Only on the very largest papers, usually metropolitan dailies, is there need for a staff or even one full-time person to handle religion. New York, Philadelphia, Chicago, Boston, and a few other large cities alone have placed church editorships on an important footing.

One of the most widely known women journalists in the United States was a church editor, Rachel McDowell, religious news editor of the New York *Times* for nearly 30 years. Among the other journalists of distinction devoting full time to covering the church in the 1940's were the late James O. Supple, of the Chicago *Sun-Times*, killed in 1950 while flying to cover the Korean war; Jo-Ann Price, of the Milwaukee *Journal;* Willmar Thorkelson, of the Minneapolis *Journal;* Alice Moldenhawer, of the New York *World-Tele-gram-Sun;* Nellie Gardner, of the New York *Herald Tribune;* George Dugan, Miss McDowell's successor at the New York *Times;* and George M. Elliott, of the Atlanta *Constitution.*

These men and women and many others less widely known do a serious job of news gathering and writing by keeping up with important religious periodicals, books, and special literature issued by church bodies, forming wide acquaintance among religious leaders, and understanding contemporary religious trends. But well-informed and trained religious editors on newspapers are not in the majority. They are more numerous, however, than they once were, because the training and educational standards of secular journalism are rising.

Church editors in the middle period of the 20th century may have their failings, but they are devoted monks and nuns by comparison with some of the gentry that held the job in the century before. Malcom W. Bingay, before he was managing editor of the Detroit *News* and executive editor of the Detroit *Free Press,* served as church editor. In his autobiography, *Of Me I Sing,* he does not flatter himself or the other men who were responsible for writing about religion and the church. First he portrays himself:

> Because I was young and innocent, it was decided that I would also make a good church editor. (He was a police reporter simultaneously.) Looking back, I am convinced that this was a very bad training for a young man of high ideals, clean, fine illusions, and deep religious impulses.
> I base my theory on the simple and obvious fact that once you have been behind the stage in a theater, the illusion is gone. When you are too close, the scenery appears to be a series of ugly daubs . . . It was a great shock to me—one from which I do not think I have ever fully recovered—to learn that clergymen are human beings with all the faults and even some of the virtues of human beings.[2]

Mr. Bingay became disillusioned when a Michigan clergyman, at a weekly meeting, invented a story about the sinfulness of his community and his own difficulties trying to save his flock. It later developed that the preacher had fabricated this for the sake of effect. When the news story was published (despite pleas for mercy) the pastor was not willing to return to his town.

Mr. Bingay went on to say:

> Church editors were always a problem for Pat Baker (the managing editor). He looked on them as unnecessary evils but kept one on the job to avoid any protest that he was neglecting the finer things of life.
> Pat Baker liked best to hire some former preacher to do the job as a good will gesture to God and the Scripps-Booth ménage . . . As far as Pat was concerned the test of a good church editor was whether he knew enough not to call a Free Methodist parson 'Father' or a Catholic priest 'Rabbi.'

---

[2] Malcom W. Bingay, *Of Me I Sing* (Indianapolis: Bobbs-Merrill, 1949) pp. 73-9.

One day there appeared on the job a gentleman who was presented to us as 'the Reverend Mr. Wilson,' who had retired from a pastorate somewhere in Iowa because, he said, he wanted to 'get into the stream of life.' This satisfied Baker that he was fitted for the assignment. He had been also a book agent, an insurance man, and a horse doctor.

We of the young set had our doubts when we saw him in action in our penny-ante poker game. He had an uncanny genius for filling an inside straight and could always produce an ace at just the right moment. As a drinker of bourbon he had a hollow leg. But he had no idea of edition time or what constituted a story.

Mr. Wilson left the staff when he was exposed as the operator of a sideline—a fake organization to teach acting, through which he mulcted vain Detroit masseurs and cigar counter girls.

Today's church editors are far more conscientious; in fact, they are given to complain about the poor co-operation they receive from many church bodies. They are puzzled by this situation, for they believe, logically enough, that newspapers and magazines, especially the former, are relatively easy to work with, for they are the more numerous, closer at hand, and not too strict in their copy requirements. The secular press also is less expensive to employ than other media and calls upon the churchman for a minimum of technical knowledge. He may not have ready skill or training in the preparation of advertising copy for newspapers, magazines, outdoor signs, car cards, or radio programs. He may not know how to write radio scripts. But he can learn quickly to prepare news and feature stories, at least in their simpler forms, sufficiently well for average publicity purposes.

The editors complain

Newspaper editorial department employees who handle church news say that churches too often fail to send in copy about their activities or to keep the paper informed in other ways, that much of the copy coming in is badly prepared, showing not the slightest idea of the newspaper's way of doing things, and that frequently newspapers are scolded for the way they handle church news when they do not deserve such treatment.

Relationships between church and press are improving, nevertheless. They are destined to improve further as church people become more aware of the problem of interpretation and as the press lets better-trained writers handle the church beat.

The American Press magazine surveyed newspaper editors in 1947, questioning them on the interest in religion in their communities, which were all in the rural areas. These editors also were asked about their relationships with churches on religious news.

Religion was reported to be on the upgrade in rural America, "but not much." It also was learned that "almost all country editors devoted some space in each issue to church news. A third of the group devoted a column in each weekly issue, nearly another third printed one-and-a-half to two columns, almost one-sixth gave three or more columns of space.

Some of the editors commented on their church news problems; half the quotations were favorable and half unfavorable. Presumably the editor of *The American Press* reprinted the opinions in proportion. Even if only half the country editors complain about the way churches handle news, a gigantic educational job on publicity still is needed in that area. What is needed among city churches is not so clear, but theirs is likely to be a somewhat better situation considering the comparatively improved financial condition and personnel in many urban churches.

"The churches seem unaware of the value of publicity," wrote J. F. Campbell, of the Hardin (Illinois) *Calhoun News.*

"We publish all church notices but the ministers seldom bring us anything for publication," came from O. E. Smith the editor of the Batavia (Ohio) *Cleremont Sun.*

"Could use more church material if church leaders knew how to work with us," declared Homer Steen of the Floyd County (Floydada, Texas) *Hesperian.*

"The editor says if you preachers keep on being late with your church notices, he's going to be an hour late to church services every Sunday!"

Reproduced by permission of
The American Press

The relationships of church and press, then, are on two levels, the philosophical and the technical. At neither level are the understanding and co-operation what they should and might be. The church complains that it does not get enough space and that the press warps the news about church and religion; the press complains that the church does not help it get the news and does not understand why it handles the news as it does. An entire book, *Church and Newspaper,* by William B. Norton, has been devoted to the philosophical side, as have innumerable articles. All books on church publicity techniques give attention to this aspect, in more or less detail. Several seminaries deal with it in church administration courses.

But far more must be done on both sides. Almost no textbooks or general courses in journalism deal with the handling of religious news or with the relationship of the church to the press. Because churchmen receive more guidance, they are moving more rapidly toward the goal of understanding with the press than the press is moving toward the clergy and comprehension of its problems.

One of the best devices available to bring about greater co-operation is the adoption by the church of a specific set of policies toward the general newspaper and magazine and in the preparation of news and other information about the church. Formation of a policy is not difficult, for it follows naturally from the work of a church public relations committee or a subcommittee of that body dealing with church publicity.

Suggested policies

A dozen suggested policies such as these might be followed by the responsible person or committee in a local church, a denominational headquarters, or some other church area:

1. Do not try to keep secrets from the press as a matter of general policy. If some reporter turns out to be untrustworthy and cannot keep confidences, there must be caution in dealing with him, of course, but do not penalize all other reporters for the infractions of one.

2. Help the press to obtain the stories it seeks about the church. These genuinely should be about the church and its official personnel, however, and not private information about members of the institution or denomination. Newspapers sometimes will try to use the church records as a source of news that they have not been able to get by other

and less dubious means. Any story which is truthful and has occurred and deals with the church belongs in the press, for the church is supported by the public and is a factor in community life. A church that helps the press get only the favorable news will immediately lose the confidence of both public and press.

James O. Supple, while church editor of the Chicago *Sun-Times,* spoke at a pastors' school some years ago at the University of Wisconsin, and told the story of a church in the Chicago area that bought an apartment building to be converted to its own use.

The press release merely identified the purchased property as being at the corners of such-and-such streets. It did not specify which corner. Now this is a very essential bit of information in which the people of all four corners would be much concerned, particularly if it meant that the flats of one of the four buildings would have to be vacated.

So, since the story arrived in the Sunday morning mail and our paper being one at which they work on Sunday for Monday's paper I 'phoned the clergyman who sent out the release.

'Dr. So-and-So,' I said, 'we received your release. Could you tell us for our story for tomorrow's paper on which corner is the building you purchased located?'

'Young man,' he said frostily, 'You should be reading your Bible. I don't do business on the Lord's day and neither should you.'

Mr. Supple had used this to illustrate his general advice that churchmen should be

as co-operative as you can with the press. Don't think that, when they 'phone you, they are out to fleece you or to trap you into a juicy heresy for the front page. Remember often that the person 'phoning you may be very ignorant of church terminology and do be patient. Also remember that the press has particular technical problems that cause it to 'phone you over things which seem to you either frivolous or irrelevant.

3. Be willing to compile facts and figures when reasonable requests are made. Not all copy about churches need be straight or spot news. Features are extremely useful in

advancing the purposes of a church. (See Chapter XIV.) Reporters who do not understand the structure of the particular church organization need help on the point and naturally are dependent upon the church personnel for research. The press should be satisfied to wait, if necessary, for this information and the church willing to provide it. Such a task may be irksome when it breaks into a busy schedule but in the long run is worth the trouble since it furthers the public relations program.

4. Do not try to censor copy. Instead, be willing to examine it for factual accuracy if it is submitted for that purpose. If it is presented only for the correction of inaccuracies, do not try to dictate the way the material shall be written or the type of heading it is to carry. That is the journalist's job and he may know better than the churchman how this should be done.

5. Do not try flattery or inducement for favors of one sort or another. In the business world the press is given cocktail parties, for example, in an attempt to curry favor. Churches sometimes send gifts to editors at Christmas time. If the news it provides is not intrinsically worth printing, it will do the church little good to use such polite bribery. If a church group or organization competes for space by flattering or bribing church editors, the violator of good practice should be reprimanded through the council of churches, the ministerial association, or the professional association on a national level.

6. Do not become overexcited about errors or omissions of church news in newspapers. Publications may print news of the Sunday services faithfully for months, then through some oversight, mistake, or necessity of the day omit a story. Far too many ministers become upset and berate the editor or reporter. If this accident happens occasionally or if a misspelling occurs, it should not be taken too seriously. The

church, too, makes mistakes in records and in its own journalism, although usually its staff has more time to be painstaking than does a busy newspaper office. A cure for overconcern at this point is the story Bob Casey, the Chicago journalist, tells in his book, *Such Interesting People*. It is about the church page of the old Des Moines *Capital*.

Every Sunday the *Capital* carried a full page of religious notices, paragraphs outlining the Sabbath services for every church in town, and there were many churches. This department was the pet of Colonel Lafe Young, the publisher who made it the personal responsibility of John Ball, the managing editor.

Mr. Ball, Casey goes on to relate, turned the editing and make-up of the page over to "a competent secretary and everybody was satisfied."

But the managing editor long had been skeptical about the reader-interest of this material. He could not persuade the colonel to cut it. Then, one Friday—which was make-up day for the church directory—the secretary was sick.

"An office boy with a long record for intelligent service took over the job and finished it quickly and without complaint," Mr. Casey writes. The managing editor was so busy he was not bothered with proofs or copy and did not see the page until Sunday morning.

The church page "looked just about as usual, the same symmetrical array of little paragraphs. But there was a difference . . ."

And then Mr. Casey quotes some of the entries:

'First Baptist Church. Rev. J. M. Pollard is in fine form today and will preach a snappy sermon on Hell.'
'Christian Church. Rev. George J. Hadley will lead the choir in singing "Everybody's Doin' It." Irene McDowell, Soloist, will yodel assisted by the eight bounding Bensons. Come and bring your lunch.'
Every paragraph had been tinged by the office boy's imagination. And there was nothing anybody could do about it . . . nothing but sit and wait for the lightning to strike. But there wasn't any light-

ning . . . No irate church-goer raised his voice. No outraged parson demanded retraction. It appeared that the page was one of those things that everybody thinks are read by everybody else.

On Thursday, Mr. Ball laid his report on the matter before Colonel Young who hadn't known that anything was amiss. The directory page was missing from the next Sunday edition for the first time in decades, and the city editor got seven more columns of space. Nobody in Des Moines knew the difference.[3]

7. Do not measure and compare space allotted to various churches or groups with the intention of registering complaints about the supposedly more favorable treatment offered the Roman Catholics or the Jews or the Congregationalists. Be sure that what the church is doing is newsworthy. If a church produces many potential news and feature stories that are ignored in favor of trivialities by apparently favored denominations, the matter might be taken up with the church bodies of the community, but never by one church directly with the newspaper.

8. Stay away from the newspaper office and the editor's quarters. Mail in copy if a reporter's weekly call is insufficient. Telephone in late material. But do not try to bring personal pressure to bear on editors and reporters. It is effective, no doubt about it, for the time being. But it is harmful in general and in the long run is resented in the newsroom. The church publicity committee should follow this policy strictly and request individual publicity chairmen of organizations to do likewise.

9. If there is a publicity plan whereby most of the copy for the press is prepared in the church building and there is more than one newspaper in the community, try to give each a differently phrased story, even if it is on the same event. Also try for variety with the photographs. Avoid playing favorites. Competing newspapers are particularly sensitive

---

[3] Robert J. Casey, *Such Interesting People* (Indianapolis: Bobbs-Merrill, 1943) pp. 37-39.

on this point. Give each an exclusive angle. Magazines are not so concerned, for they do not overlap or compete in readership so obviously and vigorously.

10. As much as possible concentrate the preparation of material in one office or person. This one man or woman should be the spokesman for the church or whichever religious institution is in question, and should be the individual to whom the press turns confidently for help. If he knows something about press and radio and has sound judgment, many of the problems ordinarily encountered in relations with communications agencies will be overcome easily if they develop at all.

11. Establish deadlines on news within the church or church organization, so that the press schedule will be met with certainty. Inform all publicity chairmen of these deadlines; if possible, give them guidance and written instructions on deadlines as well as on such matters as copy preparation and style.

12. Ask the newspaper church editor or the magazine editor for instructions on the recommended way to prepare material so that it is usable with the least editing. When a journalistic deskman finds a well-written news or feature story in the mail, in such form that it needs little more than a headline or a title, he obviously gives it preferential treatment over one that is badly-written, ill-spaced, misspelled, and generally unprofessional, for the latter causes him more work. He will print something about the news contained in the unprofessionally prepared story, but he will resent the added labor and give the story less space.

A working plan

Among the churches that have given attention to assisting their organization publicity chairmen and to putting in their hands helpful material about their responsibilities is the

First Methodist Church of Evanston, Illinois. Its program has been mentioned briefly earlier in this book and has been referred to also in volumes by Stewart Harrel and John Fortson as well as in articles in *Church Management* magazine and *Church Business*. Soon after its appointment, the church publicity committee included in its plan a single sheet of guidance for the press chairmen of organizations. Later this was expanded into a brief manual. (See Appendix I.) Every new press chairman now receives a copy, is asked to attend a meeting or two to discuss and explain it as well as the general program of publicity, and is provided with writing materials for his work. As a result, this church is treated by the Chicago, Evanston, and other publications as one that is co-operative and professional in its interpretation of itself, and it has no complaint about the lack of attention it receives from the press.

Considerable time elapsed before all of the organizations willingly channeled their news through the church office. They found it difficult to resist going to the newspaper offices to bring special pressure or to use inside tracks, such as friends on the staffs. But when it was demonstrated that such special treatment can be gained only at the expense of other groups in the church the practice was virtually halted. Some press chairmen still cannot or will not write their copy as well as it should be written, and some of it must be revamped or retyped in the office, but the majority comply with the plan. It is a working system, in use for more than twenty years, and shows what a church can do by using lay help of a professional nature and by considering interpretation important enough for regular time from staff members.

Large church organizations

Similar systems can be set up, in principle, for the benefit of larger church units. General policies and procedures need be little different, as the plan of the Wisconsin Conference described in an earlier chapter indicates. The materials may be different, but the philosophy and attitudes should not be. Indifference to proper procedures or lack of knowledge of what is needed accounts for the inadequate publicizing of large international church meetings as well as gatherings of members of the men's club of any local church.

A case in point was a state preachers' conference. At the banquet table were leaflets describing this large association of pastors, a group with 500 members. On the back page was a list of chairmen of committees and departments. Vacation schools, Christian education, field organization, and seventeen other activities were being led by committees. But there was none for publicity, publications, or public relations.

The church editor of a daily published in the city which was host to the meeting was not too sure, when he arrived in the hotel, where he was to sit at the banquet. Apparently, he said to friends, no provision had been made for him. None whatever had been made for press and radio.

That church editor, however, had been allotted considerable space by his supervising editor for the coverage of the conference. Stories each day were on an inside page, to be sure, but still it *was* space. He was asked at table if he had received any advance copies of the speeches being given during the sessions. "Two or three," he said. Several ministers at the table with him, however, questioned him more closely and learned that the committee making arrangements for the conference had either not tried or not been successful in obtaining such preparatory material.

Henry Luce, the magazine publisher, was the speaker of the evening. When he finished, the church editor of another daily approached the speakers' table. He had just arrived, having several other dinner speakers to cover at one time. He asked Mr. Luce if he could have the copy of the talk he had used; it was neatly assembled in a ring binder. Refusing, the publisher reached down to the table. He picked up a prepared release on his speech, an abstract of it, and handed it to the chairman.

"My office sent you a batch of these," he said. "Didn't you get them to give out to the press?"

The conference official made no reply but handed the copy to the reporter.

Several sidelights on this conference's publicity were significant.

An officer of the group lamented to the banqueters that one of the newspapers the day before had run a large headline on its story of the conference which put the church in what he considered "a bad light." A random remark of a speaker, uttered at a question period, had been emphasized. While the handling was not perfect, the flaw was all the conference officer commented upon.

Another officer announced that a new committee just had been formed: one on public relations. He mentioned this on the closing night of the three-day session. With a little air of having attained journalistic eminence, he said that the newly appointed chairman of the committee had telegraphed from a city across the state that he (the chairman) would like him (the officer) to "cover" the speech of that night for publicity purposes. This, it seemed to him, was being right on the job.

The incidents described here were the extent of the co-operation with the press.

What the church can do to avoid such *faux pas*, to improve its relationship with the press is a major subject of this book. Improvement depends chiefly upon proper allocation of money, training of personnel, planning, understanding of press and radio as media of communication, and the exercise of bold imagination.

Let someone who day after day works with churchmen explain the church's duty from her vantage point. Miss Jo-Ann Price, church editor of the Milwaukee *Journal* and Milwaukee correspondent of Religious News Service, writing in the Milwaukee *Lutheran,* said:

The increasingly significant actions of religious organizations in this post-World War II era make it essential that religious news be covered carefully, correctly, and objectively by the press. Pastors and laymen alike, alerted to the problem, can share in this 'home mission' field.

This does not mean the press can be 'used' for 'free publicity' by any church or number of churches. Secular newspaper editors of our American free press are under no obligation to promote any cause or institution deliberately in their news columns. They want accurate reporting of the facts and the major events of church activities. They want the dirt and the gold.

They judge a story on religion on its news value. This is equally true for stories about politics, crime, labor, finance, or medicine. Will the public—the man on the streetcar—read it?

The man on the streetcar, unless he is a member, probably doesn't give a hang about the ladies' aid of Such and Such Lutheran church. But if the pastor of the church has said something significant about human rights, displaced persons, or some other current event, he might read it. But it must be unusual.

Pastors and laymen need to become 'community minded' when they think of possible news for the secular press. And they need to understand that the reporting of church events, on the modern American scene, is not just the listing of the usual choir concerts held in the usual way and relegated to the Saturday church page or underneath the obituary column. Important as these ordinary events may be to the congregation, they have very little reading value for the general community. The newspaper seeks the 'new angle' . . . the unusual event . . . the human interest yarn. The newspaper serves the public, not an individual church congregation.

If all the ministers have to report about their churches are fellowship breakfasts—in a day when atomic experts are wondering how civilization will be destroyed by their bombs—the churches present a pretty sad picture in the secular press. The terrible part about it is that the churches *are* doing significant work in their communities.

They are making news. The problem for ministers and laymen alike is to make sure the newspapers know about these activities.[4]

What the press can do to improve its relationships with the church, from its side, was well expressed by Henry Martin, editor-in-chief of Press Association, a domestic news gathering agency in England and an affiliate of Reuters. Mr. Martin addressed the Provincial Newspapers Editors of Great Britain:

> Religion is not the only subject from which journalists seek to escape because they do not understand it or want to try to . . . Religion, without theological dry bones, can be related to life and made an interesting topic, and there is a special opportunity for journalism to harness it to local life in its many manifestations and activities . . . .
>
> Journalism can discuss the religious aspects of public affairs and the public aspect of religious affairs both at home and abroad. Journalism can show that religion is not a bolt-hole or side-show, but that Christianity is a fighting faith from which this nation has derived its most precious elements, and that it can once again be woven into not only the fabric of personal living, but into a whole philosophy of progress where the future can be ensured as well as the present saved.[5]

Denominations that refuse to permit religion to speak to all the problems of the day and insist that religion deal only with personal conduct never will gain the respect of the secular press and radio. For the communications media must themselves deal with all of life. If religion is a way of life it must examine all of man's interests and activities no less vigorously than the press and radio themselves attempt to do.

---

[4] Jo-Ann Price, "What Makes Church News Newsworthy?" in the *Milwaukee Lutheran* (March, 1949).

[5] Henry Martin, "The Place of Religion in the Post-War Press" in *Editor & Publisher* (June 17, 1944).

CHAPTER V

Church Journalism on the Air

If churchmen still must be educated and persuaded to wider use of the printing press in interpreting the church to the public, it is not difficult to understand why they are technically unfamiliar, by and large, with radio, television, and motion picture. For these comparatively new media of communication are more complex and expensive to understand and use than is the press. Consequently they are less frequently employed by the church.

Although the majority of churchmen have not availed themselves of such tools, certain leaders have seized them enthusiastically. Large denominations as well as not a few of the smaller have committees which study and at times use radio. In some instances motion pictures are joined with radio under an audio-visual aids committee and are used both locally and nationally. Television so far has remained at the service of overhead groups and relatively few local churches have been able to use it, chiefly because it is the youngest of the three media mentioned here and is just beginning to cover the nation with networks, as do the others. All three media are used through local church associations, particularly the movie and the radio.

So essentially democratic a group as are the churchmen of the United States would not embark upon the use of radio and its associated media without debate. Whereas the motion picture stirred controversy as soon as it became popular (its opponents declaring—as the remnants of the opposition do still—that it was part of the sinful theatrical life and too worldly an influence upon those persons who went into the movie houses), the radio and television are challenged more because they emphasize trivialities, are over-commercialized, and otherwise misuse an astounding inventiveness.

This book examines the church use of the new media from the journalistic viewpoint only. A broader study of one phase has been made by Parker, Inman, and Snyder in *Religious Radio*. Other volumes have treated the use of the motion picture in the church. Television is too new to have acquired such literature to any such degree. But radio and television journalism exists within the framework of the total use of these media. It is to be found in news broadcasts and telecasts that include religious and church events. Sermons, religious speeches on the air, church plays on the video screen, and services transmitted by both radio and television also are a form of religious interpretation but are beyond the scope of such a book as this.

The philosophical debate

Generalizations about church use of radio and television appear constantly in the church press and occasionally in the secular press.

The Christian Century reported, late in 1948, upon "the world's first religious television workshop" held that year at Station WRGB in Schenectady, New York, at which "14 national leaders in Protestant radio who attended emphasized the need of entering the television field at once . . . ."

Dr. Reinhold Niebuhr, the Union Theological Seminary teacher, author, lecturer, and theologian, a month later was reported by the New York *Herald Tribune* as not only having attacked the "vulgarization" of the nation's cultural standards that, he predicted, would spread into thousands of American homes via television sets, but he also was quoted as commenting on religious television specifically thus:

A televised service takes on the aspect of a spectacle, with the result that something obtrudes between the congregation and the spirit of the service. The home audience, likewise, does not get any real benefit from the telecast . . . .

To which the Confraternity of Christian Doctrine indirectly added its agreement early in 1949 when it issued the first major revision of a Roman Catholic catechism in the United States. This religious textbook declared that a person must be bodily present at the place where mass is celebrated to fulfill his obligations to the church.

On the other hand, Charles C. Barry, writing in the *Atlantic Monthly* about the same time, declared that:

The video camera has entered the houses of worship of all the principal faiths. It has brought instruction and ritual to the television audience. It seems inevitable that television will find a place as a most useful handmaiden of religion. It may indeed bring solace, comfort, and inspiration not alone to the sick and old but to vast numbers to whom religion is either a new or a forgotten experience.

Mr. Barry did go on to share Dr. Niebuhr's doubts, however, by adding:

Yet there is always danger that may intrude in the relationship between the worshiper and his church, and I therefore think that its true place in American religion will not soon be clearly defined.[1]

Churchmen as well as television industry leaders have not been sure how this new medium can best be used or whether the best ways will be feasible when discovered. They have been unable to learn from the radio industry all that is needed to settle philosophical doubts, nor have they learned at least what not to do. Inseparable factors inherent

---

[1] Charles C. Barry, "Tyrants of Television" in *Atlantic Monthly* (April, 1949) p. 43.

in radio and television are their need to earn a profit or cease operation as independent business ventures. Also hampering both sides are the discussion over whether television will replace radio, the churchman's understandable lack of technical training, the need for superior talent, and the expense. Yet churchmen do not wish to feel that they are missing an opportunity, for the possibilities on the journalistic level alone are great.

A. Gordon Nasby concluded an article on "Television in the Church" in a leading religious weekly by saying about television what had been said years before about radio.

Hitler did his job in Germany in the space of a few years because he had modern techniques and methods of communication at his disposal. Today, with television at hand, the time in which men's minds can be molded has been frightfully shortened. This is our age. Television is already a part of it. The church ought not to come too late with too little.[2]

In view of the relatively few religious radio programs and the small direct use made by the church of radio transmission, the church may be considered to be too late with too little not only for the new medium but also for the old, whose first news broadcast occurred in 1910. Yet the greatest possible use must be attempted. An examination of some journalistic means therefore may be worth making.

Organized efforts

While churchmen, through organization, may not have made the most of radio and television, they have by no means been indifferent. They have made journalistic use of the media.

The most ambitious groups have been the Joint Religious Radio Committee, the National Religious Broadcasters, and

---

[2] A. Gordon Nasby, "Television and the Church" in *Christian Century* (February 2, 1949) p. 143.

the Religious Radio Association. In 1949, the Protestant Radio Commission was organized, with the Rev. Everett C. Parker, for the previous five years director of the Joint Committee, as director of program and production. Television is joined with radio under such group study and action. The viewpoint of the Rev. Mr. Parker's organization, which encompasses sixteen denominations, was expressed in an interview with him:

> Only some mass medium of communications can reach the more than 50 per cent of the American people who do not attend church. Local radio stations are the critical field for religious broadcasting . . . and the new commission expects to aid city church councils and other local religious groups . . . .
> Television offers religion a chance to start from scratch in a new field, in which 'we must divorce ourselves from all preconceived ideas of conventional methods of presentation of a religious message and experiment with new program formats.'

Mr. Parker told *Broadcasting* that in general he disapproved of either radio or television programs originating from church. Such time, he said, and the energy involved could better be put to use in less static, more dramatic presentations.[3]

Troy and Schenectady, New York, have become strong regional centers for religious radio and television journalism, with co-operation from the General Electric Company, which has big industrial developments in those and near-by New York state cities.

"Thru the Eyes of Religion," the first religious television news program, was started in spring, 1949, over WRGB, Schenectady, the result of co-operation between the General Electric station, Religious News Service, and the Tri-City Protestant Radio Commission. The commission is comprised of the Federation of Churches of Christ of Albany and

[3] "Parker in Radio Post; to Stress Medium." *Broadcasting* (January 10, 1949).

Promoting greater understanding of different faiths: Cantor Robert Segal of the Inwood (New York) School of Observation and Practice leads a traditional Yiddish hymn during a classroom demonstration on Columbia's television program, "Lamp Unto My Feet."

Vicinity, the Schenectady County Council of Churches, and the Troy Area Council of Churches.

Religious News Service, alone, has been a dependable source of religious news for radio for years. "The Religious News Reporter," a fifteen-minute program, is distributed weekly by this news agency, which was established in 1934 by the National Conference of Christians and Jews. About 130 stations in the United States broadcast the material, which is prepared for radio and not press use.

In various cities individual churches, councils of churches, or radio stations themselves sponsor the broadcast of religious news, usually weekly. Typical was a fifteen-minute Saturday evening program of the Rev. Laurence Hosie, secretary of the Syracuse, New York, Council of Churches. When reporting national and international religious news, Mr. Hosie prepared his script principally from "The Religious News Reporter" copy and the press releases of Ecumenical Press Service. These he supplemented with local information about the church.

Using the media

The church has two principal uses for radio and television. One is to prepare or have prepared original program materials to be broadcast and telecast. Another is to use the results of broadcasting and televising in the work of the institution.

Any church can send news of itself to the nearest radio and television stations. Managers do not expect churchmen to write the copy specifically for dissemination over the air although they appreciate all soundly professional efforts in that direction. Proper preparation at least for radio is within the possibilities of almost any church, since copy is news scripts and not radio dramatizations.

Churches and church organizations can co-operate at

the elementary level of allowing their activities to be reported directly. Mortgage burnings, ground breakings, church picnics, and similar events are conventional subjects.

The second type of radio and television use comes in organizing listening parties to see or hear specific programs of interest to religious people or to integrate suitable secular programs with church work.

In either direct or indirect use, churchmen must recall that both the radio and the television industries are cautious about the mixture of religion with either medium for purposes of religious warfare. The National Association of Broadcasters includes a paragraph in its code declaring that radio "may not be used to convey attacks upon another's race or religion," and that radio should have as its purpose, when dealing with religion, "to promote the spiritual harmony and understanding of mankind and to administer broadly to the varied religious needs of the community." The Institute for Education by Radio has expanded this statement. The National Broadcasting Company and other radio networks also have set forth their policies on religion and radio. All these agencies fear inept and offensive handling.

After the warnings have been heeded, however, ambitious churchmen can study numerous technically effective radio and television program examples, journalistic and otherwise. Included are "The Church of the Air," "The Hour of Faith," "National Vespers," "National Radio Pulpit," "The Program of Free Religion," "The Upper Room Radio Parish," and the standard news programs. Less orthodox, technically excellent, but financially unsuccessful was the Protestant Episcopal Church's venture, "Great Scenes from Great Plays."

Less readily available to the church or church organization are opportunities for examining the possibilities of television religious news broadcasts. The first of these set a technical pace equalled by few secular news programs on video, which commonly show a newscaster reading from a script or teletyped news stories before the camera. The Rev. Harold J. Quigley, chairman of the radio committee of the Troy (New York) Council of Churches, described this pioneering effort for *The Church and Radio,* the newsletter of the Protestant Radio Commission.

The Rev. Mr. Quigley, minister of the Ninth Presbyterian Church, and the Rev. Richard Cummings of the First Baptist Church, both of Troy, were commentators. Both had gained their experience with the air waves as broadcasters of "Religion Views the News" over WTRY, a radio station.

The program opens with a one-minute and twenty-second movie of the First Baptist Church of Troy, showing the high tower, people going into the church, and the traffic going by. The captions, the name of the program, the commentators, the photos by Religious News Service, "News of Interest to Protestants, Catholics, and Jews," are shown successively, on a church bulletin board.

On the June tenth program, the station supplied a large map of Europe, showing the division of the "Iron Curtain." Mr. Cummings discussed for two minutes the story of the churches in the Soviet orbit. Pictures of Roman Catholic Archbishop Joseph Beran of Prague, Czechoslovakia, and Bishop Otto Dibelius of the Evangelical Church in Germany (EKID), were included. Both have severely criticized the Communist regime.

Featured next was a story on the Quakers' celebrating a year's anniversary of trying to bring about friendly relations between the United States and Russia. A picture of the Quakers receiving the Nobel prize in 1947 was used with the commentary.

Next followed a story on the investigation of the Atomic
Energy Commission. Commentary ran as follows:

A new term is being used widely these days to describe the low
punches being thrown in the fight for power in Washington, D. C.
It is 'character assassination.' Abraham Lincoln was assassinated by
a gun. The new device is the razor sharp word that cuts the heart
of the responsible public servant. Forrestal was a recent victim. The
new target is David Lilienthal.

To lighten up the program at this point, a picture was
introduced showing people going to church in overalls.
The pastor in Meridian, Mississippi, had said, "We don't
want people to stay away from church for the lack of new
clothes."

Since Mr. Cummings had attended the Northern Baptist
Convention in San Francisco the week before, Mr. Quigley
interviewed him regarding highlights of the meeting. The
proposed merger of the Baptists and the Disciples of Christ
was referred to as a "flirtation," and the five-year plan to
bring it to a successful conclusion as a "full-blown courtship."

A "woman's page" told of the appointments of women to
high positions in the church. It was illustrated with pictures
of the ordination of Mrs. Victoria Booth Demarest as a
minister of the Congregational Christian Churches, and of
Mrs. Colewell, newly elected president of the Northern
Baptist Convention. Mrs. Demarest is the granddaughter
of General William Booth, founder of the Salvation Army.
The pay-off line was:

The Moslems used to say that the women will make heaven on
the coattails of their husbands. News this week gives the lie to that
saying.

The problem of the internationalization of Jerusalem,
next treated, was illustrated by pictures showing the damage
to some of the shrines from the recent conflict, and a map
indicating the divisions of the city.

To illustrate the problem of "separation of church and state," a remarkable picture was shown of a nun, Sister Mary Josella, teaching school in Raleigh, North Dakota, but wearing ordinary clothing in compliance with state legislation outlawing the wearing of a religious garb by a public-school teacher.

The story of Dr. Ralph Bunche, former special representative of the United Nations in the Palestine dispute, turning down a job of undersecretary of state because of Jim Crow policies in the nation's capital, was illustrated by a picture of Dr. Bunche in a happier mood, receiving a medal as "father of the year."

A regular feature of the program is "pictures that tell their own story." A typical story follows:

Here is a Protestant church service in an unusual place. You could never guess this location. It is the plaza of the Imperial Palace in Tokyo, Japan. Imagine an Easter service in the palace grounds of the Emperor of Japan.

And another:

This is a new kind of paint shop. And a new kind of sign painter. Harrison Mayes is a coal miner in Kentucky, but by avocation, he is a preacher. He does his preaching, however, by brightly painted signs which he has posted in all parts of the United States, and many foreign countries. There's more than one way to preach your religion.

Seen every two weeks, the program required two full days of work (besides the initial planning), and an afternoon, the day of production, for camera rehearsal and preparations at the studio. Five scripts were required for production personnel.

The two commentator-clergymen knew that they had a big job ahead of them. Comparing their experiences in video and radio, they had this to say:

The medium of television requires more creative and technical preparation, greater financial expenditure, and extended hours for planning, writing, and production . . . .

Policy and procedure

Any religious leader or institution undertaking to use radio and television will find it wise to follow a particular procedure. It includes the basic rule of co-operating with laymen in the radio and television industries rather than attempting to go ahead without preliminary background and professional counsel. These laymen are helpful, not only because they wish to be useful to the church, but also because they know that their industry, in the long run, benefits from properly directed new users. Another step, before taking action, is to consult with the local or participating stations or the network headquarters about the religious policies they follow. A third step is to follow the policy of not approaching either industry until the church group can present specific plans. And a fourth is to be willing to change such plans reasonably if doing so obtains co-operation. A further part of the procedure is to study the facilities and offerings in the area which the church chooses to serve.

How many other churches or councils are broadcasting? What do they send out over the air? How much time do they use? When are they scheduled? Which type of programs have near-by groups found most popular? Why are certain inadequate types of programs being omitted? What does the church about to broadcast have to offer in the way of something new or better if programs are already sponsored by other churches? Which radio stations are AM, which FM, which use both types of transmitting equipment, and which are active in both radio and television transmission?

Consideration of policies should include that which the church itself will follow, not only the policy on religious news broadcasts of a station or network. How the church handles its broadcasts is of major importance. As put in the words of the National Broadcasting Company's statement, the national networks of the country "will serve only the central or national agencies of great religious faiths" and allot their religious broadcasting time to the National Council of Churches, National Council for Catholic Action, and the National Jewish Council. Great resentment of this policy is felt among other Protestant groups, such as Moody Bible Institute. They consider the National Council to be modernist. They declare that the organization they criticize should not be given a monopoly. Moody and other minority groups have countered by establishing their own stations and supporting broadcasts like Charles E. Fuller's "Old Fashioned Revival Hour" as being more in accord with their views.

The alleged monoply came about because early in radio's history there was argument over the use of religious time on the air, some of the first religious programs at times offended good taste, and others were virtually rackets. To keep peace the networks have set up a careful system of rotating attention to denominations. Some insist upon planning the entire religious program themselves; others allow church groups to prepare their own scripts.

Religious news broadcasts, when in the hands of one person representing naturally only one denomination, should be carefully planned lest they reflect an unintentional bias. A newscaster's associations incline him to bias. This is an example of the need for care about internal policy.

It is not that stations merely fear sending out vituperative sermons affronting other creeds. They oppose duplicating programs, overly sentimental broadcasts, or appeal to credulity, superstition, and fear.

If a church can pay for broadcasts or telecasts in communities where stations sell time for religious purposes, it must be careful not to arouse unfavorable reaction among its fellow-church groups. Bad public relations result from high expenditures on radio and television more than from heavy spending for printed matter, for only so many hours a day are available for broadcasts and a well-to-do church or denomination can easily monopolize this time if it wishes to do so. Other groups have been known to complain to stations with the result that in some cities no time at all is sold to churches.

Religious institutions should ponder carefully the question whether they should use radio and television at all if doing so is exceedingly expensive. If other churches are broadcasting and the ensuing competition would cut down the total response, that should be weighed. If, on the other hand, religious broadcasting is successful and popular in an area, the church making the decision to participate or not would do well to take advantage of that popularity, if there is reason to think more listening or video watching would result. If, also, no other religious body is using radio or television, an institution that does so gets in on the ground floor, so to speak. Again, if the aim is to exploit a single church rather than convey knowledge of all churches through the news, the benefits of this type of radio use will be limited.

Radio and television broadcasting is still so expensive, if more than an occasional or short regular program is desired, that an individual church perhaps might better spend its promotion and publicity money for printing or for improved equipment for its office or auditorium. Radio and television are powerful forces of communication, but their power is greatest when most needed and cannot be duplicated by less costly media. As with the use of the printing press, however, money effectively spent on all media may provide a sounder interpretation of the church than concentration of funds in any one.

Let us assume, however, that after investigation of the

situation a church decides it will be able to use radio. It will be in a position to raise the money to pay for its broadcasts or a local station is willing to allot some of its sustaining time to this church's program. What shall be broadcast in the way of journalistic material? How shall the time be planned? Churches need not, of course, confine the time they are allotted or buy to any one type of program, even journalistic. John L. Fortson, public relations director for the Young Men's Christian Association for a number of years, suggests in his book, *How to Make Friends for Your Church*, that good programs are those that are competently produced at no cost to the station, that attract a sizable group of listeners, that create good will for the station, that contribute to the public interest, and do not set a bad precedent.

Preparation and planning are needed for all the many possible types of broadcasts, including religious news programs. Common, among the journalistic, are the direct reporting programs of radio, which send out on the air the Sunday morning or evening sermon, or the sermon plus parts of the service, or the entire service. Special ceremonies in the church school, addresses by speakers at church functions, and music programs at church festival seasons are all possibilities. Of an indirect type are dramatized Sunday school lessons, Bible stories either dramatized or told, and broadcasts of the reading of significant religious documents. These may very well be individual programs or they may be used as parts of a series.

Religious programs, except for the carefully selected straight news, are not generally considered of a high order. Radio executives complain of poor workmanship in script writing, disregard for deadlines, poor singing, playing, and acting talent among musicians and stage people, lack of rehearsals, indifference to timing. Religious institutions are handicapped in their use of radio by small staffs and volunteer personnel. They therefore should not undertake elaborate programs if they will be unable to maintain them. Occasional direct reporting or regular, well-sifted news programs accomplish more than more pretentious but clumsy dramatic offerings.

A moderate-sized church in a small city, unless it be near a college with a department of speech and a school of music or has some other access to unusual talent sources, will do best to plan simple use of the fifteen minutes or half-hour of time available weekly. A mixture of interviews, panel discussions, speeches, and one or two dramatizations is good seasonal fare. Infrequently the program might be musical. Music required by other types of programs, if labor conditions locally permit, can be provided by transcriptions.

Part of planning a religious radio program is developing an audience. Whoever is responsible for the printed publicity of the church should take responsibility for letting the whole constituency know of the forthcoming series or individual broadcast. Stories about it should be submitted for publication in the local press. Newspapers sometimes do not wish to publicize radio programs; a number still refuse even to print a radio log, declaring that such listings are free advertising space. But this view is aimed chiefly against commercial programs, because so much advertising now is done over the air, and radio and television are competitors with newspapers and magazines for advertising appropriations. The attitude may not be extended to a non-profit institution like the church. The parish paper, the bulletin, pulpit announcements, posters, and even spot radio announcements, between other programs if permitted, will help call attention to the religious broadcast, whatever its nature.

Television at work

Like other citizens, churchmen can never be sure whether a new consumer industry will thrive or fail. Their interest is deep in one, like television, that affects their institution. They wonder if it will continue to do so and to what extent, or if it will disappear as a fad. In the early 1950's television was in a position of being a potentially large industry beset with technical and financial problems. Some churches availed themselves of it more promptly than others. Only the most unprogressive looked with boredom upon this striking new medium which might serve religion.

They had reason to think seriously about television when they could read statements like that of Dr. Allen B. DuMont, president of the video laboratories bearing his name. In 1948 he predicted that by 1953 television would be among the first ten industries in size in America. He declared that when television networks were available a broadcaster could enter video at a cost "well under $50,000."

Such faith in the growth of television is based in the knowledge of the rapid development of electronics, which, as Alan Barth pointed out in *The Nation* in 1944, went so rapidly during the war years as to equal a decade's normal progress.

Technical problems encountered by television early in its life as a new communication medium included several that for some time to come are likely to keep it from serving religious institutions in any elaborate, direct manner. These are the cost of programming and the cost of maintaining separate stations.

But religious television programs are beyond the experimental stage. As early as 1945 church school students at the First Methodist Church of Evanston, Illinois, took part in a Chicago video program sponsored by the International Council of Religious Education. Since then numerous religious groups have used television much as they use radio: by installing sets as entertainment or educational devices and by providing copy or talent. Operation by religious bodies of many stations may not come for some time. Use of sets in religious work is becoming common. In Chicago, for example, Roman Catholic youth organizations installed monitors as a means of keeping youngsters out of taverns, which in 1947 and 1948 were the principal users of receiving sets. Several varieties of religious activities were being televised during 1951: special events, such as large meetings or ceremonies, and even regular activities. Religious plays or motion pictures occasionally were shown on the television screen. Television news programs included bits of news of religion.

The Protestant Radio Commission alone, in 1950, its first year of production, produced 158 network and 32 local television programs. It also arranged for 51 network television programs.

Typical of the use of video by churches are these examples, reported by the Protestant Radio Commission, Religious News Service, and other sources:

Confirmation services from Chicago Temple Isaiah Israel were carried by the NBC-TV network, with twenty-four teen-age children participating in the service commemorating Shabuoth.

Similarly, Station WRGB of Schenectady, New York, televised a dedication service of the Lord's Acre Plan. Samples of the seed, the tools, and the ground were placed before the altar. Five boys who started a project which stimulated interest in their town of Pittstown, New York, participated.

Also in the eastern portion of the country was the launching of one of the Salvation Army's annual maintenance appeals by television. Rockefeller Center, New York City, was the scene of the broadcast. New York's police commissioner, a Salvation Army executive, a radio-television executive, and a journalist spoke at the meeting, which was televised over WJZ-TV. Ray Vir Den, the general campaign chairman, summed up the advantages of such handling by pointing out that:

> For the first time the general public will be able to 'attend' the opening meeting of the campaign to see the volunteers who are helping and to learn more intimately, through being able to see, something about the organization and the people in it.

Genuinely interdenominational was the program, "Lantern Unto My Feet," one on religious instruction presented on Sundays in the fall of 1948 over the Columbia Broadcasting System. Four New York religious groups sponsored this unusual TV program: Riverside Church, Fifth Avenue Presbyterian Church, the Jewish Theological Seminary, and the Corpus Christi Parochial School. Activities of three faiths were demonstrated.

On the "Morning Chapel" program, presented in the same city through the DuMont station, WABD, five mornings a week, Dr. Arthur J. S. Rosenbaum, director of interfaith activities for the American Jewish Committee, displayed a sacred scroll containing the Five Books of Moses. This document was seen for the first time on television.

When three Roman Catholic priests were elevated to the episcopacy in a 1949 ceremony from Holy Name Cathedral, Chicago, the consecration by Cardinal Stritch, archbishop of Chicago, was carried by NBC television. Receiving sets were put up in each of the 450 schools of the Chicago archdiocese. Pupils and parents witnessed the ceremony. Also on NBC television later that year was the Friendly Sons of St. Patrick dinner from New York City.

Like the motion picture, television makes both a visual and a sound appeal and therefore has double power to influence the public. It may bring religious education into the home if the fear of controversy that besets both press and radio does not throttle it. Television probably will go the way of the motion picture, which likewise combines sight and sound, but except through the news reel and the documentary film has set itself mainly to entertain.

Video differs from the film in one respect, however. It enters the home, which for the bulk of the population movies do not. Repeated studies reveal that motion picture houses are suffering in attendance and that radio listening is decreasing because of the competition from television. Religious workers can welcome the tendency for people to stay at home to stare at a television screen if what they see on the screen does not counteract religion. One way for churchmen to assure the quality of television broadcasting is to engage in it.

Motion pictures and religion

Members of the women's group of a small city church showed only moderate interest in their October meeting, when a speaker of recognized ability was scheduled.

But when two twenty-minute films were announced for the November session, attendance increased by 25 per cent. Weather conditions were the same for both meetings. Such a reaction is in line with the experience of other church groups, which has been that the showing of films can increase attendance at activities.

In a nation of eighty million movie-goers a week it may be only natural for the church public to respond like any other. The visual appeal is strong. Watching pictures, still or moving, is as effortless an occupation as can be designed for humans, short of the act of sleeping. Television's popularity can also thus be explained.

Unlike sleeping, however, seeing movies can have a

significant religious and educational value. Few media of
communication are as suggestive and powerful as interpreters of the church, yet far less use of the movie is made
than of the printing press. But the use is growing. It has
been commonplace in large churches and among overhead
church groups for years.

The reasons for limited use are not difficult to discover.
The church must buy a projector, a screen, and other supplies. If its equipment is to survive there must be control of
its use, i.e. organization rules and trained operators. Films
must be obtained and returned safely or bought at prices that
can be met readily only by groups of churches or large congregations. Rooms must be darkened.

The right films, properly shown and publicized, can bring
attention to the work of the church, to its traditions, goals,
and achievements, far more graphically than any other
medium except, possibly, television. The journalistic uses,
it is true, are fewer than those of television and radio.

Typical of the way churches can use the motion picture
for direct interpretation of their work are such schemes as
these:

An official board asked a member of the congregation
who owned a motion picture camera to take a movie of the
highspots of the church's life, the board paying for the supplies used. This film was shown during finance campaigns
and remained of permanent historical interest. Another
church made more common and inexpensive use of films
through one of its lay organizations. The program chairman,
wishing to offer variety in what was otherwise a series of
speeches or dramatizations, telephoned to a state council
of churches' motion picture library nearby and obtained two
short films. These arrived by mail the day before the showing and cost far less than the honorarium for the average
speaker.

Other church bodies have shown films provided at no cost by railways, airlines, educational groups, and industrial firms, to name the more common sources. Usually this type of motion picture has its chief interpretative value for the company or group responsible for its production. Unless it is a religious film it may not help interpret the church; but if it is not a religious film at least it may bring some un-churched citizens into the church building. Attracting crowds, however, has dubious value unless some preparations are made to take advantage of their presence. Film showings, like special use of radio and television, need to be supple-mented with promotion and with follow-up programs.

CHAPTER VI

Religion in the Syndicates

A newspaper editor inclined to add religious syndicated features to his offerings has his choice of fifty different ones, ranging from a daily 800 word column by prominent preachers to a set of what are described as "character building charts." If salesmen fail to mention what is purchasable in the way of religious materials, the editor will find a list of principal ones available in *Editor & Publisher's* annual directory of syndicated features.

Our editor could obtain still others if he knew of the existence of Ecumenical Press Service, issued by the World Council of Churches; *The Survey Bulletin,* issued by the Sunday School Board of the Southern Baptist Convention; the Press Department of the National Catholic Welfare Conference; Fine Art Features, and other, smaller groups, not all of which are included in the common lists.

Compared with what is available on women's interests (125 separate features) or the number of comics or columns (each in the hundreds), the quantity of syndicated religious materials is not great. But at least it is more than what is offered on gardening and health (about 20 each).

Despite their easy availability, comparatively few secular publications buy the religious features that are sold or print those that are free. A principal reason is that editors of secular papers and magazines are not convinced that readers are interested in that copy.

Another avenue

Churchmen, therefore, have here another avenue for interpretation of the institution they represent. Syndicated religious materials used by the secular press are found mainly on the church pages. Denominational papers and magazines print far more but even here such copy could find a warmer welcome.

The church needs to encourage its followers to note the syndicated writings and art work on religion that can be found in the general publications, to ask for more or for higher quality, and to urge religious journalists to make greater use of such materials when possible. Secular church editors need little urging, as a rule. They need evidence of reading and approval of the purchase; they need more white space and a higher quality of syndicated copy. Denominational editors frequently are not journalists at all, are unaware of the material within reach or for the asking, and do not know what the reader desires.

Syndicates, nevertheless, are an established institution in modern journalism. Dr. Frank Luther Mott, leading historian of the American press, records that the first syndicated material was a feature known as the "Journal of Occurrences," made available to newspapers in 1768. The first firm making a busines of syndicating materials was founded in 1883 by Irving Bacheller, the popular Indiana novelist, in the days when he was a Brooklyn journalist.

Religious materials were distributed irregularly in the early days by the commercial syndicates. Dr. Mott reports that a notable feature was the reprinting on May 21, 1887, in the Chicago *Tribune,* of the entire revised version of the New Testament; the controversy about the version made this newsworthy. Such an individual feature as The Ellis Sunday School Lesson, a weekly 800-word manuscript, is older than any general religious syndicate.

A general syndicate, equipped to provide its subscribers with a wide variety of religious materials, is typified by Religious News Service. A specialized group, such as Ecumenical Press Service, provides news only and therefore confines itself to one type of material.

Oldest of the general religious syndicates is the Press Department of the National Catholic Welfare Conference, which was begun soon after World War I. It is intended to serve the Catholic press of the United States; its news dispatches are used in other countries as well, with the credit log: NC.

Editors may obtain from it a news service of about 50,000 words a week. The Press Department reports that this material is collected by radio, cable, telegraph, telephone, and mail throughout the world.

A Catholic Feature Service also exists. It releases about 10,000 words weekly in short features on Catholic aspects of history, family problems, and the like. A typical release:

St. Columba and the Crane
By Dorothy Blount

Historians disagree as to why St. Columba—or Columbcille, which in Gaelic means "Columba of the churches"—went to the island of Iona, off the coast of Scotland. One story is that he was banished from Ireland by St. Molaise for the part he had played in causing the battle of Cooldrevny, between the Neill clan and King Diarmaidt; and that to atone for his fault, he had to win as many men to the faith as had perished in the battle. But worst of all, he was never more to look upon his native land.

In a curragh of wickerwork covered with ox-hide, St. Columba set sail and first landed at Colonsay; but finding that the distant hills of his beloved Erin were still visible, he went on to what is now called Port'a Curriagh—Back of the Wicker Boat. On the island he founded the famous Iona monastery.

St. Columba was kept very busy organizing his monastery and traveling all over the Scottish Highlands, converting the people to Christianity. But he was homesick for Ireland, and here's a story to prove it:

One day a weary crane landed on the shore of Iona, utterly exhausted by its flight against contrary winds across the sea from Ireland. St. Columba welcomed it as a visitor from his home, and calling one of the monks, instructed him to feed and shelter the poor bird. At the end of three days, the Saint sought out the brother and blessed him for his kindness to one of God's wild creatures. Then, going to the seashore, he released the now fully refreshed crane and bade her return to the country she should never have left.   —NC Features

Similarly NC offers a Washington Letter, the text of any important Vatican document, special articles, a Spanish-language Catholic news service, a Catholic News Picture Service, and several background features, such as an Editorial Information Service for editorial writers and a Biographical Service, described as "authentic life sketches of prominent Catholic figures."

Most widely known of religious syndicates is Religious News Service, founded in 1934 by the National Conference of Christians and Jews. It identifies itself as "the only worldwide news agency furnishing spot news of all faiths and denominations to the church press, newspapers, magazines, and radio stations."

Respected by secular journalists, this organization is run generally as is any of the large commercial syndicates. Its headquarters staff includes men and women of various creeds and religious affiliations; it has scores of correspondents throughout the world. Like NC, the RNS office releases not only straight news but also a wide variety of religious materials for publication or radio or television use.

RNS' "Daily News Report," examples of which are cited in later chapters, is the syndicate's basic release and is explained thus: "This service is the only one of its kind, covering principal developments in the Protestant, Catholic, and Jewish faiths and significant happenings of general interest to all religious groups." It includes a legislative service em-

RELIGIOUS REMARKABLES - - - By Scheel

T. M. REG. U. S. PAT. OFF.

A TEAM OF MORMONS WHO COMBINED BASKETBALL PROWESS AND PREACHING SKILL RECENTLY TOURED CZECHOSLOVAKIA. THEY WON 16 OF 17 GAMES. AFTER EACH GAME THEY PREACHED BEFORE LARGE AUDIENCES GATHERED TO WITNESS THE CONTESTS.

REV. KENNETH L. PATTON, OF BOSTON, ONCE "RESIGNED" FROM THE WHITE RACE BECAUSE HE WAS "DISGUSTED" AT RACE DISCRIMINATION.

FATHER STEPHEN BADIN, FIRST PRIEST ORDAINED IN THE UNITED STATES, IS BURIED NEAR NOTRE DAME UNIVERSITY.

Religious News Service. Scheel

bracing bills of interest to church organizations that may have been introduced into state or federal legislatures. This 10,000-word news budget is divided into domestic and foreign materials which may be purchased separately.

"This Week in Religion," a column of religious news interpretation, is used by metropolitan dailies. "The Religious News Reporter" is the fifteen-minute weekly radio program referred to in the preceding chapter; it is illustrated in the chapters on journalistic techniques. Religious news of the world is summarized in it. Special articles, religious pictures, a religious cartoon, a question and answer feature, an inspirational editorial, and some shorter features also are syndicated. The "Religion Question Box" feature is illustrated below:

RELIGION QUESTION BOX

Readers of this journal are invited to send in questions regarding the Protestant, Catholic, and Jewish faiths. Questions will be answered as promptly as possible. They should be addressed to this journal or to: The National Conference of Christians and Jews, 381 Fourth Avenue, New York 16, N. Y. Name and address must accompany questions so that a personal reply may be sent if necessary.

Religious News Service,   Release: Sat. or Sun.,
381 Fourth Ave., New York 16, N. Y.   Apr. 17 or 18, 1948

Q. Who are the Missouri Lutherans?
A. A body of conservative Lutherans organized under the leadership of K. F. W. Walther in 1847 into "The Lutheran Synod of Missouri, Ohio and Other States." It consisted originally of the congregations formed by the 700 pilgrims from Saxony, Germany, who had settled in Perry County, Mo., in 1839, and of the congregations in Ohio and Michigan served by missionaries sent by Pastor Wilhelm Lohe of Neuendettelsau.
Q. What is the Schola Cantorum?
A. A school for singers of the Papal Choir said to have been established by Pope Gregory the Great (590-604). It served to standardize the Gregorian chant throughout the western church. A

ligious Remarkables is sent to subscribers
Religious News Service for weekly release.
intended for Saturday church pages.

course of study required nine years. Teachers were sent out to establish schools in England, Germany and Switzerland.

Q. Who was Tanna?

A. One of the Jewish scholars of the first two centuries, whose teachings are contained in the Mishna (the rabbinical law) and in the Baraita (additional teachings outside the Mishna).

Q. What was territorialism?

A. A theory of church government which came in with the Reformation, but was formulated in the late 17th century. It ascribed to a temporal ruler, by virtue of his office, the right to govern the church within his realm, both in external and internal affairs— though not to impose his own faith on his subjects.

—Religious News Service

One year older than RNS is Ecumenical Press Service (EPS), whose releases are distributed from Geneva, Switzerland, and New York City. Although it reports news of many different religious bodies, its sponsorship limits its support to Protestant organizations that believe in the world church movement. It is issued under the auspices of the World Council of Churches, the International Missionary Council, the World Alliance for International Friendship Through the Churches, the World Alliance of the YMCA, the World's YWCA, the World's Student Christian Federation, the United Bible Societies, and the World's Sunday School Asociation. "To keep its readers informed of trends . . . in and about the Churches and the Christian movements" is its aim.

EPS is entirely a news syndicate. Although its copy is not as well prepared, professionally, as that of NC and RNS, it costs its subscribers far less than any similar service would cost, for its forty-eight issues were available in 1950 at a charge of only five dollars. Most of its 3,000 subscribers, EPS reports, use it as individuals, although 200 are journalists. Five radio stations use the service regularly.

Worldover Press, an international weekly news report issued from Wilton, Connecticut, under the direction of

Devere Allen, one of the leading American religious journalists, has a strong religious emphasis but is not primarily a church news syndicate, although numerous church publications subscribe to it. Its copy, prepared usually by native journalists in the countries from which the news is dispatched, is to be found reprinted in labor and other specialized journals as well as religious weeklies and monthlies and also is to be heard in broadcasts.

Porter Routh, secretary of the Department of Survey, Statistics, and Information of the Sunday School Board of the Southern Baptist Convention, sends out a condensed summary of "trends and events" in the world at large but especially in the world of religion and among the Baptists. Called *The Survey Bulletin*, this material is used mainly in Baptist publications.

Popular also among Baptist editors is the Layman's Information Service maintained by Charles A. Wells, a New York layman who edits a four-page newsletter commenting, from the religious viewpoint, on the news of the day and syndicates a religious cartoon which he draws and for which he writes a more elaborate comment than generally appears with cartoons. *Between the Lines*, Mr. Wells' publication, and his cartoon, which appears in some secular papers but mainly in the religious press, give a strong sociological interpretation to religion, as the illustration on p. 112 indicates.

The *Washington Religious Review*, a weekly newsletter published by Church News Service in Washington, D. C., is in the pattern of the "inside dope sheets" issued by Kiplinger and others but less given to speculation and forecasting than the usual attempt. Larston D. Farrar is editor and publisher. The material is intended to inform editors and others about religious news developing in Washington or secular activity affecting the church, and to provide copy for subscribers.

Added to these groups are the products of the denomina-

This is one of a series by Charles A. Wells dealing with modern religious and social problems. Mr. Wells prepares text, running from 100 to 150 words, for use with each drawing. Under the heading "The Mountain and the Toy Balloon," Mr. Wells said that "with the modern press and radio, it is possible to balloon a personality to national proportions by the magic of publicity methods, irrespective of the individual's personal worth or character."

tionally maintained offices, such as that of the director of publicity of the National Lutheran Council, Southern Baptist Convention, which sends out news stories under the name Baptist Press, or the large Methodist Information office and others referred to in earlier chapters. Such public relations offices will supply to editors, radio commentators, authors, and other persons who can use them, many kinds of materials regularly and other types of a more expensive nature than news and feature releases, such as pictures, on special request. The International Council of Religious Education has had wide success with its syndicated Sunday school lessons and commentary.

From the more strictly commerical firms come some widely used features, such as the Ellis Service's Sunday School Lesson and its "Religion Day by Day," the materials available from Fortune Features or the Newspaper Enterprise Association, Inc.

The standard religious features issued by the secular syndicates are far more widely used and known than those of the religious agencies or special syndicates. Their greater popularity is explained by the more professional manner in which the material is presented, the uncontroversial nature of the copy, and most of all by the availability of money with which to promote the features. Here follows a typical standard release:

RELIGION DAY BY DAY

By William T. Ellis

WE ARE AND WE HAVE

Europeans criticize Americans for their exaltation of "bathroom and automobile civilization." They say that we have unduly exalted merely material values in life.

That shot hits a bull's-eye. We have become the greatest coddlers of the carcass that the world has ever known. Our own grandparents would be amazed—and ashamed—to see what store we set by the appliances and accessories of life; things which they never knew nor desired. Yet they had qualities which, broadly speaking, we lack.

While man has been so cunning in ministering to his own needs on the merely physical basis, we find that God has been intent upon meeting our higher needs, our real needs, our abiding needs. That is why "the Sabbath was made for man"—for man the entity, the immortal soul.

In our hours of insight, we do desire to live life at its best, our Father; and to be rich toward God. Open our eyes to the blessedness of the Sabbath which serves our souls. Amen.

—The Ellis Service

Wire services

Types of syndicates with which churchmen may be more familiar than any of these, at least by name, are the press associations, also known as wire services. These news-gathering agencies, all of which transmit religious news and features as part of their total budget, are spearheaded by the Associated Press, United Press Associations, and the International News Service. They are designated wire services because they depend heavily upon telegraphed and telephoned communication, but they also use the mail and the radio for transmission of information.

Oldest is the Associated Press. Its present organization was formed in 1900, but preceding it were, for a half-century, similar bodies of the same name and function. The AP serves approximately 1,500 newspapers, magazines, and radio-television stations. Its form of organization is different from that of its rivals, for it is a mutually owned, nonprofit organization operated by its member publications. Members pay assessments on a prearranged budget; they must surrender their news to it for exclusive republication in each of the other member publications. The AP syndicates not only news but also photographs (by Wirephoto) and many types of written features: news summaries, columns, cartoons, special articles, and special departments.

The United Press was founded in 1907 at the instigation of E. W. Scripps (the original Scripps in the Scripps-Howard newspaper chain). International News Service was organized two years later by William Randolph Hearst. Both syndicates are operated for the profit of the owners and sell their news, pictures, and features to publications without a membership qualification.

All three have affiliations with similar syndicates in other parts of the world, maintain branch bureaus in principal cities, and employ many correspondents throughout the world.

Similarly, foreign press associations, like Reuters of England and Tass of Russia, maintain offices in this country. Also functioning alongside these wire services are other news syndicates that offer a specialized radio-telegraph-mail service. Among them are North American Newspaper Alliance and Overseas News Agency.

Church use of syndicates

The value of such syndicates to interpretation of the church obviously is great. An agency that can place a religious news story in the columns of several hundred publications simultaneously can accomplish something for the church which it cannot under present circumstances do for itself. Denominational public relations offices send literally thousands of copies of the same news release to individual newspapers. Depending upon the nature of the story, sometimes hundreds of these publications may print it. As a rule, however, such a mailing is highly speculative. It is expensive for an office to keep the mailing list up to date, to handle undeliverable copies, and to pay first-class postage on an important release that might not be taken seriously if sent in an open envelope.

Scores of publications ignore the contents of the envelope

because it is obvious publicity. But an editor who receives a religious news story via his AP, UP, or INS teletype or mailed feature delivery is more likely to print it because he knows that the copy already has been screened in a bureau office, that it has met the test of newsworthiness, and that it is concise and ready for immediate typesetting.

When an editor receives copy from a specialized agency, perhaps Religious News Service or Worldover Press, he tends to trust it more than the straight publicity with which his mail is flooded. It may be the identical story; the wire service or syndicate may have received the material originally from a publicity source, but it has been evaluated by the time the editor receives it. At least there has been a chance for evaluation. After all, the editor pays for syndicated material.

Any public relations expert for church, the entertainment world, or business, prefers to have the professional media distribute his information rather than attempt to place his copy directly. Great is the rejoicing in any publicity office when a famous magazine or giant newspaper has accepted a tip on a story involving a client and has produced a favorable piece of copy.

Thus it behooves church bodies to seek the support of the syndicates, to keep them informed and supplied with materials, and to note what is logically appealing to them. Routine news of local churches rarely has syndicate value. An extraordinarily long pastorate, a tremendous fire with great loss of life and property, a remarkable building program, or some other feature or human interest story of the sort may be acceptable, but even then most often for a state wire only, and not for national distribution. An important church convention drawing delegates from throughout the nation, no matter where it is held, commands some attention on the syndicate's wires or in its mail releases if it does not

use telegraph and cable. Only its most significant or sensational actions or resolutions will receive it, however. A
widely known speaker brings attention upon a local assembly
even if the attendance is small; a less famed speaker may
attract little notice even if addressing a larger gathering. As
a study of the basis of news selection will show, reasons exist
for all this. These the church must understand if it is to
co-operate with press and radio. (See chapters XII and
XIII.)

Religious News Service, the Press Department of the
National Catholic Welfare Conference, and similar groups
on a regional basis handle releases, both picture and text,
which might seem too specialized for the big general syndicate or press association. But they, likewise, are not interested in distributing dull and routine copy or pictures.

The final test, after all, of what is worth sending to any
syndicate is its appeal to the religious constituency as a
whole. It is unreasonable to expect the member of a church
in Boise, Idaho, to be engrossed in the minutiae of proceed-
ings at the monthly session of an official board in a church at
Corning, New York. It is even presumptuous to expect the
members of a church of one denomination in Corning to be
interested in the routine activity of the church of another
denomination in that New York state community.

Good copy—religious or otherwise—for a syndicate is
that which is of greatest interest to the greatest number of
persons who see its releases in print and picture.

CHAPTER VII

Denominational Publications as Interpreters

Since the latter part of the eighteenth century the denominational publication has been the core of all direct journalistic efforts to interpret the church to its constituency in America.

Consequently denominational newspapers and magazines have come to resemble the house organs of business and industry. Once they were important general publications that dealt with current theological, religious, and secular problems. But as journalism developed into business, even into big business, with color printing for magazines and high-speed publication and wide coverage for newspapers, the church press withdrew from the general field. With occasional exceptions the denominational publications shrank into the circle of the church to serve as news organs, builders of loyalty, and conveyors of appeals for support.

Although denominational publications on the whole still are unimpressive in appearance, dull in content, and lacking in editorial courage, more and more of them are attempting to correct these faults. The denominational boards in control of these papers and magazines now more often try to satisfy the need for better printing, smarter writing, broader outlook, and more use of photographs and art work in their publications.

Denominational journals arose as the churches realized that the secular press either could not or would not give space to the minutiae of their activities. Nor was it reasonable to expect general publications to carry the exhortations of one denomination or to give space to discussions of internal policies.

Number and other facts uncertain

The number of denominational journals never has been certain. Frank L. Mott, foremost historian of American journalism, finds evidence that in 1828 there were more than seventy weekly religious papers. In that decade there were also about two dozen magazines of religion, most of them issued by the denominations. By the 1850's the number of magazines had quadrupled, some beginning lives that were not to end for many years.

"Every denomination had its publications," he writes, "and usually a full complement of theological quarterly, home monthly, and regional weekly publications." [1]

Church magazines and papers of the mid-nineteenth century sought to deal with all the problems of their day, much as the *American Mercury, The Nation, Harper's,* and *the New Republic* do today. In fact, as Dean Mott shows by quoting from secular publications of the time, such as *Putnam's* and *Russell's,* they sometimes were even scurrilous in their expression. They behaved in a most unreligious manner when discussing such issues as slavery and doctrinal differences. At least they were forthright.

By 1870 the religious weeklies alone had reached 208. The number of religious publications in general virtually doubled, Dean Mott reports, between 1865 and 1885, more

---

[1] Frank Luther Mott, *A History of American Magazines* (Cambridge: Harvard University Press, 1938) p. 60, Vol. II.

than 650 being the total in the later year. Practically all were denomination-sponsored.

In the next half-century, while many periodicals were born and many died, the number more than doubled once again. A 1951 estimate, based on the N. W. Ayer *Directory*, the membership roll of the Associated Church Press, and the *Religious Press Directory*, places the number at between 1,400 and 1,500 and covering all types of religious journalism.

The difficulties of arriving at exact figures can be realized when one examines the attempts made to obtain dependable data. A Syracuse University student, writing to editors for their views on religious journalism, received an astonishing variety of guesses as to the number of religious publications in the United States in 1948.

From the editor of one of the largest denominational weeklies he received this reply: "I think there are no more than about 300 religious publications in the United States." The managing editor of a large religious syndicate said: "One thousand is certainly a low figure if you include various state and regional publications. We ourselves have a card index of Protestant publications totaling over 800. There certainly are more than 200 Catholic publications all told." Even the second figure was low, for the Catholic list came close to 500 and the Jewish group exceeded 150.

Circulation, another measuring stick of publications, rose and fell over the years. Before the Civil War, circulations of both religious and secular magazines and newspapers were small. For many years a circulation of 10,000 was large (the smallness of this figure can be gauged by noting that today in the United States alone fifty secular magazines and papers have more than one million circulation each and a number have three, four, or five million; one has eleven million).

After the Civil War some of the Sunday school papers

exceeded 50,000; Henry Ward Beecher's *Christian Union* went past the 100,000 mark, but the secular press already was climbing into higher figures. Except for the occasional leader, like *Our Sunday Visitor, The Christian Advocate, Upper Room, Christian Herald,* and *Extension,* the denominational publications reached no circulation heights.

Religious News Service in 1947 surveyed 70 representative Protestant and Roman Catholic newspapers and magazines. From this study it was learned that 57 of the publications gained an average of 65 per cent in circulation in the preceding seven years, the increases ranging from 10 to 500 per cent. The largest gain was reported by *Our Sunday Visitor,* a Roman Catholic weekly newspaper, which had 475,000 circulation in 1940 and 675,000 in 1947. A Roman Catholic monthly magazine, *Extension,* was second, with more than 490,000. These 57 publications had a total circulation of 4,225,000. Joseph F. Wagner Inc., publishers of the *Religious Press Directory,* in the latest edition of that guide (1943), estimated the total circulation of religious publications that accept advertising and issue circulation statements at more than ten million.

Three dailies are issued for secular circulation by religious groups in the United States: the *Christian Science Monitor,* the Salt Lake City *Deseret News,* and the Kansas City *Sun Herald.* The first is, of course, issued by the Christian Scientists and originates in Boston; the second has been sponsored by the Church of the Latter Day Saints for more than a century; the last is the newest, having been founded by a group of Roman Catholics. Unlike the other two, it is not an official publication of the church. These three papers, as well as a number of weeklies, are issued under the philosophy that the church can influence all journalism by entering the field itself, can set standards, and can provide fair and adequate coverage of religious news through such papers.

Quality is uneven

As tools of interpretation of the church most denominational publications are disturbingly uneven in quality and varied in format and content. Persons without journalistic training or experience edit most of them. Contributors frequently are not professional writers, artists, or photographers. Small budgets—which remain small because they cannot be increased or because the controlling groups are not convinced they should be larger—explain in part the lack of trained and talented personnel. They also explain the use of cheap paper and imperfect printing. Few religious magazines and newspapers can stand comparison with the newsstand publications which are their actual competitors.

The range of format and content of the whole group of denominational publications can be seen in miniature in the products of the printing presses used by the Southern Baptist Convention. This denomination, like the Roman Catholic, the Congregational, Presbyterian, Seventh-Day Adventist, Protestant Episcopal, and Methodist churches, has entered the publications field with heartiness and provides the whole gamut of publications.

At one extreme are the twenty Baptist state publications, issued under the aegis of the state conventions. Usually these are small tabloid newspapers or self-cover magazines printed on inexpensive paper, crammed with news of various state official groups, pronouncements by state or denominational officials, sermonettes, personals, editorials, jokes and a few cartoons, photographs, and routine news stories and features. As a rule the photographs are poorly reproduced. Combined circulation of these publications, which have their own Southern Baptist Press Association, was nearly a million in 1950, an increase of 400 per cent over 1940.

Occupying another extreme is *The Commission*, a carefully edited missions magazine issued by the Foreign Missions Board of the denomination. Technically directed until 1950 by its managing editor, a woman trained in journalism and experienced as a writer, it has an international circulation of 100,000. Standard 8 by 10½ inches in size and running to 36 pages, this monthly takes the world for its domain and uses photography generously and effectively.

For a time the Southern Baptists had available an independently- and irregularly-issued small magazine, *Christian Frontiers*, serving as the organ of the more socially conscious Southern Baptist leaders. Its editorial board was not always pleased with the denominational independence, amounting almost to isolationism, of the church, and advanced an unorthodox philosophy on such issues as labor-management relations and racial harmony. *Christian Frontiers* was pocket-size, with a few dozen closely and unattractively-printed pages, and managed to reach only a few thousand readers during its life in the later 1940's.

Dominating the Baptist journalistic scene are the eighty-odd magazines issued by the Sunday School Board of the Convention, the chief publishing agency of the denomination, with headquarters at Nashville, Tennessee. Almost all these publications are uniformly well-produced, as religious publications go, and include numerous pupils' quarterlies, a monthly for Baptist college students, another for members of training unions, others for persons interested in missionary education, and still others for Sunday school teachers and officers.

From other cities come additional official and unofficial Southern Baptist papers and magazines, such as the Home Mission Board's newspaper in Atlanta, the three issued by the Woman's Missionary Union in Birmingham, and the one for Baptist men produced in Memphis.

One might suppose that these more than 100 publications would reach between them virtually all the six million Southern Baptists. Prof. Frank E. Burkhalter, long director of the department of journalism at Baylor University and prominent in the publications work of his denomination, has reported, however, that "five out of every six Southern Baptists take no Baptist paper."[2]

Hardly unique, of course, are the Southern Baptists when it comes to accusations of failing to support their publications to the fullest possibilities. Whereas their Mississippi state paper, the relatively successful *Record,* in 1951 was subscribed for by about 68,000 out of 370,000 Baptists in the state, the Methodist weekly *Christian Advocate* had a circulation in the same year of approximately 320,000 in a denomination that numbered in all about nine million members.

Church publications offer complete coverage no more than does any other type of publication. In fact, on the basis of intensity of interest, they also may be thought to provide less in proportion to readers. Although the 1950 issue of the *Yearbook of American Churches* reported that about 82 million of the estimated 150 million population in the United States are on the church rolls, the circulation figure that is most optimistic, 10 million, is indeed a low proportion of the total.

Consumer magazines generally claim from three to five readers to each subscriber or newsstand purchaser. They reason that the subscriber, to begin with, buys the magazine because he genuinely wishes to read it and not out of a sense of institutional loyalty or through some quantity purchase plan set up by a church. Each copy, they have found, is read by several other persons, in libraries, public offices,

---

[2] Frank E. Burkhalter, "More Baptists Should Read Their State Paper" in *Arkansas Baptist* (September 30, 1948) p. 7.

vehicles, and family groups. Denominational and other religious publications can claim part of this extra reading, to be sure, but it must be offset by the inattention to the publication that is inevitable from its content and method of sale and distribution.

The denominational situation

One Baptist, writing in the *Georgia Baptist Children's Home Messenger,* put the denominational situation frankly in an editorial later reprinted on the front page of *The Christian Index:*

IGNORANCE AND FAILURE

To read that there are 570,000 white Georgia Baptists out of 615,000 who do not subscribe to *The Christian Index* is one thing, but to meet Baptist after Baptist, day after day, and have them tell you, one by one, that they do not read *The Christian Index* is another thing. To find countless Baptists who do not know there is any such publication as *The Christian Index* is another thing.

For nine years now, we have been meeting the Baptists of Georgia individually and collectively. As we have talked to them, we have made reference to certain things, and as we have talked, they have said, "I did not know that." To which we have replied, "It was in *The Christian Index.*" Then they said, "I do not read *The Christian Index.*" And our reply has been, "Oh."

Our feeling has been, if these good friends do not read *The Christian Index,* there is not much we can do about it.

We do not care how well educated or how well informed our Baptist people are, if they do not read *The Christian Index,* they are not educated or informed as a Baptist. Not to know what one's associates and one's competitors are doing in the business world, means business failure and collapse. Not to know what one's fellow Christians are doing, especially members of one's own faith, means ignorance to a certain extent, and certainly partial failure. We just don't see how any Baptist minister could be satisfied until his total membership is reading *The Christian Index.* That church is not a *Christian Index* reading church, cannot lay claim to being a wide awake and progressive church no matter what else it does.[3]

[3] J. L. Fortney, "Ignorance and Failure." Reprinted from the *Georgia Baptist Children's Home Messenger* by *The Christian Index* (June 10, 1948) p. 1.

Financing is varied

Almost all these papers and magazines are underwritten by denominational groups or other religious institutions; a considerable number operate at a loss but some are financially successful. Attempts to gather specific data within this disorganized area of journalism are resisted, either because of denominational competition or unwillingness to reveal facts that any democratically operated publication should be willing for its constituency to possess. So many publications are issued as part of the operations of a large denominational publishing concern that it is difficult to assess them as successful or unsuccessful financial institutions. Group publishers that do not have adequate cost accounting systems are not always aware of the extent to which certain units may be money-losing. On the other hand a few products of the denominational presses have been fabulously successful. *The Upper Room,* for example, made so large a net profit that the proceeds were used to buy a tall Nashville office building.

Financial sources, aside from the denominational capital, are circulation and advertising revenue. Circulation returns are the less important in secular journalism, as we have seen, but not in this type of church publication, despite the relative smallness of distribution figures, because advertising is not so lucrative. Advertising brings little revenue for four reasons: 1. small circulations prohibit the charging of high rates; 2. religious journals naturally refuse certain classes of accounts that are acceptable to publications that have no moral objection to tobacco and liquor advertising, for example; 3. magazines and papers that are in part sold in bulk, as are scores of religious publications, are not considered the best advertising media; 4. readers of religious publications are reached also by the mass-circulation publications and the popular radio-TV programs; 5. circulation is not concentrated geographically.

Advertising rates and volume are low. In any religious publication the copy is likely to be about church supplies, religious books and art work, schools and colleges supported by denominations, church equipment, and patent medicines. Almost none of the heavy advertising that is the bulwark of the secular publication is to be found.

Personnel is untrained

The personnel of the editorial side of the church publication is largely untrained in journalistic techniques For many years editorial executives have been, before entering journalism, ministers, rabbis, or priests, teachers, school executives, or businessmen. In some instances they received their journalistic assignments because their denominations had no other place for them. At times they were appointed to be editors, not to exercise journalistic prowess, but to carry out policy. Superannuated preachers have been known to start publications of their own, for something to do or to promote a policy. All such editors have little or no editorial skill and few have the money to hire persons with the requisite ability.

The records of the appointment of editorial personnel to denominational and religious publications in recent years are filled with accounts that show indifference to the need for professional skill. The biographical sketch of the new editorial employee invariably lists the churches he has served and the denominational offices he has held, none of which is associated with journalism in any of its aspects. Such an editor, if he uses trained editorial personnel at all, generally employs only a slightly experienced person, and one who is willing to work for a low salary.

Technical deficiencies, which competent critics never

finish pointing out in the religious press, often can be explained by the prevailing situation in the personnel. Technical improvements in the denominational papers and magazines can be made by improving the personnel.

A few steps are being taken to provide personnel with technical training. Among the more important are: 1. internships in religious journalism offered to young people with journalistic talent by the Division of Christian Publications of the Board of Education, American Baptist Convention; 2. the undergraduate program in religious journalism at Oklahoma Baptist University; 3. the three graduate programs available at the School of Journalism, Syracuse University; 4. the correspondence and extension work of the Christian Writers Institute, Chicago, and of similar groups; 5. the individual courses in religious journalism and church publicity available at several dozen seminaries and church-related colleges; and 6. the summer editorial conferences held regularly by a number of denominations.

With some logic, the publishers of church journals in the denominations insist upon their editors being members of the particular denomination or church; this insistence is necessary not only to unite the clan but also for the more useful purpose of understanding of the policies and history of the church in question. Since church periodicals generally are not financially well off they cannot pay salaries that will attract graduates of schools of journalism or men and women from secular journalism. They must depend upon trained or untrained persons willing to work under discouraging conditions; altruistic souls are no more readily found among would-be or practicing journalists than in the ranks of any other occupation.

Another personnel handicap is that the editors and other staff members are expected not merely to produce a competent weekly or monthly but also to make speeches, conduct religious services, solicit advertising, call on the sick, raise money, or perform similar duties. Except on the larger publications, religious journalists in the denominations must do such extracurricular work to supplement their incomes.

Although personnel appears to be the key to the present quality of the denominational publications, that personnel is surrounded by handicaps that would dismay the best-trained editor. Policy sometimes is an insuperable barrier to good technical work, as, for example, the plan by which church boards buy space in a publication at a reduced rate and dictate its use and appearance.

The number of persons working on these magazines and papers invariably is small, since they are not large publications. The entrepreneurs in this area of journalism are not given to hiring sufficient personnel. Nor are they in a position to provide adequate staffs. Small staffs naturally follow from small budgets.

The typical staff of a denominational magazine or paper consists of an editor and one assistant, who is a combination editorial assistant and personal secretary; a business manager, who combines advertising, circulation, and all other business duties, and several clerks. Exceptions are the extraordinarily small publications, which have one-man staffs, or one of the few unusually large magazines, which have a half-dozen editors and scores of secretaries, stenographers, and clerks to serve them, as well as a business manager, circulation director, and advertising manager.

Sources of material

Copy for their pages comes heavily from staff writers and free-lancers. Comparatively few religious publications can afford to buy or even justify the need for wire service copy and general syndicated material. Articles are contributed, ordered, or staff-written. Verse is supplied in abundance by religious poets who abound in this country. Fiction is purchased from free-lancers and through literary agents. Departmental copy is arranged for with specific individuals.

Because religious publications are so receptive to free-lance material they are excellent training ground for new writers. Their rates necessarily are low but the competition by contributors for space in them is not so great as on the consumer magazines or papers. Nor are their journalistic standards so high as to prove a barrier for every beginner. Only the best edited of the religious publications have standards equal to those of the reputable secular journals; they are not many in number.

Policy must be followed

Since the majority of the religious journals function as house organs, they tend to follow general church policy. Then, too, they are virtually private journalism, like club or fraternity publications. Although policy is considered important, discussion of it is widely permitted in this special type of publishing. Yet in the authorized publications of a denomination it is not reasonable to expect any large proportion of space to be used for opposing official policy, refreshing as such procedure might be in some instances. The degree to which policy is followed or is defied varies according to denomination. Editors generally follow official policy with little objection, not because they are forced to but because they wish to and were chosen because of known compatibility.

Publications with policies sometimes differing from those of the denomination they seek to reach are either the notably independent and outspoken periodicals like *The Christian Leader, Social Action, The Christian Register, The Lutheran,* and *Advance,* or those not sponsored by a denomination but by a group within it, such as *Christian Frontiers* (during its short life), *Integrity, The Commonweal,* or *The Catholic Worker,* the latter three within the Roman Catholic Church, or *The Witness* and *The Churchman* within the Protestant Episcopal. Carefully read in most denominational circles but responsible to none is the unique weekly, *The Christian Century,* which is independently published and nondenominational. It is almost the only religious periodical known to some national leaders, who otherwise are widely informed about the press. The *Century* operates in the tradition of the vigorous religious publications of the later years of the nineteenth century, such as *The Independent* or the *Christian Union.*

Consistent with the dominant views in the churches of America today are the policies of the strictly denominational magazines and papers. A denomination's viewpoint on all subjects on which it has taken a stand is represented, more or less faithfully, in its press. Independent publications are not necessarily all liberal or all conservative. Small publishing houses issue them as bulwarks against modernism or fundamentalism. The independent journals that might be called liberal are deeply concerned with finding the areas in which believers in certain ethical principles, such as those advanced in the Sermon on the Mount, can live up to them. Thus *Social Action* or *motive* brings the viewpoint of religion, as interpreted by one group, to bear upon all the subjects that occupy men's minds—religion, literature, politics, economics, and scores of others—with concrete proposals for individual and social action. Aided by a few official denominational journals, this group of independents forms the closest resemblance to influential journals of a century ago.

Nature of their interpretation

An interpreter of the church who looks over a sheaf of denominational publications can gain an estimate of the chances of his copy appearing in their pages by attempting to obtain an overview of that content. He also can learn what interpretation they give the church.

Such a survey was made in 1946 by examining 184 issues of 64 different papers and magazines representing 21 denominations in the United States.[4] The inescapable conclusion was that, as seen through their official and unofficial publications, the Protestant denominations in the United States are like so many national states proclaiming and insisting upon their own sovereignty.

The essence of the findings was that the major portion of editorial and news space of the Protestant press was devoted to denominationalism. Contrariwise, it was learned, little space was consumed to present the viewpoint and news of Christianity in common, that is, ecumenical concerns. Undoubtedly a survey of the publications of most non-Protestant denominations would reveal similar tendencies, since they are even more propagandistic than the Protestant groups, not so much on the basis of space as on the basis of intensity. But at the same time non-Protestant publications have broader religious interests. It would be less possible for a critic to say of them what was said of the publications of one of the major Protestant denominations after a large segment of its press had been studied:

> My dominant impression is that your denomination is interested in almost nothing but its own little doings, such things as changes in pastors, money raising for schools and churches, and the views on standard ecclesiastical and religious subjects of some of your pastors and teachers. Subjects beyond these are treated by only a few of your publications. Among them are perfectly safe topics, such as temperance or the liquor traffic . . . .[5]

---

[4] R. E. Wolseley, "The Church Press: Bulwark of Denominational Sovereignty" in *Christendom* (Autumn, 1946).

[5] R. E. Wolseley, *An Analysis of the Baptist State Publications* (Little Rock, Arkansas: Southern Baptist Press Association, 1945).

In a group of eighteen papers, for example, there was virtually no mention, in four issues of each, of religio-economic, racial, educational, musical, and religio-military problems.

The caliber of the majority of denominational publications in the United States is not unfairly represented by the implications of a letter from a reader that appeared in one:

> There is an occasional number of the _____ that brings me that peace and quiet I look for in the church. However, too often I am urged to stir myself about something; to protest against what you consider an infringement of civil liberties; to urge more rights for Negroes; to write Washington about something or other. Since these things upset me so, I am asking you to discontinue my subscription.

Limitations on improvement

Persons who have charge of publications can raise their standards little higher than the controlling boards or readers will permit. As with the secular press, the public gets the publications it wants, those for which it votes by buying and subscribing, except that in the church press the subscriber may be an unwilling or indifferent voter. If boards of control believe the constituency is unready for or indifferent to improved format, wider variety of content, or treatment of controversial subjects or if through its letters the constituency demonstrates itself to be thus unready or indifferent the result is the same: frustrated editors and cheated readers.

As many interpretations of the church are available to the world as there are varieties of publications. But minorities within any denomination have almost no publication outlet. Their views are too heretical for the official journals and so unorthodox for the large number of orthodox persons who constitute the membership that they can expect little support by going directly to the body of the church. Most of the world sees only the sanctioned publications. Thus what might be considered religion at its best or its worst—depending upon viewpoint—is portrayed rarely through the denominational publications.

Groups or persons seeking to publicize their work or their institutions must function with this background in mind.

Publications as outlets

Local churches always will find a welcome for their news stories, provided they are concisely written, in the denominational newspaper and magazine. Such publications are useful media. Regional groups that can supply features and news accounts can promote their objectives readily through denominational journals. Supervisory bodies with a great volume of material may have to pay for quantities of space, but that will be cheaper than financing separate publications; they will obtain a low rate even on advertising. Inasmuch as denominational papers have as their primary function the support of official activities, local churches and other religious institutions may avail themselves of the space at their disposal. Indeed, they should make greater use of it than they do, especially if their work is on a broad scale that brings before the readership some of the problems editorial leaders otherwise may be unable to deal with.

Even if there is some doubt that they will be used, church groups should send news, feature, and picture releases to denominational publications, which should be on any mechanical mailing list as a matter of course. Copy then is available to them. If it is examined but sometimes not used, at least it has kept the editor informed. Special stories should be sent in whenever possible; elaborate material should be arranged for in advance. (See the chapters on techniques.) Whatever is printed should be clipped from the denominational papers, as from the secular publications, and mounted in scrapbooks as part of the historical record of the institution.

Promotional possibilities

Promotion of the denominational publication within the institution naturally is desirable, the more so if the paper or magazine is worth exceptional effort to obtain wide reading. A minister or board secretary or women's group president has an opportunity to build the circulation of a publication which depends heavily on their co-operation. Representatives of the weekly or monthly may be given time to speak briefly at meetings. Sample copies, with subscription forms inserted, may be distributed at special or incidental promotion meetings. Retired ministers, enthusiastic laymen, or groups of young people may be pressed into service as salesmen, euphemistically presented as associate editors or representatives. The institution or the salesmen or sometimes both may benefit financially from such an arrangement, but the emphasis should be on the return to the church or organization rather than to the individual. Promotion should aim at genuine support from the constituency. The persons being solicited should take the publication because they really plan to read it and not merely to help a young son of a friend or out of affection for the editor; such backing is superficial and tends to be ineffective in exercising influence. Renewals are difficult to obtain if the publication has rested, unread, for weeks on living-room tables.

Everyone connected with the denominational publication—be he subscriber, reader, editor, publisher, contributor, or keeper of circulation records—should remember that the paper or periodical goes forth as the representative or spokesman of the denomination. What picture, therefore, does it paint of the church? Is it a portrayal of which the church can be proud? Is it a false best-foot-forward picture? Is it, on the other hand, a constantly unpleasant delineation? These questions are not for the purpose of telling a denominational publication what it shall print; it is a matter of urging it to realize what it already is printing.

If a different interpretation of the church is called for, it can be provided intelligently only by understanding of the interpretation currently being presented.

The Sunday school press

Printing presses have been used for many years to produce what is called most commonly lesson or Sunday school materials. So extensive has production of these publications become that they are a major part of the church publishing industry. *The Wesley Quarterly* of the Methodist Book Concern, the *Adult Class* of the American Baptist Publishing Society, and the similar materials for pupils as well as adults of other denominational publishing houses as well as such independent firms as the David C. Cook Publishing Company of Elgin, Illinois, and the Standard Publishing Company of Cincinnati, Ohio, are religious education literature rather than journalism. Publication formats are used to carry educational materials. Actually these lessons are book content issued periodically, being planned years in advance.

Principles of good journalistic practice, however, can be applied to such publications. Art work, photography, and color printing can be used. The writing, while mainly interpretative and too often editorialized, must face the customary duty of communication. Circulation problems not unlike those of other church journals sold in bulk also beset these publications intended for persons active in church school.

Commenting on these periodicals from the journalistic viewpoint, Prof. Kenneth Underwood of Yale Divinity School and managing editor of *Social Action*, wrote:

The first reaction of the professional journalist to the orthodox lesson format of our Sunday School literature would be to call for a radical change in make-up and in editorial processing. From the standpoint of reader interest the textbook pattern of presentation, the straight and unrelieved classic page format and the reliance upon one writer has the least to commend it of several possibilities.[6]

Thus in 1945 Professor Underwood recognized one of the major obstacles to improvement, also, when he went on to point out that the technical suggestions such as he had given are of little value so long as literature boards do not have sufficient money with which to hire adequate staffs of "consecrated and journalistically trained editors, make-up artists and writers," and to buy the printing that will allow them to use their technical knowledge to its fullest.

But there are signs of improvement and change in the policies of several church school literature boards, notably the Board of Christian Publication of the Presbyterian Church, U. S. A. and the Parish and Church School Board of the United Lutheran Church. The Presbyterian editors have been allowed to revamp their publications drastically, on an experimental basis, the results at this writing still being under testing. The Lutheran group has concentrated its changes on its Christian Growth Series, which makes striking use of drawings and lively typographic effects.

The need for improvement is evident in these publications that interpret the church in their own way, just as it is in the newspapers and magazines intended to circulate among the unchurched. Once again it is necessary to improve both the internal and the external media.

Non- or Undenominational publications

A *non-* or *un*denominational publication may be published by one or several denominations, by private groups

---

[6] From an undelivered address prepared for a cancelled meeting of the Editors' Advisory Section of the International Council of Religious Education.

or individuals, or by a non- or undenominational religious body. Its purpose is to appeal to all religious people, whether members of churches or not, or to large groups with a special interest that cuts across denominations or avoids denominationalism.

Examples of this type of religious journalism are *Unity, Liberty, Good Business* (issued by one denomination for general use); *Christian Life, Church Management, Church Business* (issued by private groups for general dissemination); *The Christian Herald, The Christian Century, Guideposts, Protestant World* (by private groups for general use but not for profit), and *Moody Monthly, Woman's Press,* and *The Intercollegian* (by a non- or undenominational religious body).

Several of these are published under foundation or non-profit corporation auspices, including *The Christian Herald* and *The Christian Century.*

Interdenominational publications

An interdenominational publication is a magazine or newspaper issued for the use of two or more denominations to further their common aims and may be published by a private firm or individual, a religious organization other than a denomination, or by the denominations themselves by common agreement. Examples are *Adult Bible Class* (private firm); *Bible Society Record, Ecumenical Review, International Journal of Religious Education, Christian Education, The Church Woman, Fellowship, The Chaplain, The Link* (religious organization but not a denomination); *United Church Observer* (a denomination).

These non-, un-, or interdenominational publications are not many, numbering about one hundred. A century ago this was not the case, but as religious publishing became more hazardous on the private level and as denominationalism gained strength, it was easier to leave publications to the organized church, with its ready-made reader group, other channels for arousing loyalty and consequent support. and usually greater resources. Although small, the press of this area has some of the most outstanding publications to its credit, a paradox, for the road of this group is much harder. *The Christian Herald,* one of the most widely read and professionally produced in the entire religious field, comes close to the general consumer magazine in quality. *The Christian Century* is accepted by secular journalists informed about the religious press as a leading magazine of religious opinion and is widely quoted. *Christian Life* is respected as a technically outstanding periodical.

CHAPTER VIII

Parish Publications

The Rev. Jonathan Tench preached his first sermon yesterday since he was appointed associate minister of the First Denominational Church, Richfield Avenue and Twenty-first Street, four weeks ago. His subject was "The Believing Heart."

Dr. Tench formerly was associate pastor of the First Denominational Church in Harringtontown, Pa., and had held pastorates in Martinsville, Smarton, and Slaughter Kill, Pa. Under the Rev. Donald Parton, minister, he will take over the executive duties of the church and will edit the parish paper.

This news story is based on one that actually appeared in a city daily. Although news of appointments of assistant ministers, curates, or other staff members rarely specifies duties so clearly as did this item, the duties fall to them just the same. It is a commonplace for a church to expect a new assistant to handle the parish publication.

Immediately on reading such a news story, however, these questions arise: What, if anything, does the Rev. Mr. Tench know about parish publications? What, in fact, does he know about editing? Is entrusting him with the newspaper or magazine of the parish the best procedure to produce a satisfactory result? Would Dr. Tench be so lightly entrusted with responsibility for and supervision of other operations of the church that require technical knowledge, such as its heating, its financing, its commissary, or its secretarial work? Unless he had had some experience in one of these fields or occupations he would have little to offer. Sometimes the Dr. Tenches have worked on their high school, college, or seminary paper or magazine. Usually that is the limit of their journalistic experience.

These questions are similar to those that can be raised about the persons placed in charge of the denominational publications. The parish publication is, in a smaller way, a tool for interpreting a particular local church. Since the circle of readers it reaches is much narrower than the circle reached by the denominational paper or magazine, it may not be so important that it be a first-class journalistic or publishing job. Yet if the parish publication is truly what so many churchmen tend to consider it—an assistant pastor— it surely is worth doing well if not perfectly. Actually, then, the parish publication is a transfer, in a limited way, of the techniques used in the world of secular journalism to the journalistic program of a single local church.

Every church, regardless of denomination, should consider whether it needs a parish publication, by which here is meant a weekly or monthly internal house organ and not the Sunday bulletin or announcement sheet. If a church already publishes such an organ it should examine the possibilities of improving it.

Arguments in behalf of parish publications are familiar. Stewart Harral, director of public relations at the University of Oklahoma and a writer on church publicity and public relations, summarizes the conventional ones when he writes that:

A well-edited paper will 1. advertise your church, 2. increase attendance and support, 3. reach the sick and the shut-in, 4. increase the prestige of church and pastor, 5. aid the church financially, 6. give an over-all picture of the divisions and activities of the congregation, and 7. keep non-resident members in touch with their home church.[1]

While undoubtedly a well-edited parish publication has

----

[1] Stewart Harral, *Public Relations for Churches* (New York: Abingdon-Cokesbury, 1945).

all these virtues, there is some doubt that the work and money required to issue such a publication at the very highest standard is worth the results, if other journalistic media are available. In big cities a parish journal is of greater importance than in small towns (unless the small churches can be served jointly by one publication) because there the metropolitan communication agencies cannot give the many churches individual attention, congregations are larger and more active, thus creating more news, and church members do not know one another so well. Although a country weekly is issued less often than a city daily newspaper, fewer churches are seeking space in it. The metropolitan church needs a house organ for the same reason that a business firm or an industrial plant issues an institutional publication to reach its employees as a group. It cannot do so through the general press.

Merits of different media

Whatever it has or does not have, a large church must consider the relative merits of a newspaper and a magazine as its publication. The advantages and disadvantages can be summed up thus:

THE PARISH NEWSPAPER

Advantages	*Disadvantages*
Inexpensive to publish	Ephemeral in appearance
Quickly produced	Limited in space
Cheaply mailed	Emphasizes only short copy
Timely and up-to-date	
Emphasizes news angle	

THE PARISH MAGAZINE

Dignified and appropriate	More expensive to produce
Reproduces pictures well	Low news value
Greater permanence	Infrequent in appearance
Accommodates more advertising	

A disadvantage of the magazine format, its comparative expensiveness, may be overcome by using one of the plans offered by companies that print a magazine carrying advertising and allowing space for a particular church's information in the quantity printed for each co-operating institution. This plan gives the church member a more substantial publication than he might otherwise receive, with possibly valuable religious news, features, and pictures as well as service from advertising. It includes at least as much material about his own church as he would receive in a small parish newspaper. Disadvantages of this scheme are: 1. the general material is likely to be namby-pamby and at times even offensively sentimental; 2. the full advantages of an entire magazine still are not available; 3. production conditions have been known to work against producing an entirely accurate and timely publication.

Parish newspapers or quasi newspaper-magazines, rather than the standard magazine, are most popular among American churches. The primary function of a church publication of this type is to inform the church constituency. It should emphasize news rather than views. After all, it is possible for any church to make available to its members at low cost numerous general and denominational papers and magazines conveying opinions on religious problems, but only local publications can present the local news.

Production methods

Whatever the format, this type of church publication must be produced, i.e. manufactured. Shall it be duplicated or printed? Which kind of printing? The answer lies in the church budget as well as in the congregation's taste and desires. Unquestionably a printed paper receives more respectful attention than one that is mimeographed or hectographed or similarly reproduced. Traditionally the American reading public believes a printed publication to be more substantial and professional than one produced in any less elaborate manner. If the church does not have the personnel or money for issuing a printed paper and does not wish to use any of the available group-publishing plans, a small duplicated publication provides the solution. But before abandoning the possibility of letterpress printing (impressions from type or from plates made from that type) the church should investigate the feasibility of financing the publication so that the most impressive newspaper or magazine can be produced.

Commonly the parish publication can be duplicated by Mimeograph, multigraph, hectograph, or electric typewriter. Printing from type can be by flat-bed or rotary press; it also can be planographed or produced by offset (lithography). See Chapter XI for further explanation of these tools.

Admittedly, a printed paper can be poorly produced, but it is not so easy to bungle as is a duplicated one, for generally printing is left to professionals and duplicating is done within the institution. So many persons in a church can operate a duplicating machine that there is a tendency to turn the production of the parish paper over to almost anyone willing to take the trouble to produce it. A glance at a random sheaf of duplicated publications shows that there could be higher standards of workmanship. Poor reproduction defeats the purpose of the publication. If it is smeary, so faint that the words are difficult to read, off center, or carelessly assembled, it is worse than no publication at all. A well-produced duplicated publication is worth more than a carelessly produced printed one, but it requires more individual effort in the church office or parsonage or community house. If advertising space in a duplicated publication is sold there must be special care with production.

The fewer the copies the less complicated should be the

process of reproducing the material. If the circulation is only a few hundred, duplicating is the less expensive method. If 3,000 or more copies are to be circulated, printing is not enough more expensive to deny the church the better reproduction result. But the job must be kept simple. If production costs continue to mount as they were doing in 1951, printing may become unfeasible for any but the largest churches.

Churches that publish duplicated parish papers generally produce them themselves, as inexpensively and as handily as possible. Letterpress, planograph, or offset printing demands the services of a printer, who will do the work on a contract basis. Numerous institutions solve their problem by combining their parish papers with their bulletins or by allowing a company that is in the business to solicit the advertising, edit the material, and print the publication, thereby producing a periodical which is the same for all churches except for the front page, if it is a newspaper, or certain inside pages if it is a magazine.

One such firm prepares a six by nine inch magazine containing articles of general religious interest and church advertising. Two or four pages are left blank so that the church buying a stipulated number of copies may insert its own material. Covers are imprinted with the church name and other special information. Since this publication is produced on a mass basis, it is cheaper to use such a plan than to pay for the printing of an issue entirely filled with original material.

Another concern has two hundred churches in eight large cities which send copy to the local office to be used on the front page of a standard, eight-column newspaper church publication which consists of six or eight pages of general religious news and columns as well as local advertising. The latter is not necessarily religious in nature.

Financing the publication

Three methods of financing are generally followed by local churches that sponsor parish papers and magazines. Some put the cost in the operating budget, which may have an item for printing or publicity; some solicit advertising, and others depend upon circulation revenue. Still others combine all these ways or use only two. The first plan is the most satisfactory, for it keeps the church out of the commercial world and places the publication on an independent and dignified footing. A church with an exceedingly small budget cannot follow that policy unless specially interested members of the congregation or friends contribute for this purpose alone.

Much is to be said for the subscription basis. A publication for which individuals have paid directly is likely to gain their loyalty and reading time. But churches usually are not equipped to keep accurate records on subscriptions in any quantity; the bookkeeping may cost more than the parish publication can bring in. A church member cannot be expected to pay more than a dollar a year for such a periodical, although a few churches manage to collect higher sums.

If the publication is to be financed through advertising, the pastor should consult the chamber of commerce of his community. Such a body often has an agreement with business concerns that no organization may solicit advertising for a publication issued locally without a permit from the business group. Restrictions of this type are intended to protect existing publications from racketeers, who attempt to collect money in their names, and to defend merchants from excessive solicitation. Churches at times are peculiarly conscienceless about approaching members who run grocery stores or shoe repair shops and ask them to take advertising space in their publications. If there is a clear value to the merchant, in actual sales possibilities or the building of good will, that is one matter. But likely as not he purchases space out of kindness and with a feeling that this procedure is simply a disguised method of obtaining an additional contribution to the annual budget. This unsound basis for buying advertising space will lead to embarrassment later, for when financial conditions are more stringent these merchants will withdraw their support and the paper will not survive. Only solicitation of valuable and profitable advertising will make the transaction sound and businesslike.

If the local business organization approves the plan, however, it is up to the church to assign the advertising solicitation to some layman with experience in that business. This man or woman should know how to prepare copy for advertisers who do not have enough contracts to employ their own copywriters or to have accounts with agencies. He or she should know how to schedule and place the advertising on the pages, handle the proofs, prepare bills, and other such jobs. The advertising or business manager, as he may be called, should be someone who has had a long enough connection with the church to be known in the community and to know himself what is seemly and unseemly for the church. Every transaction must be completely honest. Sound judgment as to what advertising may properly be solicited must be exercised.

Rates for church advertising of this type naturally are low, for circulations also are low, scarcely exceeding the membership of the church. In setting rates the church should consider what other institutions are charging for similar space and circulation, the cost of production and the types of advertising to be carried (classified will carry a different rate than display, for its purpose is different). But even if there is no financial advantage or only a minuscule deficit, the advantages of the printed publication over the duplicated will be well worth the investment. (See Chapter XV.)

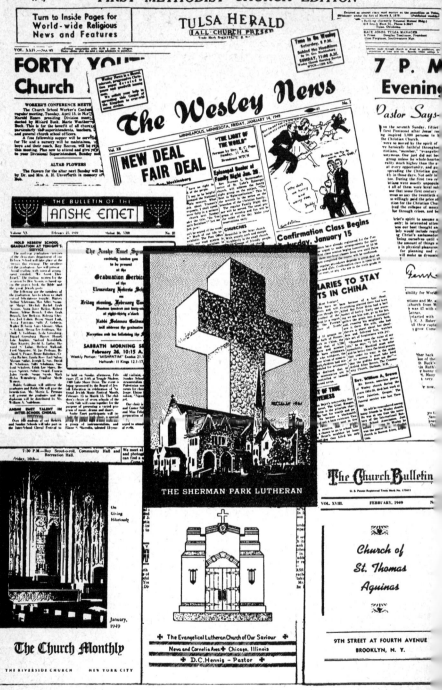

Determining content

However the publication may be produced, the next concern is with content. Main outlines of the purpose will be determined in advance. Content tends to follow purpose. If the intention is to give the church members news of the local institution, the publication obviously must emphasize that type of content. Depending upon the postal arrangements, a proportion of the content may have to be what is known as general material, that is, copy not having a direct connection with the sponsoring church. This regulation will encourage the editor to print reviews of new religious books, prayers, general religious news, and the like. So far as content is concerned, this requirement is a disadvantage also, for it reduces the quantity of local information. But it is advantageous financially, because through it the mailing cost is reduced to a fraction of what it would be otherwise.

The commoner types of reading matter (not paid advertising) used in parish publications are these:

NEWS

Activities of outside groups using the church property—parent-teacher associations, service clubs, and so forth

Community religious news

Community activities not in the church building—Red Cross, Community Chest

Committee and other official activities—board meetings

Denominational news — appointments, elections, conferences

Finance and other internal campaigns

Building construction and repair

General religious news

ere are many varieties of parish maga-
and papers, from full-sized weekly news-
rs to pocket-sized magazines. Most of
are individually produced for particular
:hes but several are sold to various
:hes, with changes for insertion of local
·ials.

Midweek or other special services—rally days
Musical and other artistic events
Organizational activities — Bible classes, men's club
Relief and other external campaigns
Purchases of equipment—projectors, furnaces, fans
Special events—forums, debates, anniversaries, conventions
Personnel changes within the church
Personal news of members
Staff reports
Sports events
Visiting preachers, speakers, leaders, and other ecclesiasts

DEPARTMENTAL
(*Fixed or Repeated Material*)

Vital Statistics:
  Accessions
  Baptisms
  Births
  Deaths
  Sick Lists
  Visitors
  Weddings
Editorials
Calendars and schedules
Bible readings
Book reviews and criticisms
Motion picture evaluations
Radio or television listings
Recommended reading
Questions and answers
Attendance records
Honor rolls—church school
Budgets

Recipes and household hints
Special pages—bishop's or pastor's
Official directories
Masthead and flag (name plates)
School and other columns
Acknowledgements of contributions and gifts
Memorial anniversaries

FEATURES AND MISCELLANEOUS MATERIALS

Poetry
News features—interviews, travelogues
Reprinted articles
Prayers
Sermons and sermonettes
Syndicated matter—syndicate releases, publicity materials
Historical and biographical articles
Letters from missionaries

Most such materials are available to editors of parish publications. Whether they obtain them depends upon the editor's time and diligence, his ability or good luck in finding reporters, writers, illustrators, and photographers within the church family. The parish paper is much like the old-fashioned country weekly in that each reader knows almost all the other readers and all the readers know the editor and he knows each of them. It is a private publication, however, and should be neither as cold as the secular paper or magazine nor as familiar as the editor might become with his closest friends.

Certain of these materials are more valuable than others. A successful editor uses good judgment in his selections and emphases. It would be unwise to stress general religious and denominational news if the congregation is loyal to general church publications and the denominational journals or if the general press locally prints a wide selection of religious information. On the other hand, if the local press gives considerable space to the church's own activities but neglects general religious news, the parish paper might attempt, in its own small way, to compensate for this lack. The objective should be to provide each member with a suitable balance of material in view of what he receives from other sources. Churchmen should consider carefully the policy of printing personal news of the "Mrs. Randolph Jones visited her cousin Angela in Norristown last month" type. In a large church this practice can become troublesome because some persons who make news may be neglected and hard feelings created or other persons may be publicity seekers and appear too frequently. Special effort should be made to report fully: meetings of all official bodies of the church, after as well as before the event, building plans, progress of finance campaigns, and changes in personnel, to mention the more common stories.

Upon the size of the publication and its mailing privilege will depend the quantity of departmental or fixed materials and of feature copy to be used. Some of this general material is available from organizations such as the American Bible Society, Women's Christian Temperance Union, and from all denominational headquarters. Other copy, like motion-picture evaluations, may be bought at a small fee from Independent Filmscores. Such standard information as vital statistics should appear meticulously. It should be correctly and properly printed. Only accurate records will guarantee its quality. It is wise to use inspirational messages, sermons, prayers, and the like sparingly. A parish paper or magazine that becomes merely a propaganda or publicity organ is soon neglected and disrespected. It must have news and other religious information.

If the format is that of a newspaper, it should be imitative of a creditable newspaper, not a technically ineffective one. Headlines should be as professional in caliber as possible, copyreading should be careful, style should be observed, the writing should be concise and although human not sentimental or kittenish. If it is a magazine the pages should be planned and pictures selected with care and properly cropped and reduced, with adequate cutlines (See Chapters XI-XIV, XVI).

The mailing problem

Mailing is a special problem related to the church publication that is not appreciated by persons who write about parish papers and stop at the point of saying that such a publication is an assistant minister. Other types of assistant ministers can get around on their own. But when the printer delivers 500 or 1,000 copies of the parish paper or magazine to the church office on Thursday or Friday a system for handling them must be ready. The only way to avoid this responsibility in the church office is to leave circulation to a firm that makes a business of mailing or to a company that prints the group or chain type of parish journal.

If the publication is prepared in the parsonage or at the church office and is to be mailed directly, as usually is the case, there must be a staff of folders. If the publication is delivered already folded, there must be wrappers; if it comes wrapped or is to be mailed unwrapped, addressers or operators of addressing machines are required. These are nice jobs for enthusiastic young people or loyal oldsters, if they can be corralled to do the job; otherwise they fall to some staff member no doubt already overworked. Papers and magazines must be sorted, tied, labeled, and taken to the post office building. A mailing privilege can be obtained if the publication meets postal regulations and specifications. Postal permits mean that the publication can be mailed by weight and without stamps. But then a genuine subscription or mailing list must be maintained in the office: here is an additional chore and one which cannot be left with safety to a changing group of volunteers.

Despite all this work, if the church finds that it must send out many postal card reminders, that its organizations are doing so or are issuing little papers of their own, and that support for activities is not what it should be, a venture into the parish paper field in a modest fashion will be worth making.

One layman of journalistic experience, who has not found any other outlet for his religious zeal, can be an enthusiastic entire staff of such a publication. If the church is near his home or not too far from his office he may do heroic service and work just as hard and interestedly at this assignment as the musically inclined members do in the choir or the housewives in the commissary.

A centralized publicity plan would add this editor to the committee in charge of all public relations and publicity work. But if such a layman is not available for the task and the church office staff can be expected to handle it, the same person who is the clearing house of external publicity might be responsible for the direction of the church paper, especially if it is small and does not require dealing with advertising problems. It is unlikely, however, that a church large enough to support a substantial publication would not have suitable personnel in its congregation.

Some existing publications

Examination of the publications issued by other groups enables a church about to establish its own to learn much. A church with a publication can obtain ideas for improvement by studying the exchanges. Scores of papers and magazines may be obtained by offering to exchange with other institutions, a common procedure in the secular press, so elaborately developed by some publications that their staffs contain exchange editors. Directories of parish journalism do not exist. Mentioned here, therefore, are examples representing various types, costs, and production methods.

NEWSPAPER FORMAT

Ascension Lutheran Church, 1236 S. Layton Boulevard, Milwaukee 4, Wisconsin, has for a number of years issued *Ascension News*, a four-page monthly newspaper, size 12 by 9 inches. An editorial board of five persons fills it with news.

The Tulsa Herald is issued by the All-Church Press of that Oklahoma city. It is a six- to eight-page standard-size newspaper printed for many participating churches. On its first page is material only about the church buying its own edition; included are the order of service, a pastor's editorial and miscellaneous news. The inside pages are similar for all churches; advertisements share the inside pages with general religious news.

One of the most widely known parish publications in the United States is *The Wesley News*, issued by Wesley Methodist Church, Marquette and Grant, Minneapolis 4, Minnesota. This 8-page, 17 by 11½ inch weekly tabloid has achieved a circulation of 7,000. Its slogan is: ". . . a liberal, tolerant, progressive Christian paper devoted to peace and goodwill among men." Issued for one of the larger Methodist churches, with a downtown city location, it is financed partly by advertising and partly by a dollar-a-year subscription charge. Generous use is made of departments, cartoons, and special articles.

From the First Baptist Church of Richmond, Virginia, comes a four-page monthly, size 8 by 11 inches, on slick paper. It is characterized by many short news stories. *The*

Friendly Visitor carries a picture of the church building as part of its heading, a familiar trade-marking device.

Typical of the papers issued by the larger Hebrew temples of the nation is *The Bulletin* of Temple Beth El, Detroit, Michigan. A four-page business letter size weekly on enameled stock, its photographs reproduced with exceptional clarity on the all-too-rare occasions that they are used.

For a quarter of a century the First Methodist Church of Evanston, Illinois, has had either a magazine or a newspaper. Most of that time *The First Church Review* has been a 7½ by 11 inch weekly newspaper ranging from four to eight pages and obtainable for fifty cents annually, just as is *The Bulletin* noted above. Also like *The Bulletin* it does not solicit advertising. News is emphasized but there also are such general materials as a pastoral prayer, a motion picture guide, book reviews, and short general religious articles received from outside sources.

Others of this general format are *The Weekly Bulletin* of the Stephen S. Wise Free Synagogue of New York, 40 W. 68 St., New York, 23; *The Baptist Visitor*, a weekly issued by the First Baptist Church, 213 N. Second Street, Seminole, Oklahoma; *The Joyce Messenger*, Joyce Memorial Methodist Church, Fremont Avenue, South, at 31st Street, Minneapolis 8, Minnesota; *St. Sebastian's Chronicle*, St. Sebastian's Congregation (Roman Catholic), issued monthly in Milwaukee, Wisconsin; *Presbyterian Letter*, Presbyterian Church of Denison, Texas; *The Trumpeter*, a weekly issued by the First Baptist Church of Portland, Oregon; *The First Methodist Churchman*, 813 S. Hope Street, Los Angeles 13, California; *The Bulletin of the Anshe Emet*, weekly published by the synagogue of that name at Pine Grove and Grace Streets, Chicago; *The Dauphin-Way Baptist*, of the church so designated in Mobile, Alabama; *The Calvary Sword*, a bi-monthly duplicated paper issued by

Calvary Baptist Church, 2202 E. Monroe Street, Phoenix, Arizona; and the *First Baptist Church News Letter* of that church in Washington, D. C.

MAGAZINES

These are less commonly produced as complete publications of individual churches. Several group production schemes similar to the All-Church Press plan for newspaper style parish publications, are available. Typical of that method is the eight-page magazine issued by Grace Methodist Church of Catasauqua, Pennsylvania. A two-color cover is used on the 8¼ by 12 inch publication, with a plate that enables the printer to insert the name of a different church for each run of the presses. About one and a half of the pages carry advertising, all of it local in origin. Little general material is printed; the bulk of the copy pertains to the church using the edition.

The Evangelical Lutheran Church of Our Saviour, Neva and Cornelia Avenues, Chicago, issues a smaller magazine, 8½ by 5½ inches produced almost entirely by Mimeograph. The cover carries a little printing. Three of the twenty-eight inside pages are printed advertising, bought mainly by neighborhood shops.

One of the most professional and impressive magazines issued by single churches is that coming from the Riverside Church of New York City, *The Church Monthly*. Seven issues cost the subscriber two dollars annually; for this he receives a periodical of polished appearance and professional treatment. The issues contain sermons preached at this famous church and several full-length articles on Riverside activities, supported by carefully selected and reproduced photographs. Size 10 by 7 inches, it is free of advertising, printed on heavy stock, and a model of churchly dignity.

Bethany Evangelical Church, 2878 N. 54th St., Milwaukee, Wisconsin, issues a monthly magazine. Size 9 by 6 inches, *The Bethany Community Messenger* is a letterpress product, and highly successful as an advertising medium, a typical issue carrying about fifty per cent advertising, or virtually half the sixteen-page edition. Its editorial content is in contrast to that of the Riverside magazine, for it is almost entirely news material.

Identical in size is *The Sherman Park Lutheran,* another Milwaukee publication, issued by the church bearing that name. Thirteen of the twenty-two pages, including covers, in a sample issue, were advertising copy; the remainder was standing directory material and news stories as well as a little general religious information of a feature type.

A hybrid printed publication is *The Mt. Olive Lutheran,* of the Milwaukee church thus named. This institution, at Washington Boulevard and 54th St., issues a six-page combination newspaper and magazine, self-cover type, with the odd size of 12 by 6½ inches. Supplementing the monthly, which also is an innovation, is the *Mt. Olive Reporter,* a two-page duplicated weekly containing the most recent news, promotional material, and reminders of activities.

One hundred and fifty thousand circulation a month is claimed for *The Church Bulletin,* a Roman Catholic group magazine circulated in the New York City area. Measuring nearly 6 by 9 inches and containing twenty pages of advertising and news material, this publication is in part particularized to the subscribing church; it is commercially produced. Catholic churches in all the New York boroughs as well as parts of New Jersey, Connecticut, Long Island, and some Hudson River shore line communities, distribute it to their members.

CHAPTER IX

Church Bulletins

Common denominator of all church publications is the bulletin, the leaflet or single sheet distributed at Sunday morning and evening services. Although it is not an ortho- dox product of journalism, it often serves journalistic pur- poses: it conveys news and information. Therefore it is another important interpreter of the church, both external and internal. Frequently an elaborated bulletin functions as a parish paper also. Then it is far more than a small piece of printing.

When it is a simply planned sheet carrying little more than order of service and the names of the staff members, the bulletin has no journalistic title, being headed only with the name and address of the church. In this form it some- times is designated the calendar or the announcer. If it is large and practically a parish paper it may carry a distinctive title, as such a publication usually does.

William H. Leach, editor of *Church Management* maga- zine, sees two main motives for the publication of a church bulletin or calendar:

1. The desire to place in an attractive and orderly way the plan of public worship. 2. To provide a dignified and effective way to make announcements relative to the services of the Church.[1]

The second can be understood to mean not just the wor-

---

[1] William H. Leach, *Church Publicity* (Nashville, Tennessee: Cokes- bury, 1929).

ship service but all activities of the church. If such wide use is made of the bulletin it supplements the parish paper and removes announcement making from the spoken portion of the worship service, enhancing that service, for it remains more dignified and worshipful in attitude when there is no mention of bazaars, rummage sales, and Gay Nineties parties.

Content possibilities

St. Paul's Episcopal Church in Syracuse, New York, prints its history in its bulletin occasionally during the year. Sunnyside Methodist Church, of Portland, Oregon, has printed a treasurer's report as well as such inspirational material as religious verse, prayers, and short prose quotations, all in four pages.

The bulletins of the University Church of Disciples of Christ, Chicago, have had pages in which the minister presents a personal message. Other churches have used the bulletin to offer the finance committee's report, sometimes with a thermometer reflecting the week-by-week progress of the every-member canvass and other times with a table of reports. Items of the church budget, in other instances, are carried so that persons in the congregation who are not members, as well as those who are, will be informed about the financial status of the church.

The content possibilities are endless. But not anything or everything should go into the bulletin. Finance campaign thermometers come close to vulgarization of the bulletin; such promotional stunts belong more properly in the parish paper or magazine. What shall be included depends upon whether the church has any other publication, the nature of the congregation, and the state of the budget. The bulletin should have whatever appropriately meets Mr. Leach's two main purposes for it. Even if there be another publication, some additional material of value to strangers is suitable, but only if in tone with the rest of the bulletin. This small publication should be as dignified and worshipful as the service itself; at its best it may be more so, providing a standard as well as a guide.

To make it so requires some knowledge of the graphic arts. Harmonious yet readable type should be selected, whether the bulletin is produced by letterpress printing or duplicating machine. The typographical dress should make this publication look like a bulletin and not like anything else. It should have its own personality, even if it is a combination parish magazine and calendar. Usually such publications are too crowded with material and marred by many heavily boxed paragraphs or filler quotations. The bulletin should be simple and readable. It is used in the church during the services, therefore its function must be taken into consideration. If it is prepared so that pages rustle as the users turn them, the result of not confining the order of worship to one sheet or a double truck (two facing pages), the bulletin is an annoyance and disturbance.

An ideal bulletin format

Although ideal printed bulletins, from the typographical standpoint as well as the financial, are not always the most practical, they serve as a goal. Church music, stained glass, and ritual also are not always the most practical, but have their place and value. So has the bulletin, if treated as an integral part of the worship service and not merely as a promotion piece.

Since this publication is a symbol of the church it should have room for the symbolism of the church, locally or throughout the world. An effective model bulletin would be one of four to eight pages, varying seasonally, 6 by 9 inches in size, with a front cover consisting only of a draw-

ing or photograph of the church steeple or some other archi-
tectural characteristic, such as an entrance; the name and
address of the institution, the names of the chief staff members, and white space. All this should be carefully distributed on the page so that the materials form a unit and are
well balanced.

The second page should be devoted to the worship service, in type harmonious with that on the cover and back
pages. If it cannot be contained on the second page (which
it cannot if the words of the choral music are printed, as
they should be when possible) it should extend over the
two inside pages those numbered two and three, and be
spaced evenly between them. Lines should be distinguish-
able and readable. Careful use of bold face and italics with
regular type will help achieve attractiveness. The main
portions or units in the service—prelude, first hymn, respon-
sive prayer, gloria patri, or whatever else constitutes the
main outlines—might be in boldface and italics, the bold
for the words like **Prelude** and **Gloria Patri** and italics for
the name of the music being played as a prelude or for the
other content of the item itself. Capitalizing and underscoring will provide such emphasis for duplicated bulletins,
while typographical normalcy can be achieved by selection
of the right typewriting machine.

If the order of service covers more than one page but
not more than a page and a half the remaining half page
can be used for brief announcements. Putting the first few
words in boldface, capital letters, or with underlining will
separate one item from the other. Headlines, box-all arrangements for items, and other devices to sharpen these
announcements will not harmonize with the worship service
typography here suggested, especially if ecclesiastical-look-
ing type faces are used in letterpress work (such as Old
English), so a simple presentation is preferred.

If the service covers both inside pages, the announcements and names of members of the official staff not already on the cover might be on the final or fourth page. Names of committee members, lists of stewards, and other such long lists can be left for occasional publication; as weekly reading matter they soon lose their value. Staff names should be at the bottom and certainly include those with whom the members or strangers might wish to deal. Announcements should be chronologically arranged and complete, so that the minister, priest, or rabbi need not supplement them orally; everything possible should be done to avoid the necessity of public corrections of errors in bulletins. Bulletins should eliminate, and when that is not possible, at least shorten, the announcement period.

Such an idealized bulletin cannot be achieved easily if it must be duplicated. But Mimeographing or other methods can provide variations in typography that are attractive. Commercial firms provide training in proficient use of duplicating machines for production of such special materials. Also, there are possibilities of combination letterpress and duplicated bulletins. A local printer can provide the printed cover only and the rest, left blank by him, can be completed by a duplicating process in the church office. He must be told, however, to use a paper stock suitable for duplicating.

Syndicated bulletins

Mention of this possible combination brings up the matter of syndicated or patent-insides type of bulletin. Some denominations, mainly the largest, provide them for their local churches; independent companies also sell them regardless of denomination. The denominational source usually is better because it is particularized to the denomination's problems and needs. Bulletins of this type can be bought by the hundred, and if desired, with printed mate-

One thing's...

St. Mark's Church
Locust Street between 16th and 17th Streets
Philadelphia · · · · · Pennsylvania
REV. WILLIAM H. DUNPHY, Ph. D. · Rector
REV. PHILIP F. FIFER, Th. D.
REV. FRANCIS W. VOELCKER, B. D.
REV. FRANK WILLIAMSON, Th. M. Vicar of St. Michael's Chapel
ERNEST WILLOUGHBY, A.R.C.M. Organist and Master of the Choir

Holy Innocents' Day
The First Sunday after Christmas
December 28, 1947

✠

Sundays

Low Mass	8.00 and 9.00 A. M.
Church School	9.45 A. M.
Matins	10.30 A. M.
High Mass and Sermon	11.00 A. M.
Nursery School	11.00 A. M.
Choral Evensong and Address	4.00 P. M.

✠

Weekdays

Mass Daily exc. Saturday	7.00 A. M.
" " inc. Saturday	7.45 A. M.
Thursday and Holy Days	9.30 A. M.
Matins, Daily	7.30 P. M.
Evening Prayer	5.30 P. M.
Litany and Intercessions, Daily	12.30 P. M.
Litany, Friday	
Confessions, Saturdays	12 to 1 and 4 to 5 P. M.

Unitarian Church of Rochester
Organized in 1829
Temple and Fitzhugh Streets
Honorary Minister
Gary J. C. Sanett
Minister
David Rhys Williams

Here Be No Man A Stranger

Love is the Spirit of this Church,
And Service is its Law.
And this is our Great Covenant,—
To dwell together in Peace,
To seek the Truth in Love,
And to help one another.

EASTER
1 9 4 8

Betts Memorial Universalist Church
677 South Warren Street, Syracuse, N.Y.
REV. ELLSWORTH C. REAMON, D.D., Minister

rial of a general nature on several pages, the number varying by the over-all size purchased, which can range from
four pages to enough for a modest parish paper. Denominational as well as nondenominational printing houses provide
illustrated covers. Discriminating churchmen, however, will
send for samples from several sources before buying a year's
stock in advance, for the art work and messages often are
sentimental or trite.

Whatever the format of this bulletin, it should be produced, if at all possible, with special financing and be in
the printing portion of the regular budget. Advertising has
no place in it, any more than an advertising announcement
from a merchant should be made from the pulpit. Members
of the congregation should not be expected to pay directly
for the bulletin, as they might for a parish paper. But if the
bulletin must be financed through advertising, copy should
be dignified and appropriate to the setting. The name and
address of the merchant is sufficient; sales talk would be
cheap and out of place.

Writing style

News stories in the church bulletin should be as brief
as good newspaper copy requires but be couched in language somewhat less cold, objective, and formal than that
of the secular newspaper or even the parish publication.

Instead of writing:

> The High School Fellowship of Savonarola Christian Church will
> meet at 6:30 P.M. Sunday night at the Church for a discussion of
> "The Gospels Come Alive"

the compiler of the bulletin might phrase it:

> The young people of the High School Fellowship will assemble

---

ny Sunday bulletins are not "home made"
are printed in a central publishing com-
and sold with blank inside pages for use
local church. Bulletins with pictures of
ocal church are always individually pre-
.

at the church at 6:30 this evening to take part in a discussion, "The Gospels Come Alive."

Expressions such as "All are invited," "Bring your friends," "Everyone is welcome," as well as cajoleries, threats, pleadings, and warnings about the dire consequences of failure to attend are out of place in such a publication as well as unnecessary and ineffective. Cheap informalities are no substitute for careful and diligent program planning. If an organization continues to schedule as speaker an ancient bore it naturally expects the bulletin to make up for the unattractiveness of what it has to offer.

Clear, dignified, plain English is appreciated in these little publications. Kittenish, improperly punctuated, and capitalized writing, like the following, actually from a bulletin, is both silly and out of place:

> All Church organizations desiring to put on Something Special at the church, are asked first, to see The Calendar Committee, of which the pastor is chairman, so as to avoid unnecessary conflicts and confusion in the matter of "Specials" of all kinds. Get A Date First.

Nothing should be in the bulletin, in other words, which the leader of the church would hesitate to say from the pulpit. The bulletin is an adjunct of the worship service and not basically an advertising or publicity leaflet.

Editing procedures

Whether it be edited by the head of the church, a secretary, or a volunteer, the bulletin should be produced as systematically as the parish paper or magazine. The one, in fact, can help the other and can be co-ordinated with it.

If the church has a public relations program, the bulletin is part of the plan. Organization publicity chairmen, when they submit copy for the outside press and radio, can be requested to include enough carbons so that a version of the news story is available for the parish paper and another for much shorter use in the bulletin. Such copy must be closely and neatly edited by the staff, if not rewritten, for it is unlikely that in the original it will be sufficiently brief and suited to the bulletin. But all the usual sources of information must be tapped. By certain deadlines the basic information needed from the ministers, the church school officials, and the organist and choir director should be in the hands of the editor, who takes the preceding week's bulletin as the basis and guide of the one to come and makes alterations as needed.

Editing an old issue first and then copying it afresh is a dependable method of producing a new issue of a printed bulletin. But that procedure is time-consuming. Instead, the editor can run off on a duplicating machine the headings or titles of the basic items for the bulletin that repeat from week to week, such as the words *Hymn No.* and *Offering*. Room should be left on this duplicated form for filling in the new facts. Thus only what is changed or is new need be written each time. Since this sheet will be larger than the bulletin, probably letter or legal size, there is less likelihood of mistakes occurring than if the bulletin itself is interlined either by hand or on the typewriter.

If the bulletin is printed by letterpress the editor can consult the printer about the feasibility of producing it and the parish paper or magazine in the same operation. That is, if both can use the same paper stock (the presence of pictures will determine this, as will the intention to duplicate part of the bulletin) and if the two, when assembled in the form, constitute the right size for printing, they can be produced at the same time and then cut apart and folded. This procedure reduces make-ready, saves paper, minimizes separate handling of the publications, and reduces the cost.

CHAPTER X

Miscellaneous Printed Materials

Dr. D. A. McCall, a Southern churchman, apparently intent on what might be called making war on the secular spirit of the day, once dropped packets of tracts over Mississippi from an airplane.

As state mission secretary of the Mississippi Baptist Convention, Dr. McCall was given a plane by the constituents of the convention so that he could suspend the tracts from parachutes and drop them in remote sections of the state. Dr. McCall, who called his cargo "heavenly circulars," himself piloted the craft, known as "The Gospel Flyer."

Thus can the church, if it chooses, use one of the several dozen types of miscellaneous printed materials. These tools for interpretation all can supplement the newspaper, magazine, motion picture, radio, and television.

Other ways, somewhat less dramatic but no less practical, are to place calendars in parishioners' homes, fans in the pews, leaflets on the corridor tables or in racks on lobby walls, booklets in mailboxes, car cards on buses and trains and street cars, posters in windows, and speakers on programs.

Nor are these all. The church also can interpret itself through news accounts sent to press associations or wire service bureaus, pamphlets left on hotel and store counters, calling cards dropped in doorway mailboxes when the pastor cannot find members of his flock at home, advertisements pasted on outdoor billboards, blotters included in correspondence, and messages via telephone and transmitted in personal calls.

Still other devices of a less conventional type are used by extremists in church publicity. One minister, preaching on "The Bread of Life," has given away loaves of bread at his services. Another, a ventriloquist, took a dummy into the pulpit with him and made the little figure interrupt him during the sermons to ask questions. Still another was able to theatricalize religion because he was a magician. Most such tricks, however, went out of fashion at about the same time that the most spectacular stunts of the circus press agent were toned down.

Each of the more conventional and suitable devices has its production problems, its own variety of content, and its special use. The decision about which to use (if any) will depend, as usual, upon the financial strength and willingness of the church, although a few cost little or nothing and others soon pay for themselves. Each is examined and discussed here, mainly from the viewpoint of the local church. Almost all are used by regional church groups as well.

Billboard advertisements: Few individual churches can afford this type of advertising. It is best financed by groups of congregations or by merchants who pay the cost of advertising all the churches in the community in this way. The bills are then posted on boards along roads leading to the community. Considering the opposition to billboard advertising in general, churches may wish to erect only small and general signs, urging church attendance or calling attention to the number of churches in the town or city.

Blotters: Like fans, blotters are small auxiliary publicity pieces but of more everyday value than fans, for blotters may be used in all seasons. Any church can keep its name before the public with a dignified blotter, either of the small type for hand use or the large, desk size. Obtainable in bulk, either type can be financed through advertising but is best handled as an investment of the church from the publicity budget.

Booklets: This piece of printed matter is more substantial than the pamphlet and, as its name implies, is a small book. Yearbooks, pictorial stories of institutions or organizations, anniversary materials, handbooks, and any number of other kinds can be issued by a church or church group. Booklets are among the more expensive products of a press or duplicating machine, but can pay for themselves, since members expect to buy them. Different means of financing have been used. An organization or the church itself can pay for production and hope to recoup from direct sales, often a sure if slow result. To be successful this method requires money on hand and a promotion plan. Or the booklet can be financed in advance, as books for general circulation were underwritten in Shakespeare's time, and not published until the cost has been raised. Or advertising can be sold—if business circles in the community co-operate and businessmen think it worth while to them to use the space—and the cost subscribed for in advance that way. A booklet, if professionally produced, can be a permanent publicity medium for the church, one of considerable value for years. It too should be neatly and carefully produced and carry a distinguishing symbol of the church or organization issuing it.

Books: Few local churches go into the book publishing business, which is left to the denomination as a whole or to a religious book publishing firm. Occasionally, however, an anniversary can be marked by the publication of a book-length history of the church or the biography of a pastor of long service. An outstanding church or minister is so good a subject for a book that a professional publishing house—and most denominations operate one or have arrangements to contract for publications—should be approached first with the idea. If it is to be a locally produced book, a large printing firm no doubt will be available in the nearest big city if not in the local community. The manufacture of 10,000 copies of an average-size bound book is far too expensive for most churches, however. Rarely can more than 500 or 1,000 be sold, even over a long period of years, so that a large order is unwise. Only if some philanthropist wishes to finance the volume and give it away should a big order be placed. Should the idea not command the co-operation of a church publisher as a safe or profitable venture for him, the volume probably should be ruled out; but not necessarily, for a distant publishing firm may not understand local possibilities. If the idea has provable local merit and the church proceeds at its own risk, whoever is in charge should obtain the advice of someone in the congregation who is familiar with book production and the machinery for distribution should be set up. The church must be prepared for the possibility of storing hundreds of copies of the book for years to come as they sell slowly. Carefully planned promotion will cut down the need for much storage space.

Calendars: Literally these are date tellers and not Sunday bulletins, also sometimes thus called. Of the small types of printed matter this publication is one of the most practical and long-lasting. Any neat wall calendar will survive a year. It is possible to buy quantities, with the local church's imprint, from church supply companies. Obviously a locally produced one, with full information about the institution, is more valuable as a publicity medium than the imprinted type, which is little more than a wintry scene, a summertime view, or a religious stereotype below which appear the name and address of the church. But the home-town printer must charge more since he cannot sell such calendars in large enough quantities to reduce the price, so the hometown product may not justify its expense. A compromise is to sell advertising space, but this policy detracts from the calendar and puts the church in a commercial setting.

Calling: Although a conventional and standard activity of any church, and the special responsibility of the ministers, priests, and others on church staffs, calling can be organized among the members on a neighborhood basis, not to relieve the professional staff but to supplement it, and to help reach friends not already members of the particular institution. Appointments may be made ahead of time or not, as experience dictates, in any selected neighborhood, since customs vary between communities in different areas of a country as large as the United States. Members of committees that make such calls will find it helpful to take with them one or two pieces of printed matter about the church: a small descriptive folder, a yearbook, a calendar, a card, the church paper or magazine, the denominational publication, or some other interpretative printed material. Families visited in such a program thus have a reminder of the visit and some reading for the future.

Calling cards: Usually this pasteboard rectangle is the minister's professional card, which he leaves in the mailbox if the person called upon is not at home. Churchmen sometimes prefer a less personal document, such as an institutional card saying, in print, that a representative of the church made the visit. Others are content to use their personal cards, adding a pen or pencil message. When printed locally and in small quantities, such cards can be expensive and tend to disappear rapidly, but they are helpful to the total program of the church.

Car cards: Car cards are a compromise over the billboard advertisement already mentioned. They appear along the upper sides of the interiors of subway cars, trolley cars, buses, elevated cars, and railway cars, chiefly vehicles that travel within cities or in limited suburban areas. Much less expensive than the larger countryside billboards, these placards can be effective regular reminders of the church's program. Copy, which usually is prepared by an advertising agency, announces services, uses symbols of the church, and harmonizes with the tone of other church literature and display in print. Related to these but used in the relatively few cities that have transportation station advertising, such as "L" and subway platforms, are sheet advertisements giving much the same information.

Fans: Practical and necessary everywhere but in an air-conditioned church or one in a constantly cool climate, fans have small publicity value as compared with booklets or even calendars. Not always are they considered in tone with a dignified church program; usually they are anything but handsome. Like calendars, they can be financed through advertising or bought in bulk quantities with the church imprint. Churches should use discretion about what is advertised and how it is presented.

Flyers: Not aviators but abbreviated leaflets, flyers generally are a single sheet carrying a message intended to promote a rummage sale, a church dinner, a meeting, or a picnic. To be effective they should be distributed widely in large quantities; hence they should be cheaply produced but not cheap in appearance. Although they can be made of inexpensive paper they should not be carelessly printed or sloppily duplicated. The tendency is to produce them hastily. Once again it must be remembered that every piece of printed matter, no matter how temporary its purpose, is a messenger of the church.

Indoor and outdoor bulletin boards: Wherever used, bulletin boards can be effective in reaching persons who may not see any of the church literature or be touched by its other attempts to interpret its work and activities. Such a board is most often seen on the church lawn or attached to the building. It announces services and especially sermon subjects. In either place it should be a publicly visible spot, preferably at a point where there is most passing traffic. Its main words should be clearly visible and readable from a moving vehicle. Smaller bulletin boards might be placed in hotel lobbies, if permitted (which they usually are if all churches are represented, with small display space for each), in library lobbies, in college commons, and similar public places. As with any other printed approach, bulletin boards should be accurate and attractive. Whatever cannot be comprehended in the time it takes to walk past such a board is lost and might as well be omitted. More specialized bulletin boards are needed in the corridors of a church than one commonly finds in use. On them may be notices of many different kinds, directories of personnel, with removable letters. Framed blackboards and composition boards that take thumbtacks are quickly altered.

Leaflets: A pamphlet is close to a magazine in format and appearance; a leaflet is related to a newspaper or poster. At most it is four pages long, usually one sheet folded, and ordinarily it is a single sheet, about 5 by 7 inches. Intended as an announcement carrier and not for permanent use, it tells of some forthcoming activity in a typographic scheme not unlike that of a poster. Or it is used for the program sheet of some event, either one or both sides carrying messages. Generally leaflets are printed or duplicated in black and white whereas pamphlets and booklets may be in colored inks. Pamphlets are mailed but leaflets, as a rule, are for hand or over-the-counter distribution, as are flyers. As with all church materials of the sort, whether letterpress or duplicated, leaflet content should not be crowded. The receiver should be able to grasp its message quickly, without having to study it. The copywriter for it, therefore, should use few type faces and try to achieve contrast between the ones he selects.

Letters: These are the heart of any direct-mail advertising or promotion campaign depending upon the printed word. The types of letters are multitudinous. Also wide is the variety in methods of production. They may be typewritten, Mimeographed, multigraphed, hectographed, planographed, printed, or handwritten. As in business, the more personal in appeal and original the more effective. Large mailings cannot be produced in a church office with the personal touch unless electrical typewriters are used; therefore most letters in big quantities are duplicated in some standard fashion. Addressing is a simpler matter. The church office can utilize any one of a number of available addressing machines. Writing letters for publicity purposes is almost an occupation in itself. If an entire finance or other special campaign is to depend heavily upon letters, the person in charge, if not a professional direct-mail user, might well study the textbooks on letter writing, seeking, however, to retain the friendliness and informality of the church family and coupling them with the word-economy and psychology to be learned from such books. Professionals, for example, advise putting the emphasis "on his lawn and not on our grass seed."

Pamphlets: Leaflets, booklets, flyers, and pamphlets are all more or less in the same family, as small pieces of printed matter go. In church circles all these have for years also been called *tracts,* but the pamphlet comes closest to the usual form for the religious tract, one of the earliest forms of religious journalism, used so effectively by John Wesley. A pamphlet is more substantial than its cousins. Like a small magazine, it may have a separate cover or be a self-cover type of publication. It may be black and white or use color printing. It can be any shape, from 7 by 9 inch magazine size to a 3 by 2 inch pocket document. It may use pictures or be without them. Any printer can produce a pamphlet, for once it becomes too elaborate it is called a booklet or brochure, and he can reject it as not being what it was intended to be. Materials of permanent value should be presented through it: the history of the church, the story of some activity that has been widely successful, such as an educational program, the description of the work of some fundamental department, like the church school. All the principles of producing effective printed matter—readability, harmonious plan, and others—should be remembered. It is wise to reproduce on pamphlet covers, preferably the first one, whatever symbol appears on other printed material produced by the church. This identifying sign can be a smaller version of the cut on the parish paper or magazine or the Sunday bulletin, such as the church seal or steeple. For the average church a pamphlet which avoids tricky format and typography is best. Pamphlets should be both short and portable. Content will determine, to some extent, what the format should be. If a sermon is to be printed, the pamphlet should be pocket-size, so that it can be carried easily in a woman's purse or a man's side pocket. If it is the story of a department or of the symbolic stones in the church building or of the church's stained glass windows or its settlement work or its missionary program and presents pictures, it should be larger, to show the pictures to advantage.

Postal cards: Naturally these are linked with letters and might be considered letterettes. If the church office uses an addressing machine the postal card is a quickly produced communicator with the entire congregation. The front can be run through the addressing machine and the message to the reader printed or duplicated on the back. That message is most likely to be effective if it can be read at a glance. Careful spacing and use of upper and lower case letters on the typewriter, addition of eye-catching drawings or symbols, and a concise style are all important. Such cards are so commonly employed, however, that a little thought in advance is valuable, for it may produce originality and hence special attention. Sometimes church groups print them early for certain types of seasonal mailings and fill in dates and places on the duplicating machine or typewriter. Postal cards are among the least expensive of publicity aids.

Speakers: Every person who speaks in the name of a church group is an interpreter of that institution, whether he realizes it or not. But the Minute Man idea is adaptable to church activities if the personnel is available. This work should not necessarily be a chore of the publicity chairman of the organization, who may or may not be an effective public speaker. Instead, it should fall upon some churchman gifted in speaking. A man or woman with a clear, well-projected voice, a pleasant manner, and the ability to make an announcement without having it sound too conventional or too freakish is helpful in making this type of interpretation effective. There also is the speakers' bureau, which may be maintained by an organization within a church body, on a local as well as a national scale. For example, the committee on world peace of a certain church offered a half-dozen speakers, with peace problems subjects, to the program chairmen of other organizations in the congregation. Public forums, roundtables, and town meetings sponsored by a church are important elements in public relations. A church which sets up such a forum on a controversial subject, encouraging the hearing of all points of view, strikes a blow for its concept of democracy.

Spot announcements on radio and television: Here is a relatively new publicity device. Radio stations—and small television stations—usually are willing to announce, at no charge, a church activity of general nature before and after some religious program. The latter may be a network or local broadcast. How many such announcements are made depends upon what religious programs are being carried and the distance in time from the events to be announced. Such time can be purchased, as well. Wording of the announcement should avoid the worst faults of radio and television commercials; what is to be said can be agreed upon with the station manager or program director.

Telephone campaigns: In a city or community where a flat rate is charged for telephone service and not for each local call a telephone committee can be a remarkably successful publicity agency. A church organization can set up such a committee, preferably of persons with time and telephone, and divide the yearbook membership list among them or prepare selected lists for each member. Every committeeman is given the text of the announcement to be made, but encouraged to relay it in a friendly, conversational manner. After all, many of the persons reached are known to the telephoner. Quick and personal, this method costs little. It can stimulate greater friendliness than is possible with postal cards or impersonal printed announcements.

Window posters: Like all printed matter, these posters have become more expensive in recent years. Unless the church has its own printing equipment or patient, skilled hand-lettering experts, these elaborate posters are not so commonly used as in the days of cheaper printing but are still popular in small communities. They provoke an ethical problem if store owners are expected to display them. Members of the church may be willing to do so on request, but

Various types of miscellaneous printed
rials used by church groups, local, reg
national, and international; the more attr
usually have clear and readable covers.

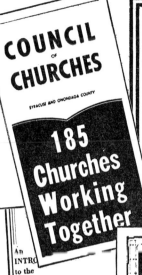

COUNCIL OF CHURCHES

SYRACUSE AND ONONDAGA COUNTY

185 Churches Working Together

CRUSADE FOR A BETTER UNDERSTANDING OF

UNIVERSALISM

Published by
THE UNIVERSALIST CHURCH

The FIRST FIFTY YEARS

The Story of
HOLY REDEEMER
Roman Catholic
CONGREGATION
Milwaukee   Wisconsin

An INTRO to the
BRYN MAWR
PRESBYTERIAN
CHURCH

Bryn Mawr, Pa.
March, 19

THE METHODIST STAKE IN
Hawaii

THE FACE AT THE WINDOW

FIRST METHODIST **MEN'S CLUB** CHURCH • EVANSTON

September 13, 1947

TO ALL MEN OF THE CHURCH:

T. Otto Nall, managing editor of THE CHRISTIAN ADVOCATE, will address the opening fall meeting of the Men's Club at a dinner-speaker meeting, 6:45 p.m. Tuesday, Sept. 23, in the church dining room.

Dr. Nall, who has very recently returned from war-devastated Europe, will speak on "Germany Today and Tomorrow". He has been managing editor of THE CHRISTIAN ADVOCATE since 1940 when Methodist unification brought the merger of seven sectional papers into one official weekly and has been identified with Methodist journalism since 1922. His message will be factual and most interesting.

Please phone your reservation to the church office (UNi. 6181), or use the handy postage-free reply card below. Reservations for the dinner must be in by noon, Monday, Sept. 22.

You are all cordially invited to attend. Let's make this a big meeting!

PUBLICITY COMMITTEE

P.S. Al Johnson, president, says, "Be on hand for this evening of fine entertainment and fellowship. There will be important announcements."

For Res

MEN'S CLUB
FIRST METHODIST
CHURCH • EVANSTON

Please reserve . . . . plates for me at the next meeting of the club.

. . . .
Phone

. . . .
Address

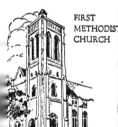

FIRST
METHODIST
CHURCH

CURRICULUM
GUIDE

1948-1949

WHY CHRISTIAN EDUCATION IS IMPORTANT

nonmembers who have shops may feel that institutional pressure is being brought to bear, as with advertising in the parish paper. The advice about preparing all such material so that it can be read at a glance is vital with these posters. They should be moderate in size, not more than 9 by 12 inches, for merchants do not wish to deface or obscure their windows with oversize cards. The content should be that of any good newspaper lead, amplified by a symbol of the church or a cut of some person prominent in the announcement. If the posters announce a profit-making activity, the firm displaying the card should be given one or two tickets of admission. By counting the number of likely outlets the number of posters needed can be determined.

Yearbooks: Much like pamphlets and booklets, yearbooks actually are a special form of one or the other of these. Organizations within a church favor annuals and yearbooks, for in them they can list their members' names, announce their programs for the year ahead, record the accomplishments of the year before, reproduce their constitutions and other official documents. The yearbook for an entire church has the same function, but is not practical with a rapidly changing membership. Such an annual publication can be as elaborate or simple as desired and can be financed through direct sale or advance subscription. It is moderately useful as an interpreter and more useful as a directory and reference book. When produced for the whole church it can carry a history, material on the ministers, past and present, reports of organizations, pictures, and souvenir content of that sort. Combining it with a calendar makes it extra-useful. Whether printed or duplicated, good workmanship should be used, since the yearbook is a twelve-month reminder of the church. Financing it through the sale of space to advertisers is common and far more appropriate than in most other church printing.

CHAPTER XI

The Tools of Interpretation

The *tools* of interpretation differ from the *media* of interpretation. The media are the outlets or channels—newspaper, magazine, radio, and the others. The tools are the machines, devices, and principally the techniques needed to create and use these media.

Such a book as this could not—nor does it need to—present a complete explanation of the tools. But there is a small amount of technical information that the churchman should possess and should understand at once to enable him to make intelligent use of the tools and to do further study. That small quantity is in this and several succeeding chapters.

The tools change rapidly. Electronics, for example, is altering journalism's tools by adding to them wire and tape recorders, faster cameras, and other inventions. Basically, however, church use of the printing press is unaffected. It is the use of radio and television that has injected the newest elements.

What are these tools? Mainly techniques of obtaining and processing news, features, photographs and other elements that the media employ. The presses, typesetting machines and other such mechanical devices will be left in the background. Churchmen can no more be expected to understand exactly how an engraving camera operates than they can be expected to know precisely how their hats or brief cases are manufactured.

Undergirding modern communications systems are the graphic arts—photography and printing. Both radio and television also use them, if to a lesser extent than newspapers and magazines. Radio has its peculiar production problems. We shall examine them as they touch the job of interpreting the church.

PHOTO-JOURNALISM

For years now it has not been original to point out that pictures have become a vastly more important part of modern journalism than they used to be. Church journalists must accept this fact. Thus we should examine at once what it means to them. Among the conclusions are these:

Newspapers and magazines are more interested in news and features about churches or church people if they are accompanied by photographs than if the copy is not illustrated.

Parish papers, denominational journals and other religious publications, while slower to accept and use photography than the secular press, use more pictures than ever before.

Syndicates, not only National Catholic Welfare Conference News Service and Religious News Service but also general feature distributors, respond to picture ideas and prints and send them to subscribers.

Radio would seem to be indifferent to pictures but it uses them as part of any public relations program. And television uses many photographs as background. Video is itself a form of photography.

Although everyone in journalism is more picture-conscious than ever before, because of the increased use of photography in publications, of movies, and of the growth of amateur photography, we know more about enjoying them than we do of taking, selecting, and editing them. Church people are quicker to see the news or feature-story possibilities in a situation than they are to see the picture possibilities. The churchman responsible for publicity or for publications work that could use photography needs to develop a picture sense as well as a nose for news.

It will be helpful to examine, therefore, the ways in which the secular press makes use of photography, some of the kinds, sources, and qualities of pictures, and their application to religious journalism.

Newspapers—all dailies and some weeklies—employ cameramen, from one on a small daily to fifteen or twenty on a metropolitan giant. Several cameras are owned by a moderate-size paper; space is provided for at least one darkroom and facilities for developing, printing, and enlarging are available to the staff photographers. Big papers have roomy studios for taking pictures in color and special black and white pictures for both news and advertising use. The Chicago *Tribune* studios, for example, are equipped to take color photographs as readily as black and white.

Large magazines also have staff photographers; they are the heart of the picture publications like *Life* and *Look*. Cameramen are much like reporters in their function but use different tools. They must work just as fast as writing and reporting newsmen, be where the news breaks, and overcome the additional handicap of dependence upon a machine that may fail, falter, or run short of supplies.

Just as they assign stories to reporters, newspapers assign pictures to cameramen—and camerawomen, for women are proving themselves highly competent in this profession. Often the reporter and cameraman travel together to a joint assignment. On their return to the editorial rooms the reporter goes to his desk and typewriter, the photographer to his darkroom. When the prints are ready they are sent, still damp and limp, to the picture editor or city desk boss. The reporter hails a copy boy to take his story to the same desk. The editor in charge decides which of the pictures—all, a few, or none—he will use. His decision may depend mainly upon the quality of the cameraman's work. A few dailies use trucks equipped with darkrooms so that pictures can be processed en route.

Staffs only one source

Their own staffs, however, are only one of the sources of pictures for the secular press. If the paper is a member of the Associated Press it may use AP Wirephoto pictures. These are photographs sent from distant points by a machine that scans the print electrically and reproduces it in the receiving office on another device. Thus a paper obtains a wide assortment of news and feature pictures of the day, much as it takes from its teletype a big selection of news and feature stories. Similar service may be bought from other agencies.

Feature syndicates also provide picture copy, by airmail if they are spot news photographs and in the usual glossy print form, by regular mail if they are not so timely and therefore can be supplied in matrix form, that is, a papier-mache or plastic impression of an engraving.

Free-lance photographers bring pictures to newspaper offices. Publicity and advertising offices provide numerous prints free, with the hope that the press will use them and gain attention for the product or person or institution being publicized.

Theoretically the staff man or woman responsible for selecting pictures for the newspaper is the picture editor. But only metropolitan sheets have full-time picture editors. On small and moderate-sized publications each departmental editor selects the pictures for his space: the society editor for her page, the sports editor for his, and so on. Someone may be responsible for assembling a picture page; that person comes close to being picture editor but he spends most of his time as copyreader, make-up editor, or in performance of some other function. He lays out a page made up of selected prints received by wire, from the staff photographer and all the other sources.

Picture editors must follow standards in making their selections if their results are to be attention-getting and attractive. Local interest in the picture is a vital test. A photograph might be of superlative quality but if what it portrays has less eye-appeal than a print that technically is imperfect it will not be given space.

Technically prints are acceptable if they are sharp and clear, with every element of importance in focus; if the detail is authentic and contributes to the realism of the picture; if the contrast is sufficient to obtain successful reproduction when the cut is made. Journalistically the photograph is valuable if it is newsy; if the news it transmits can be conveyed more quickly and effectively through the camera than by words. Artistically the photograph is first class if it has what artists call significant form; that is, it should have unity, balance, rhythm, movement, emphasis, and proportion.

Three kinds of pictures

Magazines and newspapers use three kinds of pictures: straight news, news feature, and pictorial. The first two are recognizable by their names; the third is a newcomer to our terminology and means those that are without particular news interest but are suitable for feature picture pages and special uses in advertising and fashion sections. A striking river scene, a snowy country road in December, and gulls over the water are popular as well as trite examples of pictorials.

Religious pictures

Religious activities offer many possibilities for photography. A local church publicity committee or general church organization publicity department should think of picture opportunities when laying out a promotion campaign. Let us assume that these possibilities are realized. What of expenses and arrangements for taking pictures, of types of pictures to be taken, and of ways to send them out?

The large church group seeking publicity, such as a denominational overhead organization, has staff photographers or money to pay professionals when they are needed. But a city church and certainly a rural church cannot do this. They can do something else, however.

1. Arrange with a photo studio or journalistic cameramen in the community to take pictures that have publicity value. Such arrangements vary. If the photographer is a lay churchman he may be willing to take them at cost. If he is not, he may charge as much as five dollars for each, which is too expensive for most churches if more than an occasional one is to be taken.

2. Suggest to the community newspapers ideas for pictures. When sending out stories to city editors append a note outlining picture possibilities. When telephoning to a newspaper city room about a story on a forthcoming event it is useful to mention the pictures that might be taken. On many occasions, if the event is of enough importance, the papers will come for pictures without being asked specially. The times when the church must take its own pictures are during unplanned or informal events. Then it is that the third method of obtaining pictures is useful.

3. Ask photography enthusiasts in the congregation to let someone in the church office see their photographs taken at the church picnics, dinners, or other congregational events. If this is done promptly, the church can borrow the negative and have prints made for the newspapers or community magazines.

A human interest picture, for example, taken at a church affair and not dependent upon timeliness to gain interest, is an effective publicity photograph. In its underlines appear phrases like: ". . . in this scene from a recent picnic of First Christian Church members held at Green Lake State Park."

Picture sending rules

When pictures are sent to newspapers, magazines, and syndicates, rules such as these should be observed:

1. The picture should be a glossy, because the shiny surface of this type of print is more successful than dull finishes in making engravings from photographs. But a good shot should not be discarded simply because it does not have a glossy surface.

2. If possible the picture should be 8 by 10 inches in size, but 5 by 7 inches is acceptable.

3. It should be identified completely and accurately. The print itself should be unmarked. No sharp point, like that of a pen or pencil, ever should be used to write on either side of it except in the margins or the reverse side and there only lightly. Better is a rubber stamp. Gummed paper or sheets attached by Scotch tape may be used. The reverse side should reveal the source of the picture, what credit line is to be used, and to whom it is to be returned after use. The main identification is known as the *underline;* this descriptive matter should be typewritten on a sheet as wide as the picture and fastened with rubber cement so the written material hangs below the print and can be folded over it.

Cutlines are very much like newspaper leads: they summarize what is shown in the picture, using complete names and identifications and describing the action or scene briefly.

4. When possible send different pictures to rival publications. If they are not delivered directly they should be mailed between cardboard sheets.

5. Do not expect pictures back from papers, magazines, publicity offices, and syndicates. They often will be returned but there is no obligation to do so. To make sure they are, when this is necessary, enclose stamped and addressed envelopes.

Internal use

So far we have examined only the external use of photographs in religious public relations and publicity work. There also is the internal use of photographs. Few parish papers print as many as they might; denominational publications, being somewhat more professional in their methods as well as more affluent, are increasing their use, although in some instances hardly enough for the best results.

Parish publications do not use more photographs chiefly because of the work and expense involved (certainly two excellent reasons). An additional excuse is that the church-man-editor does not believe he can spare the space. His first two reasons are far better than the third. If more members or potential members of his church give attention to the parish paper or magazine because it is attractively illustrated, the sacrifice of space no longer is a sacrifice.

Great expenditures need not be made. Now and then it is possible, surely, to spend a few dollars on a photograph and a few more on an engraving that can be used repeatedly. For example, each parish paper should have a cut, not only of the head of the local church, but also of the bishop of the area or some other official who visits it occasionally to speak or to inspect or to preside at some official gathering. The magazine-type of parish publication is especially dull if lacking in sufficient pictures.

Certain sources for photographic prints or finished engravings should not be overlooked:

1. The publicity departments of companies and organizations whose representatives are speaking or otherwise appearing at the church. If the editor knows well in advance who is to be present he can write to this publicity department and ask for mats or engravings of these persons. This material breaks up the blank-looking pages of the church house organ.

2. Failing this, the editor can approach the speakers themselves. Persons who speak or preside frequently and realize the value of proper publicity sometimes have such materials ready on request.

3. Local publications that use pictures of special interest to the church usually are willing to let religious groups borrow the engravings (or buy mats at cost) after they have been used in their publications provided: *a*) they are returned promptly and in good condition and *b*) full credit is given the source (by printing in small type a line reading: "Photograph by courtesy of the Smalltown *Daily Record Herald*").

4. Certain stock illustrative material, not photographs or engravings, but what are known as line drawings and zincs, can be purchased at a low price from firms that advertise in trade journals for the country press and in trade papers that service syndicates (*The American Press* and *Editor & Publisher*, for example). This material consists of mats of cuts or reproductions of drawings. Among stock materials are Christmas scenes and other seasonal and holiday symbols. If harmonious, they do much to make a parish publication look livelier.

In obtaining such materials, however, the borrower must be sure that his publication is printed on a quality of paper that will reproduce the borrowed cut. For instance, if the local daily is printed on ordinary newsprint, which is likely, the engravings made for it will be about 65 screen. If the parish paper is printed on a heavy, enameled stock, that halftone will not print clearly. A moderate grade of paper is best for use of a variety of engravings.

TYPOGRAPHY AND MECHANICS

Printing is the other member of the graphic arts family. Although churchmen cannot be expected to know much about typography and mechanics in journalism, they should have a little familiarity with the processes and equipment so that they can make more intelligent use of them. Non-professionals must work closely with printers and must depend upon the printers in the long run.

Religious publications are not all printed by letterpress. Scores of individual church papers are duplicated or reproduced in some way other than by letterpress. Since the less expensive types of duplication, like Mimeographing, are generally understood and since the church publicist for the most part works with letterpress produced publications, we will concentrate in this section on that printing process.

The equipment includes typesetting machines, known by such trade names as Linotype, Intertype, Monotype, and Ludlow. Copy used by most newspapers and magazines, regardless of size, is set on these machines. Books are composed on the Monotype as well as the Linotype; the former's results are more durable and stand wear better but are slower in production. Headlines and other display lines are set on Linotype or Intertype and the Ludlow typograph.

After type has been set it is assembled into pages, known as forms. The four pages of a small parish weekly will comprise a four-part form. Publications are printed directly from such forms if not many copies are needed or if sufficient time is allowed for slow printing. Daily newspapers and large magazines are high-speed productions; for them an impression is taken off the page of type, that process being known as stereotyping. In effect the page is reproduced on a curved metal plate, in reverse. This plate then is mounted on a press and inked, the paper being run across it to receive a right-side-up impression.

Photographic copy also is reproduced on plates, as are drawings and similar illustrations, such as cartoons and caricatures. The glossy photograph is the basis for the half-tone; line drawings become zincs or line cuts. In recent years photographic plates have been made of the proofs of type-set material, arranged in pages, to produce offset (lithographic) publications.

Religious journalists who are not on the production side have little contact with these machines and others that have not been mentioned but are used in production, such as the various styles and types of presses. But they must mark copy for type specifications and therefore should understand something about the uses of types.

Groups of types

Although there are hundreds of families (styles) of type, there are only five main groups: Text, Gothic, Script, Roman, and Italic. That is their historical order. Taken alphabetically, they can be described briefly.

Gothic, a name all churchmen will find easy to remember, is a bold, square, and rugged type. Popular for many years in large headlines for newspapers and magazines, it is not as readable as some other faces. It gets its appearance of strength much as do Gothic church buildings.

Italic type is recognizable at once because of its sloping appearance. Its characteristics have been taken over by all major type families. It is possible to obtain a type in regular (that is, not slanted) or italic (slanted) form. Italic is inherently delicate and effeminate; it has been used widely in church literature, which is no reason why it should continue to be used.

Roman is the largest in number of faces that can be found in one style. A compromise between the severe Gothic and the more ornate type known as Text, it appears in two main groups: old style and modern. Modern Roman types are popular in these days of streamlined publications.

Script has long been associated with the church and religion. Like handwriting in appearance, it is dignified, somewhat effeminate, and delicate; it does not stand heavy wear. Wedding and other formal announcements use it.

Text is the oldest of the five and better known to churchmen as Old English. At one time it was the most widely used type in church circles. It exudes dignity, ornateness, and churchliness, resembling the illuminated lettering of the monks of yore and being equally unreadable.

All the type faces known as Bodoni, Caslon, Cooper, Kabel, and by hundreds of other names are designations of sub-groups of the five major styles. Almost identical types may have different names because there are several type founding companies.

Marking copy

When marking copy for the printer, then, it is necessary to designate which type faces are to be used and in what sizes. Few religious journalists can do this accurately, for they know too little about printing. An unusually co-operative printer will make much detailed knowledge of the sort unnecessary. When excessively busy, however, printing houses have no time to do more than reproduce the copy in any convenient type and are content to do a passable job. It is useful, therefore, to ask the printer for a copy of his type stylebook, for it contains an impression of every face he can provide, in the various sizes and styles. Copy cannot properly be marked for type simply by selecting what the editor guesses will make a pleasant combination.

He should be sure he selects types that are harmonious. Some are easier to read than others; certain ones are less suitable for church use than others. Unless he has considerable understanding of typography the church worker does better to imitate than to invent. Examples of parish papers, church bulletins, and special printing jobs completed for other institutions provide a reservoir of ideas.

Basic formulas

Church materials editors get along better with their printers if they understand the principal terms and basic formulas of typography. These can be learned and understood best only by frequent use, as with any other special language.

Type sizes or measurements are indicated in two ways. Height is noted in *points*, a point being 0.01384 inch. This standard American unit is applied as well to some of the tools printers use in handling type. An inch is represented by nearly 72 points. The width of type is measured in *ems*. The em of any size of type is the square of its body; consequently there are as many kinds of ems as there are sizes of type. An *en* is half an em. An em which is 12 points in size is called a *pica*, which is approximately one sixth of an inch. A foot would be 72 picas.

A wide type face is called *regular*, a laterally compressed one is known as *condensed*. When extra wide, type faces are said to be *expanded*; if extra narrow, *extra condensed*.

Editors can ask printers to mark copy correctly for them

the first time a regular job is done and then compile a scale of such markings. Each time copy is prepared for printing it can be marked by referring to the scale or schedule.

Religious materials are set in the common type sizes, which range from 72 points down to 5½ points, with the usual sizes in between: 6, 8, 10, 12, 14, 18, 24, 30, 36, 42, 48, 60. Others are available, such as 11 point and 96 point, but these are used chiefly for advertising or unusual display headlines or in book matter. The extreme measurements are 4 and 144.

Letters of any one size are known as a *font,* derived from *fount.* A *series* is a range of all sizes of one particular face of type (like Coronet or Goudy). The whole series in one face is the *type family.*

RADIO PRODUCTION

Use of the tools is production. So far we have considered the production of printed matter only. But radio has production techniques, also, to which television rapidly is adding its own. In radio, production is the architecture of the program and includes its arranging or organizing, the routines it is to follow, and the direction it is to receive.

In most cities such techniques are left to the stations. The churchman active in radio might develop simple programs requiring little equipment of any sort, such as the radio speech, but any complex show, one with long distance pickups or special engineering devices, for example, had best be left to the professionals. Big stations have production direction ready to discuss details with prospective time users or buyers.

Religious broadcasting was defined by the Department of Research and Education of the Federal Council as:

Programs having as a primary purpose the promotion of participation in religious worship and activity or knowledge concerning religious subjects and events.[1]

In the interest of developing programs of the types mentioned by the department a church worker should feel free to approach the program director of a station and discuss the production of a religious program with him. The church radio planner must go with the understanding, however, that what radio stations want is competent radio, no matter if it is a religious program or a sports or any other program.

One question that will be asked by the director, not necessarily audibly, is: "Is this a good radio program?" He will not ask: "Is this a good religious service or play or speech?" A minister should not expect a radio station to surrender time unconditionally any more than he should expect a newspaper or magazine editor to leave a blank space for him to fill as he wishes each week. Such a program director or editor would have little concern for the excellence of the material that he uses if he were so obliging.

A church that has sustaining (not commercially sponsored) time advanced to it—or a church federation so favored —or one that can afford to buy time, would do well to consider the resources of the station and its own resources. Included, of course, is the nature of the station, its power relative to others, the nature of its listening group (as for example a station making a strong appeal to foreign-language population as contrasted with one appealing chiefly to a suburban audience), and the nature of its equipment. It is possible to obtain sets of recordings, cut at differing speeds, and made in varying sizes, to allow a calculated number of minutes of program material. What is the particular station's record library holding in religious transcriptions? If what is desired is not on hand, will the station borrow or buy it?

---

[1] *Broadcasting and the Public* (New York: Abingdon, 1938) p. 130.

These are simply samples of the questions that need to be raised prior to production activity.

If the church must provide its own discs it is well to know that they are available from such commercial equipment makers as Radio Corporation of America, Decca, and Columbia, as well as from various denominations and councils of churches, including the Methodist Board of Education, the Joint Radio Committee of the Congregational-Christian Church, the Department of Evangelism of the American Baptist Convention, and the Division of Christian Education of the National Council of Churches.

Church workers rarely are in a position to do all the detailed production work necessary for the preparation of significant radio programs on religion. A fifteen-minute broadcast requires considerable advance study, planning, and designing. Only the largest city churches, with full staffs, some of whose members may have had radio production experience, can be expected to write and produce their own programs. It is true that radio people do not always grasp the religious niceties. They and newspaper editors are accused of insensitivity. But since stations all must allot a certain amount of time to such public service programs as religious ones, a church is wise at least to try to use the facilities available from the radio industry.

If the church itself is permitted to plan the use of the available time and lacks a professional radio staff it should confine itself to simple programs, using transcriptions where feasible (union regulations sometimes interfere with the use of music recordings, for example) and sticking to the dialogue, speech, or dramatic programs. In the case of the latter, plays and pageants should be attempted only if suitable transcription is available.

Religious broadcasts need not always be directly useful to the local church. Such a church, or a group, might sponsor a religious program of high caliber that has no local source but in the long run will help achieve the goals of the church. In this way better programs can be produced. The results may not be immediately visible but are widely helpful. The "Great Scenes from Great Plays" program of the Protestant Episcopal Church is an illustration of this type of production. Had it not been expensive or insufficiently supported it could have demonstrated a new concept in the use of radio as a tool of interpretation.

CHAPTER XII

The Churchman as Reporter

The journalistic world makes a distinction scarcely realized by churchmen and other persons not engaged in news work. It is the distinction between reporting the news and disseminating it. Reporting is gathering, getting, or collecting. Disseminating is editing, printing, broadcasting, or in some other way presenting the news.

Nonprofessionals and novices, whether working on the job with past masters or studying with teachers in schools of journalism, used to give comparatively little attention to the gathering of news and put most of their emphasis on writing. For many years, learning to write for the press was considered a step on the road to literary success. Journalism itself was not the goal. As journalism became more of a profession in its own right the emphasis was shifted, not to an even balance but at least to provide more attention for the reporting function.

Presenting news and other kinds of information is relatively easy as compared with gathering it. The land is full of people who can write competently but few have anything to say that has not been said many times before. Journalism, religious or otherwise, needs more people who know how to ask questions that will bring the correct answers, more who know whom to see for facts, when to see them, where to find them, and the meaning of the background for a story.

In the editorial department described earlier is a staff which, on the newspaper, wire service, newsmagazine, and radio station, is built around that important yet common individual called a reporter.

Today reporters are of many kinds, especially as they tend to become experts in reporting specific areas of news. Police, society, business, and sports reporters are not new in journalism. But now science, education, and labor reporters are being heard from.

In general, reporters are classified, functionally, in two groups: *leg men* and *rewrites*. Newspapers and press associations use these terms; on other news media the functions are the same but the titles are different. On magazines the leg man may be a roving editor or a correspondent or an associate editor; the rewrite is called an editorial assistant, an assistant editor, an associate editor, or a department editor. Leg men earned their name because they stay out of the office and go about on their legs gathering news. They are not necessarily good writers, especially on newspapers, and may not even be adept news writers. But they know news sources perfectly. They have the contacts so essential to thorough and accurate news gathering. Rewrites, on the other hand, are better at writing than at reporting, but may be tops at reporting. They stay in the office, taking facts for news stories via telephone from leg men at the scene of a street accident, fire, or drowning. Or they write copy based on written materials such as letters, publicity releases, and exchanges. Frequently when a churchman calls a newspaper office to give the paper a story a rewrite man is put on the call.

Such a division of labor exists on large papers and wire services mainly; on trade journals, house publications, radio-television stations, and small newspapers the leg man and the rewrite may be one and the same. Generally a reporter must be able to gather the news as well as write it and sometimes even photograph it.

The church worker who looks to the press for co-operation should understand this system of reporting, for it accounts for certain of his difficulties. If he knows that the reporter who comes to see him may not necessarily write about the information he gathers, he can understand discrepancies that occur and place the blame—if he must place blame—on the plan rather than on the reporter. If he is telephoned to for news he realizes that the person calling may never have been in or seen the church he is to write about. But the churchman must know more. He must know how a newspaper or radio station gathers news; what system is used. A means of dependable coverage is employed by any news-gathering agency or organization. For simplicity we shall confine this description to the average-sized newspaper, typified by the small city daily.

Gathering the news

Gathering the news, in our time, means obtaining the facts about events that have occurred and, when possible, obtaining facts about events that are still to happen. Routine news is the bulk of the newspaper's material, the sort of news that occurs more or less on schedule. Spot news, on the other hand, is unexpected, unplanned, unanticipated. Since most religious and church news is of the routine type, its gathering is a special concern here.

Not for many years have reporters simply wandered around a city to find out what has happened or might occur. They go, purposefully, to where the news is breaking. City editors, the bosses of the reporters, maintain schedules, called futures books, assignment sheets, or assignment records. On them they post events in advance, depending for their clues to what will take place upon last year's paper of the same date, publicity releases, public calendars, reporters' tips, current news stories, stories of future events, and rival publications. Such a schedule records conventions, meetings, assemblies, dinners, banquets, parties, weddings, and everything else that is preceded by advance notice.

The city editor must organize his staff so that certain recurring kinds of news are the responsibility of the same person from day to day or week to week. He sets up what are called "beats" or "runs." A reporter is assigned to the city hall beat, for example. Therefore he must call at city hall regularly; often two or three times a day and telephone news to his office at intervals; he also stays in the building a long time each time he makes his visits, because many offices must be called upon. The newsman knows everyone in city hall—Peggy, the city clerk's secretary; Mayor Pembridge himself; and Art, the head engineer. From them and their companions he gets many tips to stories or officially released stories, not only about city affairs but also about other events. This reporter is supposed to keep the paper and the public informed about everything occurring at city hall or obtainable through that source.

Similar beats are set up for other standard sources: the county building, police department, social agencies, hotels, banks, hospitals, railway terminals, and, of course, the churches.

Bigger papers than those serving small cities station their reporters in other parts of the state or nation also. They work out of the state capital, at bureaus responsible for groups of counties or communities, and in Washington. Small dailies depend upon the Associated Press, United Press, International News Service and other syndicates for national and international news, religious or otherwise. Reporters occasionally may be sent on special assignments to some part of the country far from home. All such work is organized, likewise, on a pattern resembling a beat.

Collecting church news

Church and religious news—the distinction between them being that church news relates to the church as an institution, and religious news is concerned with a philosophy or way of life—generally is covered on a beat basis by newspapers. Radio collection of local church news is as yet undeveloped. Radio stations consider religious news much less important than city hall, fire department, or police department news; inasmuch as they have little time for news broadcasts, only news of the widest interest is included regularly. Radio and television news broadcasters would not know what to do with all the copy a church beat could produce for them.

Big city papers have church editors or reporters. Nearly 500 of the approximately 1,750 dailies in the United States employ them, although few devote full time to the work. Wire services, feature syndicates, and radio stations do not have such editors.

The newsman on the church beat calls upon the churches regularly for news, either in person or by telephone, if the city is not too large, receives the publicity releases or voluntarily telephoned information, and handles any special church or religious stories, such as revivals, conventions, and conferences. Sensational stories, like crime committed in churches or by church people, are left to the police reporter. This is a policy which the church editors resent, because the handling of these stories would break up the routine of their jobs.

Doris Minney, one-time church editor of a large Ohio daily, reflected the traditional journalistic attitude toward the job when she wrote:

The position of church editor was one from which every reporter on our staff shied. This I knew. But as newest member of the news force, I wanted to handle the assignment as capably as possible.

Several of the city's churchmen at the time (the mid-forties) made it difficult for Miss Minney to "handle the assignment as capably as possible." She had hardly taken over the job when she received a complaining telephone call from a minister.

"Why don't you carry my church notes at the top of your column?" he asked. "My church is one of the oldest in the city. It has one of the largest congregations. Probably you're not aware that the publisher of your newspaper is a member of my church."

Naturally Miss Minney resented this threat to use pressure. But she became accustomed to the threats, which never were carried out, as well as to other expressions of bad nature, inconsiderateness, vanity, and inefficiency on the part of the clergy in its dealings with the press. Nor did she find one denomination any worse than another.

All newspapers print church news but few print religious news. The latter is considered too abstract or controversial; the former is general and safer. A story about a change in pastorate or about the plans for the Sunday morning service is church news. One about the National Council's pronouncement on the situation in Korea is religious news. An article by Harold Fey in the *Christian Century* describing the religious background of the school situation near Cleveland, Ohio, is religious news as it is to be found in magazines, which are more venturesome than newspapers in tackling controversial topics.

Although the gathering of church news is a routine job and fundamentally simple, few newspapers do it competently. Too often the church editor is a person not well informed about church history, denominational differences, church architecture, and the viewpoint of religion. The church editorship, as we have seen, is not considered one of the prize assignments; hence the most ambitious, vigorous newsmen are not patient with its requirements.

Remembering how a news-gathering agency like the newspaper is organized and that it must operate, unless subsidized, on the philosophy that the public must be pleased, we find that newspapers gather church and religious news chiefly to induce readers to buy their papers (or newsmagazines or whatever the medium may be). Recalling how radio stations are organized, we realize that stations attempting to gather local news broadcast only that which interests listeners, not in the hope of selling such time, usually, but with the intention of winning the loyalty of the listener to that particular station.

None but this somewhat cynical attitude is realistic under a plan where, to maintain its freedom from political party or government control, the press must earn the voluntary support of the public. Newspaper, magazine, wire service, or radio station operators, employees, and owners often are motivated by keen desire to be of public service. But they can be of public service only to the extent that the public will allow them to be.

A newspaper that prints much church news in a community not interested in church or even religious news, at the expense of whatever copy the public *is* interested in, cannot survive financially without subsidy. The history of American journalism is full of instances of well-intentioned publications that failed because they misinterpreted public taste or were unwilling to gratify it.

Concepts of news

Therefore the church reporter or editor must have in mind some concepts of news to guide him. He does not walk around spouting definitions, of course, but if he is a trained and thoughtful journalist he has considered them; in any case he is guided by analysis of news made by his city editor through the force of selection.

Because churchmen more than many other persons can think in terms of abstractions we can profitably consider here what news is. The study of the anatomy of news logically begins with definitions.

Three groups or types of definitions have been phrased. They are the objective, the subjective, and the pragmatic. Commonest is the objective. It gained wide attention because it was phrased well by Willard G. Bleyer, for many years director of the School of Journalism at the University of Wisconsin. He said, several decades ago, that: *News is anything timely that interests a number of people; and the best news is that which has the greatest interest for the greatest number.*[1]

Here news is defined from the standpoint of the consumer. But untimely news copy appears in modern publications and in radio programs. Nor does it interest many persons. For example: in an issue of the Cortland (New York) *Democrat,* was a story that read:

> The quarterly meeting of the Cortland County Historical Society will be held in the Court House, Saturday, October 5, at 2 o'clock. Ralph Ames will have an exhibit of historical relics and will speak on that topic. Anyone interested will be welcome to attend. The Town Historians and other interested members will meet at 10 o'clock in the morning preceding the general meeting.

The Town Historians and a few elderly persons probably would attend this meeting. They and some of their friends might read the account, which should not be taken as an example of how to write a meeting news story.

---

[1] Willard G. Bleyer, *Newspaper Writing and Editing* (Boston: Houghton Mifflin, 1913) p. 18.

The adjoining story, headed: LOCAL MAN GUILTY IN DOUBLE FATALITY, undoubtedly was read by ten times as many subscribers for this weekly.

Therefore a subjective definition is needed. One came several decades ago from Gerald W. Johnson, newspaper editor and biographer. He wrote: *News . . . is such an account of such events as a first-rate newspaperman, acting as such, finds satisfaction in writing and publishing.*[2]

All the *suches* in this definition make it sound like part of a life insurance policy or a lease. Nevertheless the viewpoint is clear. This definition has been restated cynically to: News is whatever the city editor says it is.

Another delver into this problem evolved a more lucid and serviceable definition: Dr. Curtis D. MacDougall, journalist, teacher, and author of several books on newspaper reporting. He put it: *News is an account of an event which a newspaper prints in the belief that by so doing it will profit.*[3]

What may be the best definition of all has been devised by Dean Laurence R. Campbell, of the School of Journalism, Florida State University. It is realistic, scientific, and comprehensive: *News is the account of a current idea, event, or conflict which interests news consumers and benefits those who present it.*[4]

Even if one had memorized every one of these definitions one could not, of course, necessarily recognize news when seeing it. News has certain components or elements which, if properly understood, aid us to know what news is.

Under the heading "The Anatomy of the News" might

---

[2] Gerald W. Johnson, *What is News?* (New York: Appleton-Century-Crofts, 1926) p. 90.

[3] Curtis D. MacDougall, *Interpretative Reporting* (New York: Macmillan, 1948) p. 85.

[4] Laurence R. Campbell and Roland E. Wolseley, *Newsmen at Work* (Boston: Houghton Mifflin, 1949) p. 25.

be listed news factors, which are in two groups: *determinants* and *components*. The determinants are:

Timeliness

Nearness (or Proximity)

Size (or Magnitude or Prominence)

Meaning (or Significance or Consequence)

Policy

Timeliness: What has just happened is more newsworthy than what happened an hour ago, five hours ago, a day ago, a week ago. What will happen tomorrow is more newsworthy than what happened yesterday. Newsmen try to put "today," "this morning," "tonight," and "tomorrow" in their opening paragraphs, for they wish the reader to know that this news is not stale but fresh.

Nearness: News that breaks in Mytown is more important to me than news in Yourtown, unless my wife is in Yourtown: this is the value of nearness to reader and journalist. A wreck on a Bolivian railway line is bad news to the victims and not good news for citizens of Peoria, Illinois, or Marblehead, Massachusetts, to read about. But the interest of the latter group is casual. Had the wreck occurred in Peoria the Peorians would be intensely interested. The closer the scene of the event is to the reader the greater his interest in the news.

Size: Fire that destroys two churches is more newsworthy than that which burns only one. The greater the magnitude of the news event the greater the interest, especially in the United States, where the important building is the tallest one or the one with the greatest floor area, where the important people often are the physically largest or those with the fattest bank accounts or biggest farms. This characteristic interest in size embraces also the prominent, which is to say the widely known. King George's colds are noted faithfully in the press but the colds of George the grocer in Cornville, Iowa, are not mentioned unless one develops into pneumonia and kills him.

Meaning: In an ideal world this determinant might be the only one the press and radio should use. The inherent importance, or consequence, of an event is difficult to determine, but when determined it may become of paramount interest. The dropping of an atomic bomb on Nagasaki is more than a military operation; it has significance for all mankind. Even if the meaning of an event is not clear but a meaning appears to be latent in it, the press gives space to the story. The general public is not interested in this determinant so much as it is in others. The greater the sense of responsibility of the press the more use it makes of this determinant.

Policy: News accounts are printed if they conform to policy; that is, if the information or facts further the point of view of the publication. A newsman can detect that a certain event, while inherently unimportant, trivial, and concerning little-known persons and happening at a distant point in time and space, will be considered newsworthy simply because it furthers the official policy of the owners of the press and radio. For example. an unknown and weak legislator speaks briefly from the floor of the chamber in support of a viewpoint for which a distant paper stands. This newspaper will be inclined to play up the speech. It is a common human desire to promote the ideas and persons with which we are in agreement.

Components, to come to a consideration of what news consists in, depend upon content and include sex, conflict or combat, money, children, extremes of age, animals, and emotion. The more of these any one news story contains the greater the reader interest in it. Pictures, too, are judged by this scale. Believing in this, editors of magazines and newspapers constantly print stories and pictures about lost cats, kidnaped children, inhuman mothers, crying babies, cats cuddling up to dogs, domesticated tigers, lovable snakes, 101-year-old ex-slaves, and sums of money recovered from hiding in old mattresses.

But the use of determinants and components in judging news is a pseudo-psychological way to look at news and not the only one. Under what might be called "The Chemistry of News" is this explanation: News is not in the thing itself but in its action and reaction on human kind.

And then from George C. Bastian, one-time Chicago *Tribune* copyreader and a journalism teacher, came what he called News Arithmetic:[5]

1 ordinary man plus 1 ordinary life	equals 0
1 ordinary man plus 1 extraordinary adventure	equals News
1 ordinary husband plus 1 ordinary wife	equals 0
1 husband plus 3 wives	equals News
1 bank cashier plus 1 wife and 7 children	equals 0
1 bank cashier minus $10,000	equals News
1 chorus girl plus 1 bank president minus $100,000	equals News
1 man plus 1 automobile plus 1 gun plus 1 quart	equals News
1 man plus 1 wife plus 1 row plus 1 lawsuit	equals News
1 man plus 1 achievement	equals News
1 woman plus 1 adventure or 1 achievement	equals News
1 ordinary man plus 1 ordinary life of 79 years	equals 0
1 ordinary man plus 1 ordinary life of 100 years	equals News

This table should make clear that the determinants and components of news set up for secular newsmen a special body of standards running counter to those of ordinary vocations. It would be an oversimplification to say that the ordinary working citizen dreads accidents, disasters, divorces, and other mishaps in the human family, whereas the newsman, while still possessed of considerable human sympathy for those in trouble, welcomes them as stories for

[5] George C. Bastian and Leland D. Case, *Editing the Day's News* (New York: Macmillan, 1943) p. 6.

his paper or material to be included in a news broadcast. The greater the disaster the better the story.

Consequently newspapers, newsmagazines, radio, and other media covering general news events, tend to present a warped concept of the world, a concept greatly at variance with that which the religious person desires to see or insists is more nearly legitimate. To the church person the daily newspaper is a record of violence, hatred, conflict, and malice. If he is a typical churchgoer in the United States, however, he realizes that the record is not of the total scene but merely of exceptional happenings brought together. Even if he does not understand this, he reads his newspaper as avidly as the nonchurchman. The "good" newspaper, willing to give greater emphasis to the story with social meaning than to the one that stresses other determinants, has been notably without sufficient support from persons whose ideals, presumably, would guarantee their support. Comparative circulation figures attest to this assertion: the tabloid New York *Daily News,* which emphasizes the sensational and emotional, exceeds two million daily and four million on Sunday. The New York *Times,* which stresses the important story first, has a daily circulation of about 600,000 and on Sunday of about one million. The *Christian Science Monitor,* the embodiment of a "good" newspaper, has a daily circulation of about 165,000 (it has no Sunday edition).

The church angle

If this analysis is applied to church and religious news it is possible to understand why a reporter does not respond to the news as does a churchman.

In a local church the men's club meeting, with a visiting speaker from the world of religion, may be of paramount importance to the minister and the president of the men's club, not to forget the arrangements committee that did the preparatory work. It is of some consequence, also, to the more loyal and enthusiastic members. Vital to all of them is the success of the meeting. Hopes for a well-attended gathering mount as the occasion nears. A special offering is planned.

One hard-working member, the club publicity chairman, telephones the newspapers or has copy ready for the weekly call of the reporter on that run. On the day before and on the day of the big meeting the pastor and others look at the paper—and find not a line about their precious activity. Not a single line. There are pages of comic strips, columns of chaff and stuff about this and that, half pages of pictures of unimportant events that happened elsewhere in the world. But not a syllable about the men's club.

At this juncture the churchman must be reminded that:

1. The newspaper is organized so as to be ready by a certain hour; it is printed in parts and cannot be changed readily.

2. There are other readers besides the churchman and his colleagues.

3. These readers are interested in many subjects, finding others more attractive than church events, perhaps.

4. The members of this particular church are not all really deeply interested in the men's club function, else almost all of them would attend, which never happens. If not even all the church's people are interested, why should the newspaper assume that everyone in the city is interested?

5. The reporter may have written the story, but some editor may have eliminated it before it was set in type, for one of various good reasons, including the fact that the story already had been printed (after the first time, it becomes publicity pure and simple), may have been poorly written, lacking in certain basic facts or contrary to policy,

or was pushed aside by material considered to be of greater importance.

To cite another common experience: the reporter is given routine news, such as the story about next Sunday's service. It is Easter, let us say, and the pastor has arranged for several instrumental musicians to join the choir and enhance the music for that day. He has made a special effort. This event is unusual. Here, the churchman thinks, is really *big* news.

The reporter comes to his study—or maybe he goes to see the reporter at the newspaper office—and he finds the newsman somewhat cold to his enthusiasm. He is interested, yes, but he has fifty-nine other Easter services to report. He is worried about having insufficient space. He does not see how he can cram all the copy into the paper by publication time. His mind is on headline writing, make-up of the page, missing copy, and last-minute advertisements. It is not on what seems to him mainly an elaboration in the services planned by one church.

Obligingly the newsman takes notes on the pastor's information, nevertheless, and promises to try to add it to the existing church story from that congregation although he is not sure he can accomplish this. He goes about his work—and finds his notes the next afternoon while clearing the residue of the Easter pages from his desk. Too bad. The Rev. Mr. Jones probably will be unhappy now, but he had all he could do to get the church pages together without rewriting the Calvary Church story to include the data about the trumpets.

A quite different situation exists when the press covers the exceptional story affecting church or religion. Traditionally reporters stay away from controversial material having to do with race, religion, and rumor. The larger the paper the less is this true, but since, as we have seen, most publications are not large—there are about 200 large newspapers and 100 big magazines in the United States out of approximately 20,000 publications—this unwritten rule is generally well followed.

The mishandled story

The type of story religious people object to in newspapers is the occasional one about the preacher who runs off with the choir singer. A minister who does his work faithfully year in and year out—as most churchmen do—gets only skimpy, routine attention from a majority of the press. But let him stray, as one does now and then, and the incident receives considerable attention. By now the reason for this situation should be clear enough. The public *as a whole* is interested in the defection. The public *as a whole* is not interested in the routine activities.

As an indication of what the secular mind considers publishable religious or church news are these stories, found in the same issue of one daily paper, three in adjoining columns of a Monday issue. These stories were printed in addition to reports on a half-dozen sermons preached the day before.

HADDON HEIGHTS, N. J., May 1 (UP).—The Rev. Jarvis S. Morris preached a sermon on the parable of the pounds and the talents today and then asked his congregation to put it to practical use.

After he spoke, ushers of the Bethany Presbyterian Church passed among the congregation with plates piled high with $10 bills, $5 bills, and $1 bills—totaling $2,000.

"Help yourselves," the pastor said. "Put the money to work for the next six months. Then we shall see what we shall see."

The money had been borrowed from the Audubon National Bank to pay off a $5,000 debt on the church's mortgage and land. The pastor, whose hobby is gardening, took three $10 bills himself. He said he would use the money to make his hobby pay off. The congregation got right behind the plan and "borrowed" the entire $2,000.   —United Press

MONTREAL, May 1 (AP).—Collections were taken today at the doors of Catholic churches in the archdiocese of Montreal to aid the 5,000 striking Canadian asbestos workers.

—Associated Press

TOKYO, May 1 (UP).—General Douglas MacArthur believes 30,-000,000 copies of the Bible are needed here in Japan. He expressed this view today to Glen W. Wagner, of Washington, foreign secretary of the Pocket Testament League.

Mr. Wagner addressed students this week at several Tokyo universities, gave them Bibles, and outlined a program for distributing 10,000,000 Bibles in Japan in the next ten years.

He is in Japan at the invitation of General MacArthur and has talked with him about plans to distribute 1,000,000 pocket Testaments in the first years of the program.

In a letter to Mr. Wagner General MacArthur wrote: "This distribution of the Bible has my hearty indorsement, and I sincerely request any assistance the representatives of the league may need in the performance of their duties."   —United Press

None of these is spot news, for any could be printed as many as several days after the event. All are wire stories, with no specifically local connection, since the local area of the newspaper, in which they appeared is New York City, although Haddon Heights is not far from New York. As evidence that the editors of the New York *Herald Tribune* realized that latter fact is the position given the New Jersey account: on the first page. The others were on pages deep in the paper's first section.

Two days later, however, the *Herald Tribune's* Manhattan staff produced a local story with a church angle. This likewise was printed well back in the issue because it was fundamentally inconsequential; but a fifty dollar watch robbery in New York City ordinarily is given no space whatsoever in the metropolitan dailies. However, the robbed man was a church custodian; his wrist watch "was a gift of the ladies' guild of the church last Christmas." There is contrast enough in the situation to lift it out of the commonplace. Robbing a church employee is considered more heinous an offense, or at least more novel a crime, than robbing some other citizen.

Four youths were under arrest yesterday on charges of robbing William E. White, fifty-three-year-old custodian of Christ Church, Methodist, Park Avenue and Sixtieth Street, of a $50 wrist watch that was a gift of the ladies' guild of the church last Christmas.

The suspects were identified as

Frank Sanders, seventeen, of 32 Sumner Avenue; James De Paolo, eighteen, of 64 Steuben Avenue; William Schultz, seventeen, of 817 Park Avenue, and Frank Riccardi, eighteen, of 846 Bedford Avenue; all of Brooklyn.

The first two were arrested after a chase when Steven Galligan, a cab driver, of 30-33 Thirty-second Avenue, Long Island City, Queens, saw the attack upon Mr. White near the church and picked up a couple of policemen as the youths fled in a waiting sedan. The others were arrested later at Schultz's home.

—New York *Herald Tribune*

Church people themselves read such a story with interest; they are in no position to object to it if they respond as others do. And they should realize that so long as conduct of this type is considered exceptional by the press the church is well off.

Church people who object because newspapers gather and print sensational news, in their resentment almost always make the wrong attack upon the press. What they say is that the conduct of this particular preacher or choir singer is not typical, therefore it deserves no space at all. What they should say is that the newspaper ought to print the story but should not assign to it excessive space and should attempt to give the public an understanding of the underlying reasons for the actions reported. It is like any other crime news. The press should not exploit it, but should print it in such a manner that its publication is a deterrent to further misdeeds and that the public comes to understand the causes and to help prevent recurrence.

One day in Syracuse, New York, a medium-sized Eastern city of the United States, several members of the administration of the Council of Churches became upset about the handling of a certain news story in the morning daily, the Syracuse *Post-Standard*. But the group kept its temper and its sense of proportion. This is the story:

GLENDALE, Calif. (AP).—A Baptist minister, father of four children, yesterday blamed "disgruntled" parishioners for charges he had affairs with 40 feminine members of his church.

Dr. J. Whitcomb Brougher, Jr., 46, pastor of the Glendale First

Baptist church for 21 years and himself the son of a minister, labeled "entirely false" charges made in a suit filed yesterday in Los Angeles superior court.

Mrs. Sadie Williams and Fletcher Edgar Maxwell said they were suing for members of the church. They alleged that Dr. Brougher "has even recently been known to chase a lone young woman in an automobile in an attempt to force her to the curb on a dark street, and has been known to associate with bookies."

Mrs. Williams and Maxwell complained that they sought to bring before the church membership evidence of the "fantastic conduct" and "incredible peccadillos" of the pastor, but that Dr. Brougher removed deacons who wanted to present the charges.

(The dictionary lists a peccadillo as a light or trifling sin).

The suit also contends that Dr. Brougher "boasted" of his association with 40 women church members.

The minister, in a statement, said the action "is only a repetition of accusations brought four years ago by a small disgruntled group of members and former members of the church.

"The matter," he added, "was completely and thoroughly reviewed by a committee, the board of deacons and the entire congregation, all of whom found the accusations entirely false and without foundation."

He said the congregation gave him a vote of confidence at the time.

Mrs. Williams and Maxwell demanded a church hearing and membership election on the charge or a superior court trial by a jury.

Dr. Brougher's father is Dr. J. Whitcomb Brougher, Sr., former president of the Northern Baptist convention. The elder Brougher, now retired, formerly was pastor of the First Baptist church of Oakland, Calif., Tremont temple of Boston, Mass., and Temple Baptist church of Los Angeles.

—Associated Press

The ministerial group said it thought that as news this story was greatly overemphasized, since the minister in question had no local connection, since the incident occurred at the other side of the continent, and since the editors had included a one-column, three-inch engraving of the minister involved, run a three-column-wide headline on the story, and placed the whole account prominently at the bottom of the first page. They explained that any clergyman proved guilty of such charges should by all means be given publicity. They were *not* saying that the story should have been killed or omitted. They *were* saying that it simply should not have been spread over the first page so blatantly.

Further analysis of this particular issue of the Syracuse paper would have given these ministers additional reason for concern if not for complaint. On the third page was an article headed: ACTION SCHEDULED FEB. 4 ON MERGER OF TWO CHURCHES. Its lead was: "A new step in the proposed largest merger of American Protestant churches in 10 years was revealed yesterday."

This story was worth front-page position from the standpoint of importance, significance, or meaning. The other story had no great importance, but it had other determinants and components, including prominence (through the elder clergyman), timeliness, sex, age, conflict, and emotion. If both were placed on the first page, which would the clergy read thoroughly; which would the lay churchmen read through, and which would the nonchurchman read?

The news gathering process

The process of gathering news is the same whether it be used for newspaper, radio, magazine, press association, or some other medium. All reporters work more or less the same way. They all must interview human sources, consult documents, typewrite their copy or telephone their information, check for accuracy, watch for libel, have authority for what they say—and avoid ulcers. In the United States all reporters, unless they be employed by the specialized press, have the same news standards. If they work for the religious press they have different standards but only because they are gathering information for readers with specific, evident interest in the details of one particular subject—the church or religion.

This difference can be understood further by comparing the news gathering activities of Religious News Service and one of the secular press associations. RNS sends its members detailed accounts of news made via speeches, resolutions, and other events occurring in church and religious circles. The secular agency, like United Press, sends out to its subscribers only what interests the average American citizen, an indistinguishable entity who may or may not have religious interests.

The churchman who expects to prepare copy for the press or to deal with the press in any way needs to bear all this difference in mind. It is summed up in the term *reader interest*. The American citizen is not overwhelmingly interested in church or religious news, either in print or on the radio.

Before World War II the Federal Communications Commission sampled the listening to various types of radio programs. During the week of Dec. 11, 1938, for example, only 5.15 per cent of the total listening time went to religious and devotional programs, as compared with music, which was first with 52.45 per cent. After the war another survey, made by private groups at the University of Denver and Columbia University, showed that at the end of 1945 religious broadcasts were eighth in rank on a list of eleven kinds of programs.

Such a survey of newspaper reader interests as that being made continually by the Advertising Research Foundation shows that religious news stands low in the scale, although no total figures have been compiled. Religious or church news never appears in the lists of most-read stories, although crime in religious circles or freak items like four-year-old "ministers" performing wedding ceremonies command much attention. A typical reader interest result is that of a study made of the Niagara Falls (New York) *Gazette*. On page 30 of the issue for the day studied, in a prominent position at the top of the first column on the left, appears a story with a headline beginning: PRESBYTERIANS PLAN TO BUILD NEW CHURCH HERE. Only 12 per cent of the men readers and 14 per cent of the women checked in this study read this story.

Radio "reader" interest

Radio has its reader interest problems, also. *Listener interest* is as difficult to gratify and control as *reader interest.* Dr. Paul F. Lazarsfeld of Columbia University, a student of both reader and listener interest, has made an important discovery as a result of examining studies of what the American public listens to. He made his point after citing evidence that serious programs are not ordinarily listened to by people on a low cultural level. When they are there is a reason:

One of the main reasons that people on the lower cultural level listen to serious broadcasts is their interest in a special cause with which they are affiliated.

Dr. Lazarsfeld's observation can mean that the church may gather religious news for dissemination to religious people who, although many may be at a low cultural level, may not read much but will listen and that their religious loyalty may be used to gain their attention more effectively through the ear than through the eye.

Invariably religious programs are serious. The American public as a whole does not listen as much to serious programs as to entertainment broadcasts. Hence this general problem becomes an acute church problem, to be corrected, possibly, by study of the factors that are important in listening as well as in reading.

The churchman should know something, for example, about the value of a frame of reference in broadcasting news of church and religion. His journalistic sense will come into new use in radio at this point. For instance, churchmen are urged in this book to include in news releases full names and identifications and to supply background material. Providing such facts equips the reader or listener with a frame of reference. Everyone is interested in hearing or reading about something of which he already has knowledge, however incomplete. One's own name is of intense interest when seen or heard. Whatever interests us becomes part of us. Radio or press work that can touch upon that interest becomes part of the frame of reference of the reader or listener.

Announcers of musical programs habitually tell listeners something personal about the composers. Speakers are introduced not only to provide authority for what they are to say but also to make them part of the frame of reference of those who are about to listen.

In gathering news about the church and religion for use by the secular press and radio the churchman should:

1. Not expect press and radio to do what is unreasonable, especially uneconomic.

2. Make the best of his news sources by draining them thoroughly.

3. Prepare the hearer or reader to be interested.

4. See that his news reaches the outlet promptly and in good form.

5. Judge the local situation by local conditions.

Churchmen as city editors

The local church secretary, the publicity committee chairman, or the director of public relations for an overhead organization is in effect the head of an editorial staff. The secretary is the city editor, reporter, copyreader, and mail clerk all in one; if she supervises some such news gathering plan as explained in Appendix I she has reporters (publicity committee chairmen for the organizations of the church) from whom she receives copy regularly more or less as does the city editor of a newspaper or the news editor of a radio station. A publicity committee chairman gathers news in turn from the members of her group or his organization, whether it be within the city limits only or sprawling across the nation. A director of public relations for a religious body of national or international scope is like an editor of a large magazine, with the joint responsibilitiy of gathering and disseminating the news as well as using it in publications issued under his aegis.

From the secular city editor the church journalist learns to be systematic, orderly, and thorough. If he wishes to save himself travail he sets up schedules, keeps in touch with his reporters, gives them suggestions from time to time, and tries to keep them interested in their work. He must add to these duties the publicity functions, which include redistributing the information and illustrations gathered for him to the surrounding press and radio outlets, checking on their use, and keeping records of what was sent when and where.

Church sources

Reporters who cover beats for the secular press must know where to find the news. Rarely does it come to them. More certainly is this the situation with the churchman who acts as city editor-reporter. He generally has an unpaid and untrained staff and is himself a journalistic neophyte. He can assume that his reporters readily take "No" for an answer and that they have little skill at recognizing a news story when they see it. Clearly, anyone responsible for collecting information about church activities must know first of all the sources of the news.

A common generalization of the journalistic world is that there are no bad subjects, only bad writers. Thus it is with the church world and journalism. There are no churches which cannot be interpreted by press and radio, for the newless church is no church at all. The person responsible for revealing information about the church, be it symbolized by the Bethany Church or the Disciples of Christ or the

Foreign Mission Board, is limited as to subjects only by his diligence and imagination and budget.

Since the pastor, priest, secretary, or volunteer worker most often is responsible for this duty, the sources of information should be easy to tap. For all these functionaries (even the volunteer, who should be an old-timer) know the church membership, keep track of organizational activities and the schedule of the church, and are aware of its traditions and history.

Everything and everybody in a church is a source. Even a small congregation of only eighty members and a minister with two or three points or charges is fruitful not only with spot or routine news but also with innumerable features. Churchmen may need to be reminded of their sources, but more than that they need additional hours in the day during which to do their journalistic work, once they see the possibilities.

How shall the churchman proceed to tap sources? A procedure that fits a small rural church does not suffice for a downtown metropolitan institution. A large church should keep a futures book, that is, a notebook or dated calendar pad. In this are listed all the known news possibilities. Once used, such a record is useful for a succeeding year, for at the beginning of a new year the standard events, such as seasonal services, finance campaign activities, and appeals for special offerings, can be listed in advance and anticipated by adequate preparation. As current stories develop they also can be noted. For example, St. Mary's Ushers' Club today decides to have a special meeting two months hence. The club publicity chairman is expected to notify the office of that intention. The office, in turn, tells the church's "city editor," who records the forthcoming event at the proper place in the futures book, thus assuring that advance stories are sent out about the meeting and printed in the church's own bulletin and parish publication. Possibilities for pictures also are indicated.

A tiny church would need no such elaborate system. But the minister, its only official, should develop the habit of marking possible news stories on his personal calendar and at least notifying near-by newspapers and radio stations.

An overhead organization's news department cannot, of course, concern itself greatly about small, local activities, although it should support and stimulate them with materials and guidance. Such local information is useful chiefly in the area where the event occurs. Digests of it may appear in a publication issued by the board for its constituents. The chief news-gathering activity of an overhead church body deals with the major policies and operations of the group: a large international conference, appointment of new directing officials, and shifts in procedure. The publicity director or chairman of such a group has widespread sources. He uses the channels of communication employed by the headquarters officials; he is himself often of major rank in the organization so as to insure the co-operation of persons in the field. He calls upon specific individuals for particular information that is assembled into news and feature stories. His "beat" is the outer reaches of his organization. It may be the world, just as the minister's "beat" is his congregation and community.

To enumerate the sources is a book-size job. Everything that happens is a news possibility, although not everything that happens is worth presenting to readers or listeners, inasmuch as it may be trivial or incomplete, i.e. unimportant news. Applying the tests of what determines and constitutes news, as explained earlier in this chapter, may help separate the more newsworthy from the less.

Realistically speaking, although all that happens has some possibility as news, church bodies have too little time and too few employees to process everything into copy. Therefore they must select only what has the widest appeal or is inherently most important. Note that the standard here is not stated as being what the institution would like to see printed. Such a policy does not deal fairly with press and radio, and by following it the institution becomes a propaganda agency rather than a news disseminator.

A brief checklist of sources may be useful as a reminder of possibilities:

ORGANIZED NEWS SOURCES

(Including a few examples)

Church, Sunday school: All religious education activities.

Clubs: High school, Young people's, Men's, Ushers', Married couples, After College, Mothers', Boy and Girl Scouts, Camp Fire Girls, Girl Reserves.

Committees: Board of missions, Overseas relief, Equipment, Finance, Care of the church building, Personnel, Peace.

Musical organizations: Senior choir, junior choir, children's choirs, college choir.

Official groups: Board of deacons, Official board, Church Council, Board of stewards, Official committees.

Societies: Sisterhood, Women's, Young People's, Holy Name, Women's Association, Women's League.

GENERAL NEWS SOURCES

Pastor, priest, reader, leader, rabbi, or other chief officer: Speeches, journeys to meetings, radio and television appearances, exchanges, publications.

Other church officials and staff members: Similar activities.

Personnel: Changes in staff, visiting preachers, priests, superintendents.

Institutional: Historical anniversaries, co-operative activities in the community, co-operation with overhead church bodies, support to mission field.

CHAPTER XIII

The Churchman as News Writer

All communications media employ the written word, but three of the foremost—the motion picture, radio, and television—add the spoken word.

This book is not the place to consider the techniques of preaching, calling, and general lecturing, also important nonjournalistic media of spoken communication and interpretation. Therefore in this chapter we shall examine only the ways by which churchmen can use the written and spoken word as employed by press and radio. Here we shall consider the patterns of news and the formulas needed in preparing copy for printed and spoken use.

Although the techniques of news *gathering* are virtually the same, regardless of outlet, the techniques of news *writing* differ according to whether the information is to be used by newspapers, press associations, radio, television, or magazines. Since the likely use the average reader of this book will make of his newswriting skill is for newspapers and radio stations, the techniques for those two agencies will be examined in more detail than others.

News writers for press associations write for a larger and more varied audience than do those aiming their material at other media. Copy for them must be of considerable public interest, especially if it be about religion or the church, if it is to appear in the reports at all. News of an annual conference, for example is carried by wires to papers receiving Associated Press, United Press, or International News Service reports because reader interest is more than city- or county-wide. Such copy has meaning for persons of the particular denomination sponsoring the conference in all cities within that conference, which may include several states. A local church board of education meeting story will be read only by the congregation of that church and hence receives space in none but local papers, if there, and practically never on the wire services. Leads must be short, must carry a dateline (RICHMOND, Va., Jan. 15, —) and must subordinate the local angle.

This local story, for example, might have state-wide possibilities:

The congregation of Quinn Chapel, A.M.E. Church, Wabash Ave., and 24th St., will observe the 102nd anniversary Sunday of its founding July 22, 1847.	Dr. Russell Brown, of St. Louis, Mo., will be guest preacher in the pulpit of the Rev. T. Deans Scott, pastor for 14 years. The present church is 58 years old. —Chicago *Sun-Times*

If this were discovered to be the oldest church of its own or any other denomination, not merely in Chicago, but also in the entire state, the wire services might carry a squib reading:

CHICAGO, July 21.—The oldest church of any denomination in Illinois will observe its 102nd anniversary tomorrow here. The congregation of Quinn Chapel, A.M.E. Church, Wabash Ave. and 24th St., will celebrate the event with special services, at	which Dr. Russell Brown, of St. Louis, Mo., will be guest preacher. The pulpit regularly is occupied by the Rev. T. Deans Scott, pastor for 14 years. Quinn Chapel was founded July 22, 1847. Its present building is 58 years old.

News is found in magazines as well as newspapers—not only in the newsmagazines but also at least in rear sections of trade journals, professional periodicals, and other specialized publications. A church worker has frequent opportunity to write the news for the magazines of the church and religion. *The Sign, Christian Century, Christian Advocate, The Churchman, Advance, Christian Register,* and scores of other denominational or religious magazines print both straight and interpretative news stories. Few churchmen, on the other hand, have a chance to write for *Time, Newsweek, U. S. News and World Report,* and the other newsmagazines, which carry religious or church news departments that are staff written. The writing here is group journalism, to begin with; that is, several persons work on a story. News of religion is left in the hands of a highly experienced journalist with exceptional knowledge of church matters. In other respects writing news for magazines is so much like writing it for newspapers that the two can be considered together.

Writing for newspapers

The standard news story organization has been represented for many years by a pyramid or a series of rectangles. These two structures still are correct for the bulk of the news writing being done for the press of the United States. There is a slow tendency to depart from them, but most news material that churchmen handle for newspaper and magazine publication should be arranged in these two conventional patterns, for they still dominate.

The pyramid is an inverted one, standing on its tip. The broad area at the top represents the summary of the news. The point is the location of unimportant details, the news having been told in gradually descending order of importance. Literally, that is to say, the facts, ideas, and sentences are arranged so that the most important (newsworthy) information is seen first by the reader, the moderately important next, and the least important last.

The rectangle makes graphic the story construction for news of more or less equal importance through the length of its presentation. Here the minor elements are sparse or almost lacking; such construction is reserved for exceedingly short, significant news accounts.

Not all of the thousands of newspapers and magazines that print news cleave to the inverted pyramid pattern, but most of them do. By thus presenting the highlights of the news first, the press uses what can be called the anticlimax form. The summary of the news that results is known as the *lead* (pronounced *leed*). The reverse of this is the climax form, a pattern used for feature stories. Here the news is left to the end, more or less as in a surprise-ending O'Henry short story. Using a religious news story as an example, the inverted pyramid and regular pyramid (climax) patterns behave thus: (Inverted first)

NASHVILLE, Tenn.—A complete survey of Southern Baptist theological needs in respect to curriculum and geographical population trends will be undertaken by the Southern Baptist convention committee on theological education.

Dr. John H. Buchanan, pastor of Southside Baptist church, Birmingham, Ala., told of his group's plans for study in a report to the Convention's Executive Committee here. Porter Routh, statistician for the Baptist Sunday School Board, and Dr. J. E. Dillard, retiring director of promotion for the executive committee, will work with an employed impartial consultant in the survey, Dr. Buchanan said.

—Religious News Service

If, however, this story were handled in the climax fashion (which it should not be, since this subordinates the news) it would read thus:

NASHVILLE, Tenn.—Dr. John H. Buchanan, pastor of Southside Baptist church, Birmingham, Ala., made a report to the Executive Committee of the Southern Baptist Convention here.

Dr. Buchanan, chairman of the Convention's committee on theological education, said that the committee will make a complete survey of Southern Baptist theological needs in respect to curriculum and geographical and population trends.

Porter Routh, statistician for the Baptist Sunday School Board, and Dr. J. E. Dillard, retiring director of promotion for the executive committee, will work with an employed impartial consultant, Dr. Buchanan said.

The difference is more evident to the eye than to the ear, but it is that the news is imparted swiftly in the anti-climax or summary lead form and more slowly in the other. This fact will help us to understand why journalists use one or the other. If the news must be told without delay, because it is important or at least attention-getting, then the first form is used. If, however, the news is subordinate to the way the story is to be written or to its entertainment or pathos or other emotional content, the second is used.

Reasons for summary lead

There are at least six reasons why the press—exclusive of radio—continues to use the standard, anticlimax form:

1. The news can be read quickly. The reader needs only to glance over the opening paragraph or two to know what happened.

2. It avoids repetition in writing. If the essence of the story is crowded at the top the news writer can hang the rest of it on a simple structure, since he has established clearly the Who, What, When, Where, Why, and possibly the How.

3. It makes editing the copy easier. A story in this pattern can be copyread swiftly, for the desk man knows where to find each element and check it.

4. It can be headlined readily. A good summary lead provides the content for an accurate headline. The copyreader's job of bringing the essence of the news into a small area already is started for him if the lead has been handled so that it is complete.

5. It can be contracted or expanded readily. Having been built with its most important elements placed first, the news story can be cut from the end without serious harm, as the last portion contains the least important details. Likewise, it can be expanded easily by adding new or necessary details at any point.

6. It can be written swiftly, a virtue of any news writing pattern. After a time the newsman composes all accident stories, all obituaries, many church stories, and all other common stories more or less along the same lines and does not have to build each anew.

The five "W's"

Newsmen for years have been indebted to Rudyard Kipling for a jingle that helps remind them to write complete introductory paragraphs for their news stories. It reads:

> I keep six honest serving-men;
> They taught me all I know;
> Their names are What? and Why? and When?
> And How? and Where? and Who?

The satisfactory summary lead answers as many as possible of these questions. It does not do so by cramming them into a gigantic first paragraph. The lead can be thought of as the first few paragraphs, not simply the first.

Not all the five "W's" and the "H" can be answered by every lead section. *When* and *Where* and *Who* generally are known and readily supplied. *What* is the main subject of the news. A speaker said thus and so: that is the *What* of a speech story. A house burned: that is the *What* of a fire story; two persons were killed when a car overturned: that is the *What* of an accident story. *How* and *Why* are not so easily provided, or even necessarily newsy. *How* an accident took place cannot always be readily determined, for there may have been no witnesses and the victims may be dead. *How* a sermon was delivered is inconsequential; naturally it was by a churchman speaking from a pulpit. *Why* is rarely included because the newsman seldom knows why an accident occurred or cares why a sermon is delivered (that is, he does not care because the purpose is obvious). Yet the *Why* is an important part of the news without which many a story is incomplete. Pastor X resigns, the news story says, but it does not go on to explain *Why*. Readers can jump to conclusions, usually erroneous. Churches, consequently, are wise if, whenever possible, they include the *Why* in their news material. Rumors, gossip, and misinformation are estopped when the reasons are included in the news.

The Bible is a popular example of the validity of the modern summary lead. James L. Verhoeff, editor of the Blytheville (Arkansas) *Courier News,* anaylzes the Bible's own "lead": the first sentence of Chapter 1 of Genesis.

"In the beginning, God created the heaven and the earth."

Said Mr. Verhoeff, in an article on news writing published for religious journalists:

> Apply the five W's for a first paragraph for a news item and we find:
> When—*In the beginning*
> Who—*God.*
> What—*created*
> Where—*the heaven and the earth*
> Why . . . .
> Only the Why is lacking, and it is easy to supply, for it was given by the author of that first book of the Bible. The Why of the creation was to give "man a place of abode before and after death."

Patterns less popular

Arguments against the patterns of news writing, including the use of the five "W's" and the "H" in the lead, are numerous. Although practically all secular newspapers and religious journals continue to practice the standard forms, objections to them are mounting. These are the major objections:

1. The pattern is losing its usefulness, since radio has taken the edge off spot news.

2. The headline tells the main news, therefore the news story need not summarize again.

3. Pattern writing makes for dull writing; stories tend to sound more or less alike; readers consequently do not read what they are not already interested in.

4. The summary approach makes for heavy and long-winded opening paragraphs which are neither readable nor clear.

5. Summary leads make it more difficult for the news-

paper to perform a function beyond presenting the news, that is, explaining its meaning.

Churchmen in communities whose editors share these objections soon can tell what news writing style is used and therefore prepare their own copy to conform to it.

A church example

This lead comes to the desk of the church editor:

Children and parents of the Primary Department will share in a beautiful service of worship.

Under the direction of Mary Parker, this service of worship will be one of the outstanding events of the year.

What is wrong with It? Everything. It is incomplete. *When* will the service be held? Both hour and day are needed. *Where* will the service be held? The name of the church must be inserted. And that adjective, *beautiful!* Editorializing does not belong in news stories. *Beautiful* is a dubious word under any circumstances. Two persons can look at the same scene or painting and disagree about it right down to the adjective. Facts always are more convincing than adjectives, especially in news accounts. *How many* children and parents? *What* is to take place during the service? Is someone to speak or play the organ? Specific, concrete details are needed.

News writers must try to get the main facts, then, into the opening paragraph or two, and in addition learn to arrange these facts in the most attractive order. A guide to the order is understanding of the reader. What does a reader usually want to know first? What will attract a reader's eye most quickly?

Further work is needed on the example cited. It would not, however, do to begin thus:

At 9:30 A.M. Sunday, in the chapel of the First Evangelical Reformed church, Primary department children will give a demonstration worship service.

This wording would not serve because the emphasis is on *When*, which ordinarily is routine and unimportant, as it is here. If many news stories stressed *when* the publication would be dull reading. *When* must not be omitted, however, only subordinated.

The next try produces:

> In the chapel of the First Evangelical Reformed church at 9:30 A.M. Sunday, Primary department children, etc.

Where, however, is no more important or significant than *When*, in this story. Therefore it likewise should not be over-emphasized. The second attempt is a poor specimen of a lead. Instead the writer looks for what gives the story distinction or difference from preceding stories of the same type; he seeks for that which will catch reader attention. The interesting elements in this story are what will happen. The action of the story usually provides the material to be emphasized. What a committee will do, who is to speak, and the like are the best material. Time and place usually are standardized in church news.

Therefore the lead might be recast to read:

> Primary department children will give a demonstration worship service at 9:30 A.M. Sunday in the chapel of the First Evangelical Reformed church.

Or, still better, with the reporting of more facts:

> Nineteen children, all members of the Primary department of the First Evangelical Reformed church, will take part in a demonstration worship service at 9:30 A.M. Sunday in the chapel.

Such clumsy news writing as the first attempt at this Primary department story is produced by denominational publicity offices as well as by local churches. There is excuse for the latter, since personnel is not trained for journalism. It was a national office, however, that released this slightly disguised story, beginning thus:

All of the thirty-one members, except five, of the Executive board of the Denominational church met in regular and annual session in Center City December 13.

Perhaps the outstanding feature of this meeting was the climactic offer of Secretary John D. Jones to finance the production of a proposed cinema portraying in a graphic way the principal episodes in our Denominational history during the past two hundred years, the premier showing to be given in Center City on Tuesday evening, May 8, in connection with our 200th anniversary. . . .

An editor who received this dull, wordy story struck out seventeen of the twenty-five words in the lead, killed fifteen in the second paragraph, inserted three words, combined parts of each of the paragraphs, and added a new sentence to subordinate mechanical details. After the surgery the story read thus:

A motion picture portraying the principal episodes in Denominational church history during the past 200 years will be shown next May in Center City.

The Executive board of the denomination will direct and the Educational board will finance production of the film. Premier showing will be May 8 in Center City, in connection with the anniversary. Plans were approved at a recent meeting of the Executive board.

Leads are classified not only by their emphasis on the facts they contain but also by the choice of words. They are effective if thought is given to the grammatical form of the opening. Leads also are categorized by material. Church people, however, need not be too much concerned about such refinements. If they can prepare news stories with a few variations of adequate summary leads, they will be doing far more than has been done through the years. Only the large church or religious organization with a specialist engaged to handle its news need go beyond this.

The body of the news story follows logically the arrangement of the materials in the lead. If the opening paragraphs present the facts in descending order of importance, as they should, the rest of the story must follow suit. If the reader is supposed to read as he runs he must be able to gather the main secondary facts as soon as he has read the lead and not have to wade through the whole story to learn them. The news writer must judge what is of importance and either leave the unimportant out or place it toward the end, where it can be cut, if necessary, without harm to the yarn. But he should not imitate the cub reporter in the classic story. Often scolded for being too detailed, this time he wrote:

A shooting affair occurred last night. Sir Dwight Hopeless, a guest at Lady Penmore's ball, complained of feeling ill, took a highball, his hat, his coat, his departure, no notice of his friends, a taxi, a pistol from his pocket, and finally his life. Nice chap. Regrets and all that sort of thing.

English and style

There are several other elements in news writing of which the churchman should be aware. They are news English, news style, and copy preparation.

For journalism, the best writing is that kind which communicates most successfully. Writing that communicates facts and ideas to the masses of the people must take into consideration their capacities. Psychologists, theologians, and other specialists have a private language, which they can use in communicating with each other but which cannot be understood by the world at large. Journalists cannot use this language. Therefore they avoid such shortcuts and use, instead, short, simple words, sentences, and paragraphs. The news writer does what, in fact, the most successful churchmen do in their speaking: makes himself understandable to all readers.

Churchmen who write for the press and radio can profit from study of Rudolf Flesch's book, *The Art of Readable Writing*. Secular journalists already have taken its content to heart. Dr. Flesch has been engaged by the Associated Press and other journalistic groups to test the English in their materials. Book publishers, advertising agencies, and public speakers have found useful his essentially simple system of testing writing and his formula for producing easily understood English. If his findings are not taken too literally they can have a remarkably beneficial effect upon both writing and speaking.

In essence, Dr. Flesch's suggestion is that the average word be short, that sentences rarely go beyond a stated length, and that at least a minimum number of personal words and sentences be employed. He has set up a table for readability against which any piece of writing may be checked.

Newspaper and magazine editors follow a particular typographical style when they prepare copy to be set in type. Publications sometimes have their own style rule books or guides. (See Appendix III.) The news writer who prepares copy for one secular newspaper need study only that paper's style sheet or the paper itself to learn its practices in abbreviating, capitalizing, contracting, and the like. If he writes with the hope of seeing his copy in more than one publication, which is likely in the community supporting more than one, he may not have time to prepare each release in a different style. If there *is* time, he should tailor as many as he can. At least he should be consistent in whatever style he uses. For example, an editor who receives copy like the following is tempted, especially if it is routine and unimportant, to toss it into the big wastebasket beside his desk:

Plans for a picnic at Green Lake on Saturday, have been made by the Married Couples Club of the Second Unitarian church.

Busses will leave for Green lake at 10 A.M. Sunday morning from the Yates hotel. Reservations for space must be made with Mrs. Bertha Lindemer, secretary of the Married Couples club.

This is the second picnic of the season for this Second Baptist

Church group. Others are planned for later this year, also at Green Lake.

To begin with, this is a commonplace story. Plans always are being made for something. The reporter might have noted how many couples are expected to go or mentioned what entertainment is planned for the picnic. But *Green Lake* is written with a capital *L* at the beginning and end of the story but with a small *l* in the middle. The word *church* after *Second Baptist* likewise is inconsistently capitalized, as is *Club*. The expression "at 10 A.M. Saturday morning" is redundant. If it is A.M. it must be morning. Hundreds of such errors or inconsistencies are corrected in preparing copy for printing in the city daily. Church workers who want their copy treated hospitably are wise to reduce to a minimum such infelicities as those illustrated. The simplest way is to follow a style book.

If language is to be alive it must change, must reflect common usage rather than authority. Its purpose is communication. For many years, for example, church editors of secular publications and editors-in-chief of religious journals have battled over the expression *reverend*. The battle is an unimportant one in the atomic age, but has become well publicized.

Technically to speak or write about a man of the cloth as "a reverend" is incorrect. To write *Rev. John Jones* also is incorrect. Both are incorrect because the word *reverend* in each instance is used as a noun whereas it is an adjective. The logic of the correction can be realized if we substitute a parallel word of respect, *honorable*. We do not say "he is an honorable." By the same reasoning neither should we say that "He is a reverend," or talk about "the reverend." We say "The Honorable John D. Jones, representative from Pulaski"; we do not say "The speaker tonight is Honorable John D. Jones." The word *the* is imperative.

John A. Womeldof, of Princeton, West Virginia, writing in *The Presbyterian Outlook,* quoted this poem by Bishop Douglass H. Atwill of the Episcopal Church in support of an attack on the misuse of *reverend* which had been made by the General Assembly of the Presbyterian Church:

REVEREND

Call me **Brother,** if you will,
Call me **Parson**—better still.
Or if perchance, the Catholic frill
Doth your heart with longing fill,
Though plain **Mister** fills the bill,
Then even **Father** brings no chill
Or hurt or rancor or ill-will.

To no D.D. do I pretend,
Though **Doctor** doth some honor lend,
Preacher, Pastor, Rector, Friend,
Titles almost without end
Never grate and n'er offend;
A loving ear to all I bend,
But how the man my heart doth rend,
Who blithely calls me **Reverend.**

Churchmen can continue to try to turn the tide of usage, but it is likely that the *the* will remain ignored on bulletin boards, in church advertising, in church news stories, and even in the journals that are fighting to restore the little word as a preliminary to *reverend.*

It should not be necessary, whatever the style and usage churchmen may follow, to plead with them to follow some prescribed method of preparing copy for the printer, whether the printer be in the composing room of the newspaper, the print shop that has the contract to produce the parish paper or magazine, or the plant operated by the denominational publishing house. Church editors and others who handle copy from church sources complain, however, that there is appalling lack of uniformity and no concept whatsoever of what is likely to be acceptable and useful to the press.

That copy must be readable, so that it can be edited and then translated into type, cannot be disputed. The best way to achieve physical readability is to typewrite or at least write clearly and legibly by hand. It should be equally obvious that leaving space between lines and providing for adequate margins on all sides of the page are helpful to the person who must process the copy.

Everyone who writes news, therefore, should follow a few simple rules when he sets his stories on typing paper. (See Appendices I and II.) Following such rules as these will enable anyone to meet the requirement of any type of publication. But such regulations for preparing copy are not necessarily acceptable for radio (to be discussed later).

Prefabricated copy

Denominational public relations directors and publicity chairmen, taking a cue from men and women who do such work for business groups, sometimes send out prepared news stories to ministers, with blank spaces left for insertion of the local angle. Either enough copies are supplied for local release or a model story is written, with the suggestion that the pastor copy it, with adjustments to suit his conditions.

An example of this procedure is the following story, prepared by C. E. Bryant, while he was director of publicity for the Southern Baptist Convention. Headed "Local Pastor Wants 'Every Baptist a Tither,'" it was printed in *The Baptist Program*, a promotion publication. Beside it was the explanatory material, reading: "A Story for Your Paper. To the right is a suggested news story many pastors will want to complete and then hand to the editor of their local paper." Here is the story:

"Every Baptist a Tither," a slogan adopted by the Southern Baptists at their recent convention in Memphis, Tenn., is beginning to have local as well as national meaning, according to .... pastor of the .... Baptist Church.

The Rev. Mr. .... said that the slogan has become one of the major 1948 emphases of the local church, and that he hopes the goal it suggests will be achieved by the congregation at least by the time 1949 church pledges are made this fall.

Tithing means the giving of 10 per cent of one's income to the Lord's work, Mr. .... said. The principle was taught and practiced throughout the Old Testament and endorsed by Christ in the New Testament, and has long been accepted as a minimum standard for Christian giving.

The average church member gives much less than the tithe, however, according to the pastor. Although many members do tithe conscientiously, many others give so little to the church that gifts average slightly over 2 per cent rather than the biblical 10 per cent, he said. The average Southern Baptist contributed only $21.07 through his church last year, while his tithe would have been $97.

If all Baptists tithed there would be no financial worries in the denomination, but while agreeing to this the pastor added hurriedly that spiritual blessings "which come in this obedience to the will of God" outweigh all other rewards of tithing.

Viewed from both financial and spiritual standpoints, the tithing emphasis is expected to be the basis for a great forward movement throughout the denomination. Dr. C. E. Matthews, superintendent of evangelism of the Southern Baptist Home Mission Board, believes that many recent signs point to a spiritual revival throughout the Southern Baptist Convention territory, and Dr. M. Theron Rankin, executive secretary of the Southern Baptist Foreign Mission Board, has expressed hopes for realization of a greatly expanded foreign mission advance in 25 countries of the world.

Editors sometime object to such prefabricated journalism but, especially in one-newspaper towns, enough are willing to print or broadcast these stories to justify use of the idea. It is not a perfect method of publicizing religion, but it is better than no effort at all.

The busy or indifferent user of canned stories only fills in the blanks by hand or on the typewriter. The churchman who wants them to be most effective not only fills in the blanks but also retypes the whole story. If he delivers the copy to the newspaper or radio station office he can say that it is based on a national release or he can attach a memo to that effect; the alert editor knows the difference anyway.

The tests of publicity material are its newsworthiness or its strength as a means of obtaining advertising to complement it. Ordinarily the owner or editor of a publication does not care too much about the form or source so long as the story is local, legible, and legal. His test is: will it have any readers or will it have more readers than this other piece of copy that is competing with it?

Radio-television news writing

Church workers may have the opportunity to prepare all types of scripts for radio and television use, especially as FM stations increase in number and as AM stations use more local news. In sending out accounts of religious activities, church people should include on their mailing lists the radio and television stations in their area as well as the newspapers, press associations, and religious journals that circulate there.

It is not feasible to expect the average city church to prepare copy especially for radio news programs. In present circumstances the news editor of a station, or its newscaster, is willing to prepare his copy from the regular news releases that go also to newspapers. But he would be more likely to use a news release from a church group if it were tailored for radio use and if he did not have to make major changes.

Radio and television news writers usually have had newspaper news writing experience. They come to this special application of their training with a knowledge of reader interest. They are aware of the factors or components of news. What they must learn—as must the churchman who tries to write for radio and video—is a new group of patterns. They must learn to write for the ear instead of the eye.

Radio listeners also are newspaper readers. They are persons accustomed to stopping to reread what they do not at first understand. They have had the help of headlines in summarizing the news. Cartoons, pictures, diagrams, graphs, and charts have helped them comprehend the news.

Newswriters for radio must recognize the difference in listener reactions. The listener can ignore the program and switch to another if he pleases and the radio speaker does not know this has happened. Listeners may be sophisticates or sophomores, but the program must be intelligible and attractive to both. Consequently all the strictures about simplicity, brevity, and straightforwardness of style in newspaper and magazine news copy go tenfold for radio and television. Radio news stories are more simple even than those for the press. Radio, it must be remembered, has an absolute limit on what it can present that is far more rigid than the space restriction of the newspaper. A news program generally is only five, ten, or fifteen minutes long. The highlights of the news must be compressed into those few minutes; several minutes, in fact, are used for advertising.

As with news for print, news for hearing must be accurate, in good taste, and dramatic in so far as its content will allow drama. Unlike the news lead to be printed, however, the summary lead will not serve. It has the same purpose, this radio news lead, but because the medium of communication is different, it must be constructed differently.

Radio leads

The radio lead should not put all the important facts together in the first paragraph or two, as does the news story for print. It should start, when possible, with familiar words, not strange names of places or persons. Trick openings, possible in newspapers, like the question or quotation lead, are not successful on the air. They cannot be distinguished from commercials. Nor does the radio lead have to be structurally perfect. It can consist of descriptive phrases instead of grammatically complete sentences. The latter, too, whether incomplete or complete, never should be involved and circuitous. They should all be short, running between fifteen and twenty words. The present tense is the more effective; it is more acceptable for radio than for print because radio news is reported soon after it has occurred. This stricture applies less to routine than to spot news. It affects the writing of church news for radio with less pertinence than other and more general types, such as legislative action, accidents, and obituaries.

Radio and television stories are so terse that they offer almost no structural problem. Usually they consist of little more than a lead and rarely run more than three hundred words. When they do, they present the facts in descending order of importance. Second and third paragraphs are likely to be more important in writing for the ear than for the eye because the lead is not crowded; vital information has been left for the body of the story

These typical radio religious news leads and stories illustrate the brevity and informality of the copy written for listening:

SPRINGTIME IS TRADITIONALLY A TIME OF RELIGIOUS FESTIVITY AMONG JERUSALEM'S MOSLEMS AND JEWS. BUT THE PALESTINE CONFLICT PROVIDES A DEPRESSING BACKGROUND FOR THIS YEAR'S CELEBRATIONS.

GREATEST DISAPPOINTMENT TO PIOUS MOSLEMS HAS BEEN . . .
✿   ✿   ✿

AND IN NEW YORK—THE PRESIDENT OF THE FEDERAL COUNCIL OF CHURCHES CALLED UPON THE UN TO TAKE ACTION FOR THE PROTECTION OF JERUSALEM.

SPEAKING FOR THE CHURCHES CO-OPERATING IN THE FEDERAL COUNCIL—CHARLES P. TAFT, THE COUNCIL'S PRESIDENT, URGED . . .

❋   ❋   ❋

RELIGIOUS MUSIC HAS BEEN BANNED FROM ALL SCHOOLS IN MEXICO.

AN ORDER TO THAT EFFECT HAS BEEN ISSUED BY THE NATIONAL INSTITUTE OF FINE ARTS—THE AGENCY WHICH ACTS FOR THE MEXICAN GOVERNMENT IN MATTERS AFFECTING MUSICAL INSTRUCTION IN THE SCHOOLS.

SHARP REACTION TO THE ORDER WAS IMMEDIATELY FORTHCOMING. ONE MEXICO CITY NEWSPAPER CHARGED THAT THE INSTITUTE IS CONTROLLED BY COMMUNISTS. AS A MATTER OF FACT—THE NEWSPAPER SAID—THE INSTITUTE HAS REWRITTEN A LINE OF THE MEXICAN NATIONAL ANTHEM SO THAT MENTION OF THE NAME OF GOD WOULD BE OMITTED.

—Religious News Service

Radio has its own style rules, although they are few and highly individualized, and its own methods of copy preparation. As the copy is to be read and not used for printing, there is little concern about capitalization and abbreviation, as compared with the newspaper and magazine. Reasonable consistency is expected, but there is no attempt to achieve perfection. Style is used to achieve smooth and easy reading performance by the newscaster. Consequently round figures always are more desirable—and understandable—than exact or fractional figures. The number *3,171* is avoided, unless human lives are involved, and *31-hundred* is used instead. *Quarter of a million* should be written instead of *250,000* in a story saying that that number of persons became members of a denomination the previous year. *Almost 25 per cent* is preferred to *24.8 per cent*. Only a few of these rules are to be found in radio writing textbooks, for there is little standardization.

Rules for preparing radio manuscript are not unlike those for printed copy. Clean copy is essential. Since it is to be read—and is supposed to be transmitted without stumbling—interlinings and other alterations are a handicap to the newscaster. Margins should be left on all sides. Paragraphs are indented, as for newspaper copy, but some radio stations prefer indentations that begin half-way in from the margin, instead of only five spaces. Wire copy for radio arrives typed completely in capitals, for the teletypes that serve both newspapers and radio stations are more efficiently operated if they do not have to be shifted for upper and lower case. Local copy, that which the churchman might produce, is written in ordinary typing. Double or triple spacing is expected. Different stories, no matter how short, should be on separate sheets.

The tone of copy prepared for eye or for ear can best be realized by comparing church news written first for the newspaper and then for radio, as in this example:

NEWSPAPER VERSION

New York,—(UP)—The number of Roman Catholics in the United States, Alaska, and Hawaii has increased 866,049 in the last year, it was disclosed today in the official Catholic directory for 1947.

The newly published directory said the 1947 population Catholic total was 25,268,173.

An increase of 1,490 priests over last year was reported to bring the total in the three U.S. areas to a record 40,470.

The directory reported a total of 738,314 infant baptisms in the past 12 months, led by 39,126 in the Chicago archdiocese.

The denomination reported its largest archdiocese was Chicago, with a Catholic population of 1,716,536. The Boston archdiocese ranked second and New York was third. The largest diocese was Brooklyn, with 1,111,446 Catholics.

RADIO VERSION

There are now almost 900-thousand more Catholics in the United States and possessions than last year.

That was the figure released today in New York by the official Catholic directory, which is published in that city.

The new directory said that the Catholic population of the United States, Alaska, and Hawaii now is more than 25-million. . . .

CHAPTER XIV

The Churchman as Feature and Article Writer

A church school's request for a lion is not news, but it is the basis for a feature story.

Parishioners who help build, paint, and clean a new church building are not creating a news story, but a feature deemed worthy of a three-column picture and a story on the first page of one of the country's biggest dailies, the New York *Herald Tribune*.

The church has been a popular source of such features for the press, for it is in contrast, in so many ways, to the other modern social institutions. It is not operated for profit, it has its own code of conduct, and some of its members dress or live in unusual ways.

News is the beefsteak of the journalistic menu; features are the salad or dessert. No one is harmed by not learning from the press that the Maryknoll Fathers in New York are looking for a lion to send to Kyoto, Japan, where a missionary would like to add it to the newly organized zoo. But the reader is amused, entertained, or informed by the little story. What is more meaningful to the editor is that he stopped to read. Feature copy provokes reading if it is something different, unusual, and off the routine track. It offers relief from the dominantly unpleasant fare which gains most space in the press or time on the air. As part of a mosaic of accident, lockout, fire, and crime stories it offers needed contrast.

Almost every category of feature story is available in the church. The chief types are human interest, historical, biographical and personality, explanatory or interpretative, how-to-do-it, and scientific.

Human interest features

The human interest feature is short, at its best when it reaches no more than 250 words and hovers around 150. It emphasizes emotion. Its ingredients are pathos, humor, pity, novelty, sympathy, and contrast. Religion, being deeply concerned with emotional experience, readily produces such features. They tend to be personal—the word *human* in the name is taken literally—and therefore must be used with care. The large religious organization can exploit this type of feature more safely than can the local church, for it is more impersonal, being further removed from the persons featured. Here are some typical subjects for such features:

The oldest and youngest members of the church, synod, denomination, or other administrative unit.

Incidents involving children, such as unusual remarks or actions that occur in church school.

Humorous occurrences, such as take place during a religious meeting, but only when not derogatory to the church.

Incidents that take place on the church's property, occurring to persons or organizations assembled there.

The following story of a war bride is an example of a human interest feature that had so many of the desired ingredients that it was distributed nationally by the wire services. It did not originate in the church, that is, the church in question did not itself prepare an account of the situation for press use. But the incident took place in a church, in part, and therefore is associated with the church and religion. The story, nevertheless, has no effect upon religious life one way or the other. So highly readable was the story that few newspaper readers and radio listeners overlooked it. The first account reproduced here was the original story; the second is known as the follow-up, i.e. the latest development.

CHICAGO (AP)—Rosanna Peveri, who came here from her London home to marry the Chicago GI she met during the war and then left him standing at the altar, says she is ready and willing to marry him now.

"I felt so homesick," the dark haired 24-year-old English girl said in relating why she answered "no" at the scheduled marriage ceremony Sunday when the priest asked, "Do you take this man to be your lawful wedded husband?"

Her intended bridegroom, Peter Vasquez, 26-year-old express company worker, was not sure if there would be a wedding.

"If she's not certain," he said, "it wouldn't be a good idea."

But Miss Peveri, who said she left home over her family's protests to marry Vasquez, said: "I made a silly mistake. I know I want to marry him. I came over here for that."

Vasquez, his marriage halted, went through with the reception and guests at the church went to his home for a party. Miss Peveri, who is staying at his home, joined the crowd and danced with Vasquez.   —Associated Press

CHICAGO (AP)—Rosanna Peveri, the unpredictable English bride, yesterday said that her final decision in her international romance with ex-GI Peter Vasquez was "I'm definitely not getting married."

Rosanna, 24, traveled from London alone, against her parents' wishes, she said, to wed Vasquez, 26-year-old express company worker. But the trip to the altar last Sunday gave her qualms. In the middle of the ceremony she said "no."

That decided Peter. The marriage was off, he said, since "if she's not certain, it wouldn't be a good idea." Then Rosanna exercised her woman's prerogative again. She decided she wanted to go thru with it after all.

But Peter left his parents' home, where Rosanna was staying, to live with friends. After a day's thinking it over, Rosanna made her negative decision, which she said was her final one.

"I've just gotten to feel that he's not really worth worrying about," she declared.

Asked if she would return to Giovanni Castellani, the man she left behind in London, Rosanna said, "It wouldn't be right to marry someone you didn't love."   —Associated Press

The religious press itself makes rare—too rare—use of human interest stories. Because they are not easy to come by, human interest is provided, instead, by borrowed or stale jokes. Typical of the human interest story as found in church journals is this; invariably the purpose is to preach, to draw a moral. Inasmuch as almost everything in the religious publication has that purpose, the feature offers too little contrast with the surrounding material.

When R. G. LeTourneau, Christian industrialist, spoke at York, England, during his recent trip to dedicate the new factory at Stockton-on-Tees, a prominent Chinese businessman sat in his audience. Interested, he came to the LeTourneau, Ltd., office in York and was presented with a copy of *God Runs My Business*, LeTourneau's life story.

What happened then was told by the businessman in a letter to Mr. LeTourneau: "The most blessed part of my trip to England came from reading the book *God Runs My Business* which Mr. R. F. Nelson gave me at Stockton-on-Tees. I started to read this booklet that afternoon in my room at the Travelyard Hotel. I read to page 30 where Mr. LeTourneau was quoted as saying, 'I got out of bed and ran to her bedroom. "Mother," I said, "it is settled. Now you don't have to pray for me any more. I am saved and on my way to heaven!"'

"By that time I could not read on. I just knelt down and prayed. Then, I got up, took pen and paper, and wrote to my wife, 'Mother and daughters, you need not pray for me any more, for our Lord has answered your prayer that I will be submitted to His will now.'

"So my problem of spiritual paralysis was solved in the twinkling of an eye. Praise His name! I can imagine how happy will be my wife, daughters, and fine Christian friends, who have prayed faithfully for me for years and years."   —*Christian Life*

Historical features

Wide use is made by both the secular and religious press of historical features. Every newspaper in the country has at one time or another carried a series of short historical articles on the churches of the community or an occasional article on a church anniversary.

Typical features of this type, in addition to histories of specific buildings, congregations, or institutions are histories of:

Equipment in the building, such as furniture, the altar, stained glass windows, carvings, and even particular special rooms. One church was given a sedilia, a clergy-stall. A short historical feature was prepared about it for both the church and community papers.

Organizations within the church—the women's groups, a revered church school class, and the like.

Activities, publications, or projects connected with the church, such as a settlement or mission.

Unless they are in a series, all these stories should have a news peg, that is, a tie-in with current news. For example:

Grace Episcopal Church, whose 110th anniversary will be celegrated with a dinner in the community house tomorrow night, was founded by throo . . .

Biographical features

The biographical-personality feature is popular reading because human beings are deeply interested in other people, an interest that church people possess even more intensely than many others. This feature can be handled either as a series or as an individual story. Treatment in series form must be indulged in cautiously, however, for omissions of persons who should be included occur readily and provoke criticism and discontent.

Some often-used subjects:

Biographical or personality sketches of the ministers, priests, rabbis, or other executives of the church as well as national figures in its overhead groups.

Such sketches of the oldest members or the member of the board of stewards (as a typical organization) longest in service. This feature is an elaboration of the human interest, which is more timely and considerably shorter.

Sketches of persons who are retired or of new church employees or of employees who take a responsible place in general church work.

A biographical sketch deals chiefly with the chronology

of the person's life, the record of his accomplishments, and the accomplishments of those immediately surrounding him, such as his family. A personality sketch emphasizes the subpect's appearance, habits, foibles, interests, activities, and only briefly his biography.

Usually these features are better newspaper and magazine stories than they are copy for radio. Radio and television prefer to interview the protagonist and let him tell his own story.

When Charles Clayton Morrison retired in 1947 as editor of *Christian Century* magazine, *Time* published a combination biography and personality sketch. This magazine, which actually is as much a newspaper as a magazine, illustrates a trend in modern biographical writing: informality, brevity, and candor.

Man of the *Century*

An outstanding career in U. S. Protestant journalism was drawing to a close. Dr. Charles Clayton Morrison, 72, editor of the *Christian Century*, decided that it was time to retire and turn the magazine over to his longtime managing editor, Dr. Paul Hutchinson. Last week, Dr. Hutchinson prepared to take over. Dr. Morrison will stay on the staff as contributing editor of the weekly magazine that he has made into Protestantism's most vigorous voice.

A slender, decorous man with old-world manners, Dr. Morrison wears gold-rimmed glasses that do not quite hide the fire in his eyes. Even in his youth, he never lacked for words. Like his father, he became a minister of the Disciples of Christ, a denomination originally formed by Presbyterians who wanted less sectarianism and more church unity. Once in his preaching career Dr. Morrison, in the pulpit of a church he was visiting, discovered a clock with a warning sign: "Do not preach over 30 minutes." Dr. Morrison preached right on past the deadline.

In 1908, he went to the public auction of a struggling little Disciples of Christ publication (circ. about 600). No other prospective customers showed up, so Dr. Morrison got the *Christian Century* for $1,500 cash.

As he explains it now, Editor Morrison never really gave up his pulpit: "I was simply acquiring a larger pulpit." From the first, the distinguishing characteristic of the *Century* under Morrison was its intellectual vigor. It rose to its present circulation (40,000) in a time when Protestantism was so mired down in social reform that it tended to forget theology—a time when the intellectual world often looked on religion as a misty-minded form of escapism. In such an era, the *Century* dared to speak of Christianity as a way of life, and stuck to the truths of Christian gospel.

Beacon in a Fog. While most other Protestant publications were displaying their intellectual poverty either by clinging stubbornly to dogma or retreating headlong before the advance of secularism, the *Christian Century* remained stimulating and profound; it eventually became a beacon of level-headedness in a fog of misty thinking.

On strictly theological issues, such standards led the *Century* to oppose fundamentalism (when fundamentalism v. liberalism was a burning issue), to crusade for unity among Protestants (in 1917 it abandoned its affiliation with the Disciples of Christ and became frankly non-denominational), to take a position that was pro-ecumenical but anti-Roman Catholic.

But Dr. Morrison's belief that Christianity is responsible for the character of civilization also prompted him to apply Christian principles to the whole area of current events. The *Century*, at various times, campaigned for the League of Nations, for prohibition, for NRA, for the rights of labor. Sometimes it campaigned itself into positions that many readers thought untenable (e.g. attempting to be both crusading and pacifist in support of the Kellogg-Briand Pact, the *Century* naively hoped that a pact to "outlaw" war could, in fact, outlaw it). But the *Century's* alertness, firmly backed by the principles of evangelical Christianity, never degenerated into sterile intellectualism; and whatever side it took, the *Century* always came up with a challenging case.

The Integrated "We." For 39 years, Dr. Morrison's pulpit has kept growing: *Century* readership has increased steadily, almost from the time he took over. The paper is now owned by the "editorial family" (the names listed on the masthead), with Dr. Morrison as chief stockholder. Like very few butcher-paper weeklies, it pays its own way without patrons.

Behind the *Century's* editorial "we," consistent readers have come to recognize the Morrison touch: a subtle blend of scholarship, sweet reasonableness and hard-punching prose. But Dr. Morrison attributes the rise of the *Century* to no one man. Editorial conferences, he says, are always "a highly integrated collective mind" engaging in "an informal continuum of conversation."

New Editor Hutchinson, a Methodist with a D.D. from both DePauw and Garrett Biblical Institute, and a *Century* veteran for

23 years, has no intention of changing the weekly's vigorous liberalism, its anti-denominationalism, its habit of speaking its mind. His biggest policy change, he says, will be a greater attempt to appeal to the laity. About 25% of the *Century's* readers are laymen; Editor Hutchinson hopes to boost it to 50%. Says he: "I'd like to keep our theological editorials short and crisp. Now, Dr. Morrison's editorials on theology are certainly impressive, but a bit overpowering."

Searching and often inspiring—as well as overpowering—Dr. Morrison's editorials have been the chief factor in making the *Christian Century* one of the few publications in its time, lay or religious, which combine high intellectual standards, humanitarian crusading and a basically Christian orientation.

—Courtesy of *Time,* Copyright Time, Inc., 1947

Local newspapers also use the biographical feature. This Monday-morning story, one in a series called "A Reporter Goes to Church," gives combined coverage to a service and to a pastor. It is reproduced only in part, for the first few paragraphs indicate the pattern of the story:

In his Sunday sermon, the Rev. Frederick Butman, pastor of East Syracuse Methodist Church, told his congregation: "The right spirit must be created before the deed."

Possibly this was the thought that was uppermost in the minds of a group of Methodists who, in the early days following the turn of the century, established the East Syracuse church.

They quickly put in effect a program . . . .

A native of Syracuse, Mr. Butman attended . . ..

Taking his theme from Jeremiah, entitled "The Inner Life," he said that . . . .

—Syracuse (N. Y.) *Herald-Journal*

Exploiting personalities

In preparing the biographical and personality feature particularly, church journalists must beware of overexploiting themselves or their subjects. In every community are religious persons who constantly are quoted or interviewed. Sometimes these men and women are deliberate publicity seekers. More often they simply are accessible, reasonable, and co-operative.

Marjorie Moore Armstrong, speaking before the Associated Church Press annual meeting in 1949, while she was still managing editor of *The Commission* magazine, reported on a survey she made of the church copy in three major newspapers. She found that secular church editors find it comparatively easy to deal with the Roman Catholic Church and difficult to deal with Protestants, as has been indicated in other parts of this book.

"A reporter has to make twelve phone calls to know what the Baptists are doing and only one call to know what the Roman Catholic Church is doing," she said.

Other church journalists support or deny this for their particular localities, but the result of a co-operative attitude may be that the churchman who reveals it finds himself featured frequently in biographies or personality sketches. Envious colleagues may suspect him of being a publicity-hound. What is more likely is that they themselves are abnormally unco-operative or publicity-shy.

Professional journalists can detect space-grabbers and make use of them. But this is no reason for the rank and file churchman to compete with them. The feature story actually is less important as a medium of exploitation than the day-by-day stories that mention one person repeatedly.

A churchman should consider whether he wants his church to be known as the Third Congregational or the Elm Street Church, or to be called Dr. Simpson's Church or Rabbi Myers' Synagogue. If the church is built chiefly around a personality it may suffer when that personality no longer is there to carry it into prominence. A churchman should be willing to do his part with press and radio, but when they exploit him to the damage of his congregation or of himself he should be wary.

Explanatory features

The explanatory feature, also sometimes called the interpretative or expository, is more widely used in religious magazines than in secular publications, and practically not at all over the radio. When found in newspapers it may be in the form of a special article written for a syndicate or handled by the church editor for a Saturday or special issue. It borders on the impartial editorial. Because it can be an important device for gaining understanding of church action, it should be more widely used in the secular press.

Some typical stories are:

An explanation of a change in policy made by a church group.

Exposition of a resolution passed by a church organization.

An interpretation of trends in the religious world.

When Pius XII decreed excommunication, in mid-1949, for Roman Catholics who "knowingly and freely . . . defend and spread Communism" the press printed numerous articles explaining the meaning of the act.

Explanatory features need not deal with such ponderous or complex subjects, however. Far more orthodox an example appeared in the St. Louis *Post Dispatch.* Keith Wheeler, one-time war correspondent for the Chicago *Times,* wrote a 2,000-word article about the tallest church in the world: Chicago Temple. He explained the activity of this church, described the building, and gave a few words of its history. The tone is revealed in this reproduction of the lead and a few succeeding paragraphs:

As anyone who has ever occupied a Loop hotel room on Sunday morning can tell you, one of the easiest landmarks to find hereabout is the top of the Chicago Temple First Methodist Church.

The bottom of it is a little more obscure and some people who have lived in Chicago for years have never consciously seen the Gothic church door surrounded by haberdashery and jewelry stores amid the metropolitan uproar at Washington and Clark.

In several respects the First Methodist is a unique house of worship. It claims to be . . . .

—St. Louis *Post Dispatch*

The meaning of a local church merger was made clear in

a feature that appeared under the by-line of a staff writer for a big-city paper but concerned the union of churches in a small town. Here is part of the story:

BY CELESTINE SIBLEY
Constitution Staff Writer
DEMOREST, Aug. 18—The spiritual descendants of the Pilgrim fathers and the spiritual descendants of John Wesley have joined forces in Demorest.

For the first time in Georgia and possibly the first time in the South, a Congregational Church and a Methodist Church have become federated. It is a moment, religionists hereabouts feel, that may point the way to languishing and dying small-town churches everywhere.

(There follows the story of the actual merger: when begun, the difficulties encountered, and the views of members and leaders of both churches on the significance of the plan.)

—Atlanta (Ga.) *Constitution*

Radio and television features

Radio and video make an entirely different use of features than do other media. A long historical article is far more effective when presented as a play; it would be dull to listen to someone reading such copy. Consequently neither radio nor television has the slightest interest in the lengthy scripts found in the press. Direct reporting is their forte.

The churchman who has a feature idea suitable for radio may take the suggestion to the radio station manager. Let us say it concerns the oldest member of his church. Instead of being written about, this man or woman may be interviewed on the air. A segment of the anniversary celebration of a large church can be televised, much in the same manner as the motion picture's coverage through news reels.

Short, written features have their place in radio religious journalism. The human interest feature, even if intended chiefly for reading, can be made part of a radio news program. Religious News Service, Ecumenical Press Service, and the other denominational or general syndicates usually include in their budgets several items of news that qualify as features. Here are the leads only of several examples:

THE REV. REUBEN FORD—LUTHERAN PASTOR IN MINNEAPOLIS —IS A PREACHER WHO PACKS TWO SERMONS INTO ONE.

ARMED WITH AN EASEL AND COLORED CHALK—HE DEFTLY TRANSFORMS SCRIPTURE TEXTS INTO EXPERTLY DONE SKETCHES. HIS USUAL PROCEDURE IS TO . . . .

❀   ❀   ❀

WHEN A MINISTER HAS PREACHED SOME NINE THOUSAND SERMONS HE MIGHT BE EXPECTED TO RUN OUT OF IDEAS.

BUT NOT DR. LUDWIG J. PEDERSON OF MINNEAPOLIS. AT THE AGE OF EIGHTY—HE IS THE OLDEST ACTIVE MINISTER IN THE EVANGELICAL FREE CHURCH ASSOCIATION.

AS FAR AS SERMONS ARE CONCERNED—DR. PEDERSON SAYS . . . .   —Religious News Service

—Speaking of atom bombs—Dr. Malcolm Dole, famed atomic physicist of Northwestern University, will speak on "The Possibilities of Atomic Power" at St. Matthew's Parish House, Lincoln and Haven Streets, in northwest Evanston next Friday evening at 8 o'clock . . .
                —WEAW, Evanston, Illinois

Radio's religious news writers and broadcasters depend heavily upon news prepared originally for print. These next two stories, distributed by Religious News Service for publication, are readily adapted to radio use as features:

SEATTLE, Wash.—Seattle's fisher-folk are on their annual voyages to the banks in the north after a church service in which they were given Godspeed, faith in a safe return and their honest labors blessed.

It was the 18th annual fishermen's festival in the Ballard First Lutheran Church, originated by the pastor, the Rev. O. L. Haavik, who was a fisherman himself years ago in his native Norway.

Gnarled hands that hold the fishing lines were folded in prayer, keen eyes in seamed faces, usually lifted to sun and spray, were lowered, and voices that roll out over the boom of the sea were lifted in hymns, as the fishermen sang:

"Lord of the everlasting hills,
"God of the boundless sea;
"Help us through all the shocks of fate
"To put our trust in Thee!"

"There are the ships that will not sail again," Mr. Haavik told the fishermen and their families, who crowded his church. "There are the fishermen who will go down to sea no more. Yet, go in Christian faith and, confidently and courageously, experience God's blessing and peace upon your labors. God be with you! Amen."

Songs of the sea were sung by the 65-voice Norwegian Male Chorus. An address of appreciation was given by Capt. Konrad Uri, president of the Fishing Vessel Owners' Association.

The narrative qualities of this story make it easy to alter for radio use. It already is informal in tone and rich with personal references. More difficult is this next, a straight news story laden with specific detail.

PHILADELPHIA—An abandoned church 115 years old in the Cumberland County town of Newburg near the Pennsylvania state capital at Harrisburg has been sold on the auction block for $350. The church pews brought $82 and the fine old metal bell $6.

The congregation, which organized in 1832 as part of the Middle Spring Presbyterian charge, has been drifting far and wide to other churches over the years. The purchaser has not decided whether to raze the building and salvage brick and lumber, or remodel it as a home. A collapsed ceiling blocks off the bell tower, and the question remains how can the bell be gotten down.

Epitomized is the larger question: what becomes of old church buildings, long revered as landmarks?   —Religious News Service

A rewrite for radio would bring this result:

WHAT HAPPENS TO ABANDONED CHURCHES?

THE ANSWER IS—PROBABLY WHAT HAPPENED THE OTHER DAY TO A 100-FIFTEEN-YEAR-OLD ONE IN PENNSYLVANIA.

THIS OLD PRESBYTERIAN CHURCH HAS BEEN IN THE CUMBERLAND COUNTY TOWN OF NEWBURG NEAR THE STATE CAPITAL, HARRISBURG. THE CONGREGATION — WHICH ORGANIZED IN EIGHTEEN THIRTY-TWO AS PART OF THE MIDDLE SPRING PRES-

BYTERIAN CHARGE—HAS BEEN DRIFTING AWAY TO OTHER CHURCHES OVER THE YEARS.

ACCORDING TO THE RELIGIOUS NEWS SERVICE STORY ABOUT THIS FROM PHILADELPHIA—THE OLD CHURCH HAS BEEN SOLD ON THE AUCTION BLOCK FOR 350-DOLLARS. THE PEWS BROUGHT EIGHTY-TWO DOLLARS AND THE OLD METAL BELL SIX DOLLARS.

THE PURCHASER HASN'T DECIDED WHETHER TO RAZE THE BUILDING AND SALVAGE THE BRICK AND LUMBER OR TO REMODEL THE PLACE AS A HOME. A PROBLEM IS OFFERED BY THE BELL. A COLLAPSED CEILING BLOCKS OFF THE BELL TOWER, SO THERE WILL BE TROUBLE GETTING THE BELL DOWN.

Articles

A question arises at once as we face the subject of articles: How does feature writing differ from article writing?

The feature, first of all, is closely associated with the newspaper; the article is considered to be an ingredient of the magazine. There are technical differences as well. These are disappearing, however, as both secular and religious magazines print more and more of the kind of copy once found exclusively in the newspaper and as newspapers, especially on their editorial pages, publish what used to be copy for magazines alone. Five technical distinctions remain, however:

1. The magazine article usually is longer and more detailed than the newspaper feature. More time is available to prepare it; therefore it is possible to do careful research.

2. The article can be couched in more elaborate language, with longer sentences, a wider vocabulary, and more allusions. Readers expect more complex and profound material in magazines than in newspapers, which are here today and gone tomorrow. Magazines cost far more an issue, have greater permanence, and are treated as the storehouses of longer-lasting material.

3. Magazine articles usually are signed. Consequently they are likely to contain more opinion than the feature, which puts the emphasis, in most instances, on narrative instead of on argument.

4. Staff people write the feature for the newspaper; the magazine article frequently is contributed by outsiders (free lancers).

5. News features must be timely, relating to the news of the day and therefore incorporating a news peg; magazines want timely articles, of course, but are willing to use some that are timeless in the sense of being attractive and interesting reading when they appear.

Distinctions like these should be impressive to religious journalists. Churchmen are interested in ideas and facts more than are persons in many other walks of life. If the magazine article gives them a better opportunity than the newspaper feature to present complicated ideas and complex collections of facts, they should use this form with enthusiasm. The churchman ordinarily is a serious-minded person; he appreciates listeners or readers who take him with equal seriousness. Although the modern magazine is everything from the latest *Superman* comic book to the *Annals of the American Academy of Political and Social Science*, typically it is neither of these extremes any more than it is typified exactly by the consumer magazine, the trade journal, or the religious weekly.

Types of articles

Like the news feature, the magazine article falls into specific classes or types: biographical and personality, confession, historical, adventure, argumentative, explanatory, and discussion.

Certain ones, it will be recognized, are the same as the feature types: the biographical and personality, the historical, and the explanatory. The magazine version generally is longer and more thoroughly and carefully developed. For examples of the personality article the "Profiles" to be found in *The New Yorker* magazine may be examined; several volumes of them have been published. *The Saturday Evening Post* and *Collier's* print biographical-personality articles that also frequently find their way into the anthologies. Historical articles in magazines are more interpretative and thoroughgoing than there is time or space to make them for the newspaper. The expository article in the magazine is varied, for it may be on "How to Tend a Church Furnace" or on "The Meaning of Palestine." Each tries to make some situation clear to the reader. The management and shelter magazines print the how-to-do-it type, the quality and idea magazines explain the meaning of events.

First of the types not usually found in both media is the confession article; this, despite its name, is not merely copy for *True Confessions* magazine. It is the anonymous article that relates to a human situation, on the basis of one person's experience, such as "Why I Don't Like to be a Preacher's Wife" or "Confessions of a P.K." It is a type of social problems copy with a serious intent, seeking to throw light on an intimate, personal experience.

Religious journalists who write about journeys to famous shrines are contributing the travel article; an extraordinarily exciting trip might qualify as an adventure article.

Although the argumentative and discussion articles are closely related they are not the same. The argumentative takes a position and seeks to win support for it. Hundreds of such articles are used by the religious press every month. Often they are sermons in print, literally the Sunday morning or evening dissertation typed and sent to an editor. This is a natural form for churchmen to use but also an all-too-easy way to get into print. Surveys of religious magazines show them stuffed with these typed-up sermons. Often the copy is wordy and dull; few such articles say anything new. They are patchworks of undisputed ideas, comment from the current press and popular leaders, rehashes of news events, and moralizings used interstitially to keep them together. They originally were written for the ear and not the eye. They are loose-jointed, lack documentation and authority, make broad generalizations based on the limited experience of one person. There are exceptions, to be sure, but the majority of these sermon-articles are an appalling collection of platitudes and truisms.

Discussion articles differ from the argumentative in that they do not seek to win a debate but simply to present all arguments on all sides. They are like a sermon that does not propose action but outlines a situation and offers the views of various authorities.

Few such articles are found in religious journals but are encountered frequently in secular magazines. They are safe to print, for they are educational rather than propagandistic.

Marketing articles

What standards might the editor of a religious publication set up for the articles he accepts or rejects? What opportunities does the churchman have to write and prepare articles that interpret the church and religion? How does he go about marketing the copy? How does he know if magazines are interested in his material? How should a churchman go about using his sermons as the basis for magazine articles, if he is not merely to retype them?

Magazine articles have distinct patterns similar to those for news and feature stories. Because articles are longer their construction is more difficult; much material must be maneuvered, outlining is essential, and a specific architecture is needed. Two of the more formal patterns, two designs into which articles readily fall, are a guarantee of successful communication of the ideas or facts to be transmitted. Both use the triangle, one with it on its base and the other with it on a tip.

In both methods of construction the article is in three parts. In the first pattern the triangle being on a tip, broadside up, the writing begins with a general statement (Part I), followed by word pictures, incidents, anecdotes, and examples that illustrate the generalization (Part II). That may occupy as much as 25 to 50 per cent of the article. The remainder (Part III) is comprised of minor details, interesting but not vital. The ending clinches the general statement with a new reference to it. The second form of presentation opens with a specific example or illustrative incident (Part I). There follow word pictures and incidents that expand the idea suggested in the lead section (Part II). The third and final part, the base of the triangle, is a general statement, summarizing the idea of the whole article.

Here are examples of the two constructions, using the opening passages to indicate the style of article architecture.

First is an article which begins with a broad general statement:

Returning home recently from a birthday party given by one of his schoolmates, my little boy rushed in the door, "Mommie—Mommie, look what I got! Candy cigarettes!"

The real problem before us is not the atomic bomb, and never has been. The real problem is modern war, in which weapons of all kinds have become so effective that victors and vanquished are almost equally destroyed.

(From here the author, Harold C. Urey, goes on to evaluate specific policies that take account of the destructiveness of war and concludes that world government holds a possible solution to the problem posed in the opening. He proceeds then to analyze world government theories.)   —The Christian Century

Maxine Lock, writing on "Cigarettes for Your Children," chose to begin with an incident:

Returning home recently from a birthday party given by one of his schoolmates, my little boy rushed in the door, "Mommie—Mommie, look what I got! Candy cigarettes!"

I took the package to see for myself . . . .

(The author tells of examining them, speaking to persons who sell these confections to children, of the manufacturers' tie-ins with tobacco firms, of the views she has come to hold about such candies, and about similar commodities, such as imitation liquor bottles, and concludes with this statement:)

Unless we as Christians become indignant at the liberties which the commercial and worldly interests take in attempting to seduce our children and young people to their ways, we shall continue to fight a losing battle against sin.   —*Christian Life*

Deductive and inductive reasoning, familiar to all who have studied debate and homiletics, are thus applied to article construction. In the first, the writer goes from the general to the particular (deductive), and in the second, he reverses the course, moving from the specific or particular to the general (inductive). A helpful experiment is to take any collection of articles, such as the pocket magazines or digests—*Coronet, Reader's Digest, Magazine Digest, Catholic Digest*, or *Religious Digest*—and test each article to see which pattern it follows.

Outlines needed

Magazine articles, more than newspaper features, should be outlined thoroughly, especially if the writer is not accustomed to the patterns for writing journalistic material. The standard—A.B.C., I.II.III., 1.2.3., *a)b)c)*—form can be used advantageously. Workable schemes for outlining are explained in Brennecke and Clark's *Magazine Article Writing* and in Bird's *Article Writing and Marketing*.

The churchman who outlines his sermons in advance and constructs them according to some logical plan has a start on converting his sermon manuscript into a magazine article, even if it is only an article of opinion. But he is wise if he simply reads his sermon again and then puts it aside. He should plan an article as an article, for he will have a different group of readers than he had as listeners, persons possibly of different education and variable responses to ideas. He may wish to be more or less personal in the article than he was in the sermon. He may have space to introduce more evidence or facts than he had time for in the homily of the morning.

Once his information is assembled and he has outlined the article, the church journalist is ready to begin marketing it. Notice that it is not suggested that the article be written and then sent out. Most professional article writers are asked by editors to prepare certain articles or themselves suggest to editors that such an article be prepared, at the writer's risk.

The Rev. Charles Heimsath, for example, published an article in *Harper's* while he was minister of the First Baptist Church in Evanston, Illinois. One day while he was in New York he had called on Leo Hartman in mid-town Manhattan. He outlined an idea for an article to Mr. Hartman, then editor of the magazine, who told him to attempt it, but made no guarantee of acceptance. Dr. Heimsath was able to write it satisfactorily. Later this article became the basis for a book. Had he written the script and mailed it without first making an inquiry he might not have placed it in that magazine. Interest in the material is aroused in advance by querying thus. Special instructions can be obtained from the editor about the form, length, or content. If the publication has a manuscript on hand much like what is proposed, the writer is saved unnecessary work. Arguments against this method are that it slows up production of a timely article and that it does not permit the manuscript to sell itself to the editor.

When the writer is ready to mail the finished version of his article to an editor, he should prepare the final draft in the form for all copy, as already explained. How does he know where to send his brain child? Alert church people are familiar with some of the journals of their occupation. Those they read most closely they should understand best. They will know the policies of these publications better than do the market guides that list addresses, manuscript lengths, and such details.

If the churchman reads *Social Action, The Christian Century, The Churchman, Presbyterian Outlook,* or *Advance,* he knows that an article declaring that the Federal Council was a dangerous, subversive organization will not be considered seriously for publication, for it is counter to the policy of these journals. If his reading is wider than the church press he knows that most secular magazines do not want out-and-out propagandistic articles on church or religion. Some periodicals will print explanatory articles. A concise report on the status of the church unity movement or an explanation of why church attendance is increasing or decreasing, as the case might be at any one time, will be of interest to magazines like the *Atlantic Monthly, Coronet, Harper's,* and *Tomorrow.* Human interest articles about church life, especially if not controversial, are acceptable to *Pageant, Coronet, Reader's Digest,* and other magazines making an appeal to large numbers of middle-class citizens.

The writer, in other words, must decide what reader group would be most interested in what he has to say and send the article to the magazines that serve that group. He may query more than one editor but should send the manuscript to only one editor at a time.

Addresses may be obtained from market guides. The March, July, September, and December issues of *Author & Journalist* magazine; the annual published by *Writer's Digest* magazine, *The Writer's Market,* or the similar guide issued by *The Writer* magazine, *The Writer's Handbook,* contain this information as well as data on kinds of material desired, rates of pay, deadlines, and the length of copy.

The principal but by no means all the religious publications appear in such guides. In general the religious press appreciates receiving manuscripts—superior ones, for it gets plenty of the inferior type—but is not in position to pay well for them. Fifteen to fifty dollars is about the range for articles. An incident which has come out of church life may sell to *Reader's Digest* for $200, although the article is only 200 words long, while the church magazine article that runs to 2,000 words does well to bring $30.

But the churchman writes for more than pay, welcome as the check is. He writes to influence people, he considers the printing press and the radio or television set an adjunct to the pulpit.

Well-paid or ill-paid, the churchman turned feature or article writer is using another tool to interpret the work of the institution he represents. If he succeeds in providing effective interpretation, that, like virtue, is its own reward.

CHAPTER XV

Advertising the Church

Today churchmen do not oppose the policy of advertising the church so much as lament the lack of money to pay for space or time in the press and on the air.

Not so many years ago, however, there were vigorous opponents of church advertising. The Rev. Bruce S. Wright, in 1930 pastor of the Asbury-Delaware Methodist Episcopal Church of Buffalo, New York, attacked paid advertising in an article in the influential weekly of his denomination, *The Christian Advocate*. He declared:

I do not advertise because I am running a church, not a circus. Somehow I cannot connect display advertising with glorious gothic architecture. I cannot synchronize the ugliness of display 'ads' with the beauty of holiness. I cannot harmonize the idol of publicity with the altar of the living God. A circus comes to town, and it needs must advertise . . . . It must acquaint the populace with the new stunts it has to present, its spectacular features, its horseback riders, and daring trapeze performers . . . . A church does not move in at dawn and out at midnight. A church is a settled part of the community life . . . . I cannot advertise, in the blatant sense of the term, because I am called to be a prophet, and not a vaudevillist . . . . I do not advertise . . . . because I love the church universal.[1]

In contrast to these words are those of J. F. E. Nickelburg, executive secretary of the American Lutheran Publicity Bureau, who spoke three years later in Chicago before an International Walther League convention.

---

[1] Bruce S. Wright, "The Publicity Panacea" in *The Christian Advocate* (March 20, 1930).

The church should use newspaper space for both items of news and insert paid advertising. Why? We have more than 63,000,000 unchurched persons in these United States. We can reach the great number of these, all our prospects, by the public press.

Mr. Nickelburg then asserted that the first advertisement had been written 3,000 years before Christ and inscribed on a sheet of papyrus. It was the offer of a reward for a runaway slave. Likewise, he added, "man ran away from his Creator" and advertising will get him back.

The case for advertising

Advertising, per se, is no more to be condemned as an interpretative tool than are propaganda, water, fire, or food to be blamed for the abuses made of them. *What* is advertised and *how* the advertising technique is employed are subject to criticism, within the church as well as outside.

The Rev. Mr. Wright's arguments come down to the assertion that to advertise a church is undignified, unnecessary, and unethical. Church advertising, however, need not be undignified. It often is, but it can be otherwise if persons in charge of it exercise good taste and discrimination. News of churches, radio references to church activities, and church parish papers sometimes are in bad form, also, but this does not mean that such media should be ignored.

If church advertising is unnecessary, so are all other publicity techniques. Not until religious people are convinced that they need make no further overtures to the unchurched is advertising to be discounted.

Some advertising also is unethical, to be sure. Now and then a denomination launches a paid national or regional campaign which misrepresents itself or its opponents. Occasionally a local church advertises unethically; that is, it alleges that a visiting speaker is more prominent than he actually is or that an evangelist can perform miracles. These abuses the church can correct from within.

Proponents of paid advertising by the church can cite biblical support: "Because I will publish the name of the Lord: ascribe ye greatness unto our God" (Deut. 32:3) and "And the gospel must first be published among all nations" (Mark 13:10). Naturally these passages do not rule upon the point that publishing shall be paid for. It is not to be overlooked, however, that opponents of church advertising are entirely willing to accept the free space of newspapers and magazines that print editorial copy about their institutions. Thus they demonstrate no real objections to publishing; they quarrel with the cost or the nature of what is published.

Church advertising, like radio scripts, news stories, or sidewalk bulletin boards, is only one part of a general program of church interpretation. It is important to stress this point because churchmen tend to expect paid advertising to perform miracles by itself. It is, however, merely one more reminder. It keeps the institution in the spot where the seeker after information is accustomed to find it. It enables the church body to obtain a given amount of space or time in which it may say what it wishes in the way it desires and as frequently as it can afford.

Ways to advertise

Churchmen desiring to use paid advertising may do so in many ways. They may buy display as well as classified space in newspapers and magazines, purchase spot announcement time on the air, and use car cards, billboards, motion picture trailers, and space in the publications they or their denominations sponsor. Each advertising medium has its own problems; some already have been considered in Chapter X. Here we shall deal only with the widest use of paid advertising by the church: in secular publications.

To begin with, there must be clarity about terms. Church

editors of newspapers have the experience, the year around, of hearing clergymen say to them over the telephone that they have "news they wish to advertise." Or a minister comes to the news rooms with a story which he calls "advertising." "My advertisement," he later says if for some reason it has been omitted, "did not appear in your account of the Sunday services."

These churchmen are confusing editorial matter and advertising matter. Material which the press prints without charge is not advertising. (Sometimes an obliging publisher or editor prints advertising but does not bill the church; in that case the church has received a gift equivalent to the value of the space.) It is reading or editorial matter. The press has the right to decide what shall appear in such space, that is why it uses its judgment about printing copy. It is under no legal compulsion to print church news. On the other hand, material which the paper prints only in space for which it makes a charge is advertising. Usually this copy has commercial value to the institution buying the space. The press expects the church to pay for space if 1) The material is a repetition of news already told (published free in the news columns) and 2) If the church wishes to call special attention to its information in the form that advertising usually takes.

Purposes of advertising

The church makes use of advertising for one of the three sales purposes of advertising: to sell ideas, services, and goods. It concerns itself mainly with the sale of ideas. The expression *to sell* is not too happy here. The church does not wish to force upon people the ideas, that is, the philosophy, it represents. The psychology of fear is being eliminated from religious work. Commercial advertisers at times employ advertising to frighten people into using commodi-

Almost 600 American newspapers print the weekly "Support the Church" ads syndicated to them by the Keister Advertising Service. Local business firms usually meet the cost by small block ads at the bottom of the page.

ties. The citizen is warned of all sorts of infirmities, lacks, and weaknesses that he must be sure to avoid if he is to survive as a respected member of society. While there still is an element within the church that depends heavily on gaining converts by arousing individuals to fear regarding their spiritual future, this strategy is no longer dominant in most groups.

In "selling" its ideas, therefore, the church should use the advertising techniques most suitable to its purpose. Religion as a way of life is neither a soft drink nor a motion picture. Persons who respond to sensational advertising will not be deeply affected by religion. Yet church advertising need not be dull.

It has two functions, one short-term and one long. Short-term advertising is intended to stimulate interest in and inform the public about some immediate event or activity of the church. Long-run advertising is employed to keep the existence of the institution in the public mind. Churches may learn from the world of business the value of long-run advertising. During World War I many firms did not advertise, for they were not producing their commodities. The public had forgotten these brand names by the war's end. New companies or the old ones that had kept their slogans and packages and company names alive through what is called institutional advertising had captured the business. During World War II newspapers, magazines, and radio carried advertising from motor car firms that were not then producing automobiles but in these advertisements kept their trade names before the public.

Short-run advertisements have their long-run values, also, but the content of the copy diminishes the cumulative effect. When a resident of a community sees an ad in a Saturday paper about a Sunday morning service he is advised of the immediate objective of the copy but also sees a symbol of the church.

Long-run copy is the "card" type, carrying little more than the name of the church, its minister's name, the address, and a few other basic facts. This type appears in publications as well as on bulletin boards. It is static but it can avoid dullness. If the space permits, it carries a small cut of the church building or a fragment of a scene from a young people's meeting. An appealing quotation breaks the monotony.

The decision to advertise should be made on the basis of the advantages to the church, not on the advantages to the publication or whatever medium is considered. Newspapers and community newsmagazines at times ask a church to buy space because they are giving the institution space for news and they need the church's financial support. This is not the best reason for advertising. If the church news is not newsworthy the publication should feel no obligation to print it. If the publication cannot find legitimate, economically sound support in the community because it is needed, it should not try to function as a business at the expense, in part, of a public institution such as the church. When the publication is new, conditions are different. Once a paper or a magazine has had sufficient time to find its place in the community it should not depend upon appeals to community institutions for survival.

Measuring results

A church will gain advantage from paid advertising if the readers of the publication or radio listeners can be reached through this advertising. The larger the numbers thus reachable the greater the advantage to the advertiser.

Immediate results of using paid advertising of the church cannot be calculated readily. A department store can an-

nounce a sale and count the number of persons who inquire
or make purchases. Shoe stores can mention over a selected
radio program a sale on a particular style of house slipper
and measure the effectiveness accurately. Too many factors
enter into the behavior of church people, however, to determine readily the correlation between their actions and a
particular advertisement.

A churchman may announce a sermon topic in the public
prints and find seventy-seven more persons attending the
service than the week before. It may have been the paid
advertising that brought them but also it may have been: 1)
the bulletin board on the lawn, 2) the fact that the day was
cool and pleasant or warm and dry, 3) the fact that it was
not a holiday week-end of any sort, 4) the return of students
to the near-by college, 5) the attractiveness to parents of
special events in the church school that morning, 6) the
special music previously announced to begin that day and
to continue for the remainder of the season. Probably all
these factors, plus the paid advertising, accounted for the
increase.

Even if advertising alone is able to draw strangers to
the church in large numbers, the institution must have a
program to retain their interest. Advertising, by itself, is no
magician's wand. Like church publicity in general, it must
be part of a planned public relations program.

What to advertise

What, then, shall be advertised? The church should put
into its paid space its most attractive information: what it
is doing. This may include, in so far as money and space
permit, facts about the Sunday services, the week-day meetings, and special, seasonal activities. If the church has a
modest budget it should mention a different activity each
week, on a rotating basis, rather than crowd the small space

at its disposal. As with news story copy, the emphasis should be upon the institution and its work and not upon any particular individual. The name of the church and the titles of sermons should be visible first, not the name of the church's leader.

To avoid monotony and to direct the response, the church should vary the advertising in space and frequency from time to time. Within the limitations of the contract, a normal program of paid advertising is the buying of space weekly, in which the basic program of the church is presented, and the purchase of a larger advertisement at appropriate seasons. In the larger space the special event can be emphasized.

The kind of church involved is another consideration in writing ad copy. Downtown churches naturally wish to appeal to transients and will include a few lines issuing to them a special invitation. Suburban churches in residential areas benefit more from the label type of advertising, which acts chiefly as a reminder of their existence. A rural church that is one of several served by the same pastor has fewer facilities for communication with its members, and can use paid space to highlight ordinary information.

Producing the copy

The mechanics of church advertising can be as simple or as complicated as the church makes them. Since religious workers usually know little about advertising and its preparation, the publication selling the space is prepared to suggest the typographical dress for the advertisement. A well-managed newspaper or community newsmagazine has developed, over the years, a series of patterns or models from which the church can pick. Certain type faces are more suitable for church advertising than others. What type shall be used and what other typographical devices should be employed depend upon the advertisement's size and the variety of printing materials available.

If the church staff includes a person experienced in the advertising business—or if a volunteer with training or experience is available as adviser—the church office can prepare the copy, guided by the style books of the periodicals in which space is being bought.

Layout is the principal element in advertising production. The copywriter uses it to show the printer a chart of what he desires in the advertisement and to guide himself in producing the most effective copy. The best advertising in the commercial world conforms with accepted principles of design and presents a simple, unified message.

Church advertising layouts understandably avoid the appeals of commercial copy. Dignity and sobriety are inherent in religious copy. Without dependence on sex, excessive personal adornment, and the too common desire to keep up with one's neighbors in the purchase of household commodities, church advertising must try to be compelling, interest-arousing and convincing, and to stimulate action. All this it can hardly do, any more than the building in which it is housed can produce a commotion equal to that of the carnival down the street.

Its reminder function, therefore, can be discharged most readily by dependence upon straight copy without embellishments or the use of colored inks. Ornaments are kept to a minimum, being used mainly to bind the advertisement into a whole. Masses of type are arranged so as to achieve balance, all parts of the material are kept in proportion, writing is concise yet original.

Classified advertisements

Suggestions so far made for copy preparation hold for display advertising, which runs in size from entire pages of a publication to as little as a space measuring one inch deep by two inches wide. Classified advertising, familiarly called "want ads," is little used by churches except in the conventional manner: when seeking a new sexton, offering rummage for sale, or publishing legal notices. The area need not be small merely because the unit generally used is not large. The classified columns offer an inexpensive medium by which persons who may not read display church copy can be reached.

The Rev. Cecil A. Baker, while pastor of the Tiptonville (Tennessee) Methodist Church, made successful use of classified space in the Tiptonville *Lake County Banner,* a country weekly. He scheduled a series of sermons called "Stories of the Beginning" dealing with familiar biblical figures.

The week before each sermon was to be preached at the evening hour his church bought from one to three small classified ads. The copy read thus:

What happened to Adam's boys? or Wanted: Information as to the whereabouts of Eve's sons. We'll find out about them at the Methodist Church Sunday night at 7:30.

Did Adam get back into the garden of Eden? Come to hear the story at the Methodist Church Sunday night at 7:30 and find out.

Want to take a long journey with Abraham? You can go along if at the Methodist Church at 7:30 Sunday night.

You think you are a businessman? Learn much from Jacob at the story hour at the Methodist Church Sunday at 7:30.

The Rev. Mr. Baker also gained the co-operation of the publisher of the *Banner,* a member of his church, and of the advertisers in the paper for the insertion of a few lines in regular commodity display advertisements.

A Tiptonville clothing store allowed this churchman to include, without charge, three lines in a quarter-page advertisement of fall clothing for women, men, and boys. They read:

Story Hour—Story Hour—Story Hour—Story Hour
Methodist Church—Methodist Church—Methodist Church
Sunday at 7:30—Sunday at 7:30—Sunday at 7:30

In the large ads placed by the Western Auto store, through its local distributor, this imaginative minister was able to place two lines reading:

Tiptonville Methodist Church invites you to the story hour Sunday night at 7:30. This week's subject, Jacob.

Contracting for space

Advertising copy is scheduled to be at the newspaper office by a certain hour of a specified day, proofs are to be delivered to the church by another deadline, and returned to the publication at a designated time. As with all other printing, copy should be correct to begin with. Changes that can be avoided should not be made in proofs, for worse errors may be committed in making the alterations (and frequently are). Besides, making changes in the proof can be expensive because it is customary to make a charge for alterations beyond a certain percentage.

It is customary to draw up a contract between the church and the publication (or the radio station, if time is being purchased) setting forth the terms of the advertising agreement. As a rule the same space or time is used, usually weekly or semi-weekly, and changes are made in sermon subjects, names of speakers, and other variable information, the general framework of the advertisement remaining the same for long periods. Special rates are usually offered but this does not involve any necessity for a special contract form of any kind.

A typical contract form is this one, used by the Syracuse (New York) *Post-Standard,* a morning daily with a Saturday church page. The conditions appear on the reverse side of the order form.

Daily   THE POST-STANDARD   Sunday
                         Syracuse, N. Y.
                        ADVERTISING ORDER

You are hereby authorized to publish our advertising as indicated below, and subject to the conditions printed on the back of this order.
.... lines each week for .... weeks within one year at .... cents per line. Starting date ....
In the event more or less space is used than is called for by this order, advertising used shall be paid for as per the rate schedule in force on this date.

Accepted for | Advertiser ....
     The POST-STANDARD CO. | Address ....
.... | Signed by ....
Salesman .... | Date ....

CONDITIONS GOVERNING THIS ORDER

The Post-Standard reserves the right to cancel this order at any time for non-payment of bills overdue, or for any reason whereby continuance of this order would be detrimental to the interests of The Post-Standard or its readers.

Errors in advertising must be called to the attention of The Post-Standard on the date of publication, and The Post-Standard shall be held liable only for errors committed by itself to the extent of space occupied by such errors.

Terms . . . net, ten days following presentation of bill.

The Post-Standard reserves the right to revise the rates in this contract on 60 days' written notice, in which event the advertiser may adjust his schedule without penalty if he so desires.

Group advertising

Newspapers like to interest merchants in a community in paying for the advertising space used by churches. Every church—or a logical, related group—under that plan is allotted a small area regularly. The merchants' names are listed separately from the advertisements of services and other religious data.

If there is no other way to obtain advertising space this method is helpful. But it is only an expedient. It does not keep the church independent. Presumably the grateful parishioners thereafter will trade with these merchants, an obviously commercial motive marring the good will inherent in the plan.

Such unified efforts also are made by the churches alone,

a far superior method than reliance on the business community. No one church can buy the space that all together purchase by paying pro rata. Most commonly this is done for joint activities—a Lenten series or a program of some other religious meetings.

In many communities newspapers have special rates for church advertising. A few forego profit to enable churches to use space. The Syracuse *Post-Standard,* whose contract is illustrated here, puts churches in a special classification. Its charge, in 1949, was fourteen cents a line as compared with fifty cents a line for commercial sports and twenty-four cents for amusements advertising. The paper's transient (basic, short-term) rate was twenty cents.

A typical rate arrangement for group advertisers is the church page of the Clarksburg (West Virginia) *News,* a community weekly. In 1948 twenty-two business concerns paid $2.50 weekly for the spaced allotted to churches. The same space—170 inches—would cost one advertiser $59.50 at the regular 35-cent rate. All Clarksburg churches were presented. Surrounding the advertising space were local news stories about churches and releases from Religious News Service. This paper charged regular advertising rates, otherwise, to the Clarksburg churches, which used display for advertising revivals, speakers at special rally days, and visiting preachers. The president of the Ministerial Union set up a schedule for sermonettes by local churchmen to be printed on the church page.

Group advertising need not be confined to newspaper or magazine pages. In Paducah, Kentucky, in 1946, the Ministerial Association sponsored a Go to Church campaign. Newspaper space was bought, but also an arrangement was made with a company that leased outdoor signs to give the use of one on each of the eight highways into town. The association purchased the signs to be placed on the boards, spending about thirty dollars. The signs remained in sight from six to eight weeks. Small car windshield stickers, stories in all parish papers and bulletins, pulpit announcements, and other means of interpretation supplemented them. The participating churches financed this venture according to size and ability to pay.

CHAPTER XVI

Editing the Materials

Dwight L. Moody once said: "If we cannot do God's work with all the knowledge we would like, let us at any rate do it with all the zeal that God has given us."

Sensible counsel for religious journalists also is contained in II Timothy 2:15, as translated by Moffatt: "Do your utmost to let God see that you at least are a sound workman, with no need to be ashamed of the way you handle the word of the Truth."

The primary point—the point at which sound workmanship and zeal tell most in religious journalism is in the editing of materials.

Need for editing

All copy dealing with the church and religion would be improved if more churchmen followed professional procedures, not only of gathering and writing material, but also of editing the manuscript that results.

The conscientious editor of a denominational publication himself must do such editing or see to it that someone on his staff is capable of doing it. "Must" is used here to mean that if he himself is incapable he should try to get the best results by obtaining the assistance of trained personnel. Actually, however, church papers and magazines are guilty of railroading their copy; that is, of simply placing it more or less unedited in the hands of the printer. The "responsible" editors in such a procedure might accurately be designated irresponsible editors. They excuse this procedure by saying that they have not the time, or knowledge, or judgment to edit their copy. Few editors exercise their function as little as do the heads of some religious journals.

The pastor, priest, or rabbi responsible for the publications issued to interpret the work of a local congregation or the secretary or layman to whom he delegates the responsibility, also should make necessary improvements on copy for the parish weekly or monthly, the church bulletin, and special printed pieces, like yearbooks. Few churchmen or laymen know enough about editorial duties and techniques to do the necessary work without instruction. The seminaries do not teach the procedures. Only the occasional churchman who once was an advertising man, a newspaperman, a magazinist, or a publisher knows how to go about editing manuscript.

A denominational secretary with similar responsibilities is likely to have professional assistance available. Yet the necessity to do better editing exists even here. While in general, nationally circulated material is technically better than the usual locally produced printed matter, perfection has not been reached in the editing procedures of overhead church offices.

The religious editor of a newspaper receives copy from church groups. He uses editing techniques on that copy. But if the persons who dispatch it use certain of these techniques themselves before it is mailed or delivered, the copy is much less subject to change or refusal.

All churchmen with editorial duties want, at least theoretically, to be aware of the best ways to edit material. Editing is part of the preparation process. Understanding of how professionals handle manuscripts makes better editors as well as better writers among religious journalists.

Steps in editing

Editing copy includes these steps: 1. correcting errors; 2. improving grammar; 3. keeping copy to a consistent typographical style; 4. marking it for type size and style; 5. checking for libel, bad taste, or other infractions of journalistic standards; 6. writing headings and captions.

Copy editors find it helpful to use certain hieroglyphics that are a form of rapid communication with printers. Known as copyreader's symbols, they are not to be confused with proofreader's marks, with which churchmen are better acquainted.

This phase of editing commonly is called copyreading. It is differentiated from proofreading. The symbols are alike in a few instances, but are not all the same. Their aim is different. The proofreader works on proofs of type that is set from copy. The copyreader marks the copy *before* it is set in type. Proofreader's symbols are used to note where the copyreader's symbols have not been followed, as well as to catch other mistakes. Proofreader's symbols are used in two ways: for newspapers and magazines they are written in the margin of a galley proof and connected to the error with pencil lines. For slower types of printing, such as books, the proofreader's corrections are made on the margin of the proof but are directed to the error, not by a line, but by a caret.

Forty-two principal copyreading symbols are used. They are reproduced in this chapter. These can be learned best by repeatedly using them. There is no need, however, to learn and employ all of an elaborate system intended chiefly for large publications produced at high speed. But if the user simplifies this set of symbols and gives the printer copies of the simple version for his machine operators he will become a more efficient editor. Printers usually are familiar with most of the symbols.

Symbol	Meaning	Symbol	Meaning
∧	Caret	⋎⁗	Insert quotation marks
ℬ	Delete	;/	Insert semicolon
✗	Broken letter	:/	Insert colon
ꟼ	Turn over	?/	Insert question mark
#	Insert space	-/	Insert hyphen
]	Move to right	ⓈⓅ	Spell out
[	Move to left	!/	Insert exclamation point
][	Center	tr	Transpose
⌒	Close up	wf	Wrong font
⌣	Less space	stet	Let it stand
⊓	Move up	rom	Set in roman type
⊔	Move down	bf	Set in **bold face type**
⊥	Push down space	ital	Set in *italic* type
=	Straighten line	Caps	Set in ROMAN CAPITALS
‖	Align type	sc	Set in SMALL CAPITALS
⊢⊣	Em dash	ld	Insert lead
/3/	3-em dash	lc	Set in lower case
▭	Em quad	[ ]	Brackets
¶	Paragraph	( )	Parenthesis
No. ¶	No paragraph; run in		
⊙	Period		
⌃	Insert comma		
⋎	Insert apostrophe		

These are the conventional symbols to be used when editing copy for a newspaper or a magazine. They need not be employed, except in making corrections, on copy going to the secular press, but they should be used on material sent to the printer working for the church.

The seriousness with which the secular press takes the use of these symbols may be realized by observing the copyreader's routine in handling manuscript. Briefly described, it is about as follows:

A story (news copy, feature, article, or other material) comes to his desk from the chief copyreader or some other supervisory editor. He glances through it to grasp its sense and start his mind working on the heading. Then he settles down to reading the story (*story* in journalism does not necessarily mean fiction, but any manuscript), word by word, line by line, paragraph by paragraph. As he goes along, the copy editor writes the symbols into the manuscript where they belong. Each paragraph is emphasized with the paragraph mark. Deletions are made, words inserted. If special type styles are to be used, such as boldface leads or an opening section set in a size of type different from the body of the article, he indicates this on the margin. If the lead is to be set two-columns wide, he marks that also. When this copy reaches the printer, that workman knows just what he is to do to translate the copy into the type in the way the editorial department wants it. The symbols have given him instructions; they have done so with few words, since the code replaces explanations. Instead of writing in the margin the sentence, "Please set the word 'mission' in italics," the copyreader has given the signal for the use of italics by underscoring the word with a straight line.

Certain basic assumptions and understanding make this system of communication possible. The composing room or print shop knows that all copy is to be set in body type to a standard width and size unless marked otherwise.

Keeping records

The copyreader or other editor responsible for copy keeps records on it. Church publications, especially small ones, often are handled without adequate record keeping. Recorded should be the amount and kind of copy sent to the printer. The record may be kept by listing the number of units by headlines or titles; so many of such a size, with stories, so many of another. Or it may simply list what is sent by the slug line (subject) or length, in either estimated words or approximate length on the basis of 100 per cent for a column, or whatever other simple form of copy control is used.

If, for example, a minister has a small printed parish paper which he has to fill completely each week or month he may avoid overset expenses by assuming 100 per cent for each column of his publication. Eight pages with three columns each will add up to 2,400 per cent for the whole publication. Certain basics must be deducted, as the flag (name) on page one, the masthead inside or on the back page, the space allowed for addressing, and whatever other standing or regularly appearing and unchanging material is used. As copy is sent to the printer, possibly in takes (small sections of about three 50-word paragraphs) each portion should be listed by per cent. If, for instance, the column is 10 inches long, and accommodates 500 words, then a 250-word article is five inches long or half a column deep. Headlines and titles can be measured lineally and be given a standard or permanent percentage (a 1-inch deep headline would be 10 per cent, since it is a tenth of a column). A unit that is half a column deep is worth 50 per cent. As the editor comes close to the total 2,400 per cent he is cautious about selecting additional copy for use in that issue, especially if he has a normal amount of different-length reserve material already on hand for emergency use.

Only if the church journalist edits a large publication which uses teletype copy (wire or press association material) need he worry about the special methods employed in editing copy off the ticker. Wire copy comes from the teletype written entirely in capital letters. To shift from upper to lower case letters would delay the sending process and run into confusion because the copy is used by publications with different styles of capitalization and abbreviation. The copy editor who handles wire material therefore must underscore, usually with one, two, or three small lines, every letter to be set in capitals. The letters already are in capitals, but he emphasizes the capitals. Everything else is set in lower case even though the copy is in capitals.

Headlines and titles

Large or small, every publication uses headlines and titles. Church publicists, since they prepare stories for newspaper and magazine use, should be aware of what happens in headline and title writing because such understanding brings quicker comprehension of the reasons for the mistakes occasionally made in print through faulty headings. The churchman responsible for a parish paper can improve the use of headings if he studies their production.

The function of the heading in a religious publication is no different from the heading in any other: to guide the reader through the periodical or paper, to help dress up or ornament the publication, to enable the reader to grasp the information quickly, and to induce the reader to stop to read. Since few religious publications appear on newsstands the selling function so important to newspapers is reduced. It reappears, however, in the home or office where the religious journal is in competition with secular journalism. Modest headings are required by the nature of the material.

Writing the heading

The tools of the headline or title writer are paper, pencils, a schedule of headings, reference books, particularly word books, and manuscript on which to build his heading or caption.

A news story, let us say, is before the heading or title writer (on newspapers he is the same copyreader who edited the manuscript; on magazines he is an assistant editor; on church papers he is the man or woman of all work). He began to assimilate the contents of the manuscript when he first read it for correcting. If it is not marked by a superior with the size and style of heading it is to receive he uses his own judgment. A model of the heading selected appears on the chart, which is a collection of all headings used by the publication, whether they be headlines, titles, or captions. Each is numbered or lettered, i.e. keyed, and only the number or letter is used in referring to it. Beside the sample is the count, that is, the number of units of space for each line of type in the heading. This number varies according to the size of type in the heading.

Glancing at the chart, the writer learns that the particular head desired consists of two lines counting twenty units each. Part of his chart is a head counting-in system: a table showing that punctuation counts so many units, numerals so many, and so on for all the elements in addition to the alphabet. The experienced editor knows from memory both the head schedule and the counting system and can compose the heading almost in his mind, write it, and then need to make but few changes. But the neophyte should list the main words in the story as a starter on the heading.

Headline writing follows certain principals. The heading is a complete sentence in the newspaper; in the magazine, where it is called a title rather than a headline, it sometimes is complete but also may be a fragment of a sentence, a label like "On the Trail" or "And so we left . . . ." It must be a positive sentence, built around short, crisp verbs. It should avoid the passive voice. The top line, when possible, should make sense but this is not imperative. Key words should not be repeated in any part of the headline. The count, except in the flush left style, should come within one unit of perfection. That is, if two lines of twenty units comprise the plan for the heading each line should be not less than nineteen or more than twenty-one in size, to preserve the balance and pleasant appearance.

The copyreader writes the heading on a piece of paper separate from the manuscript itself unless the head is small enough to be set on the same machine as produces the body type. This separate sheet is sent to the operator of a type-setting machine used exclusively for setting heads of large size. The head copy, when ready for setting, should look like the accompanying illustration.

He puts the first two words, in this case "Father Basil," on the original story, in the space left blank at the top of the first page of manuscript, so that the headline and the story come together properly in the print shop. The slug on the story is "Basil," the material copied on the manuscript from the head sheet ("Father Basil") is called the guideline. The copy editor checks again to make sure that the lines count properly, because in this style if they are more than a unit off they may be unsettable and the printer will return the copy for adjustment, causing delay, or make arbitrary and not necessarily acceptable changes. If the lines are too short the headline will look ragged and create white spots that mar the general appearance of the publication.

Headlines for all types of publications for many years were printed in step form, that is, each line was set in from the left-hand margin the same number of spaces so that the whole appeared like a series of steps. In recent years, however, a style called "flush left" has gained popularity in church as well as general publications. Here the lines of

Basil

#5

Father Basil Turulo Retires
As Pastor at St. Josephat

Basil

#6

Father Basil Turulo
Retires as Pastor
at St. Josephat

type are pushed to the left so that the left-hand margin formed by the type is straight, running beside the column rule or column space, and the right-hand edge is ragged or uneven. Writers of headlines of this style need not count their units so meticulously; mainly they must be sure to stay within the outside limit, which may have variations of from one to six units between lines.

Publications that do not use headlines print captions and titles. Generally titles are a few words intended to lure the reader without revealing the complete import of the material. Typical titles in religious journalism are "Thoughts on the Mass," "The Half-Past Seven Child," "Are You a Glum Mum?", "Long Road to Heaven," and "The Experience of God." Titles need not be written on separate sheets but may appear together on one page of manuscript. They must be marked according to the type style used by the publication and stay within the physical limits of the page and the agreed-upon typographical style. Editors may follow the routine of writing all the titles that are in the same style of type together on one sheet, keying them with numbers to the original copy.

Captions are the titles over pictures and other illustrative matter, but they are passing into disuse as more and more publications run their pictures over the margins or prefer that the picture run even with the top margin. Underlines, also called *cutlines,* are the descriptive and identifying words under illustrations. Generally in a different style or

The headlines for news stories to be sent the printer (not to be sent with publicity copy, however) should be put on sheets as shown. At the top is the dress for the ordinary stepped headline; below is the same wording written for the flush left head. The word at upper left is the slug; the number indicates to the printer the size, style, and width of the head; the side lines remind him of the step or flush setting, and the short line under the head is the dash used by some papers.

size of type from the body type, they are written on separate sheets and never on the illustration or the article it illustrates. They serve as legends and identifications.

Make-up

Make-up has to do with the arrangement of the materials on the type page. Any publication is easier to read if some orderly pattern of arrangement is followed. Newspapers have several sets of fixed patterns for their front pages—balanced or unbalanced—for example. Study of the first page of the New York *Times* shows all the major patterns (except one: the circus) developed to mechanical perfection. Inside newspaper pages also are planned by well-produced publications. Magazines, being issued less frequently than newspapers and having more time for planning, follow few standardized patterns and instead have been an expression of the individual skill of layout artists.

The principles of make-up operate in both newspapers and magazines, although in a different manner. Both seek for harmonious, appealing, and pleasant results. They want their pages to be readable, they want to plan them so that no optical difficulty is placed in the way of the reader who has consented to give to them attention which might have been bestowed, instead, on sports, radio programs, the movies, or television.

Religious journalists can profitably study these general procedures and apply them to their own publications far more than they now do. A small parish paper should be neat and readable if these virtues can be achieved without much additional expense and labor. But this takes planning and attention.

An area in which planning is used professionally is in dummying the publication, a step which is partly editing and partly production. Dummying is the natural result of using a make-up system. Newspapers and magazines have different ways of dummying. One is to sketch on a prepared blank the general appearance of each page, penciling in each major element at the proper point. Headline numbers and slugs are written in the space to be occupied by the story they represent. Pictures are roughed into position. Thus the bigger stories, the cartoons, and other units of content are drawn on this blank, called a dummy or layout sheet. Publications that carry advertising, record the paid-for space first; the editorial department must accommodate itself to this plan because the advertising is sold by position, whereas the editorial or reading matter can be placed anywhere, at the discretion of the editor.

The other system, used by magazines, is to take proofs of the set type, trim off the margins, and paste them on blank sheets the size of the publication or on old copies of the publication itself in precisely the position in which the material is to appear. When completed this dummy looks generally like the finished production; the elements, both big and little, are all pasted into the spots where they are to stand. Unfortunate juxtapositions of copy and art work are then more readily detected and the printer has a specific guide for the placement of materials.

In carrying through either system the journalist must have a plan if his pages are not to look thrown together. Many specialized journalists, not least of all those in the church, leave this make-up operation to their printers. Conscientious print shops, staffed by men and women who know something about editorial production, provide a satisfactory result most of the time. But the editor of a church publication should know enough about make-up so that he can design pages himself and place the emphasis where he thinks it belongs.

Unless he is told, how is a printer to know what should be given the best position when he receives a batch of copy for use in a church publication? The dummying method is the most efficient way to tell him, because he and the editor can see the results in advance. To make-up properly the editor must have a list of the materials in type, including the headline and title sizes, the picture dimensions, and the amount of body type in each unit. Otherwise he or the printer may omit material inadvertently.

Proofreading

Proofreading both precedes and follows page dummying or diagraming. The editor's first opportunity to check the typesetting occurs when he receives galley proofs, so named because the tray holding the type (about the length of a newspaper column) is called a galley. Several sets of proofs are sent to the editor. One is for reading, and is on white paper. Another is on pink, blue or some other color, and is the overset (unused) material left over from a previous issue. The editor is expected to read these carefully, i.e. check the proofs against the original copy, which the printer returns to him for the purpose.

An editor without an assistant is at a disadvantage in proofreading, because the best checking is done when one person holds the copy and another the proof and they read one to the other. Without a secretary to help him, the editor must verify at least dates, proper names, unusual words, and quotations against the original copy, reading straight through only the proofs. The degree of care to be exercised is determined by the quality of work ordinarily received from a particular printer.

Corrections are marked on the margins of proofs as already described. After these corrections are made, the printer returns the original set of proofs with new ones for further reading. This procedure is followed as often as necessary to achieve perfection or as frequently as agreed upon in the contract between the publisher and the printer. Lower printing prices are granted if the number of sets of proofs is kept low. If the printer does high-quality work few sets are needed. If his work is not efficient and the contract specifies only one or two sets of proofs, the editor may regret the low cost because his publication is marred by uncorrected errors.

When the type is clean, as printers say of corrected material, proofs on colored paper are sent to the editor. Whichever type of dummy is used—the paste-up or the diagram—will determine his use of the fresh proofs. For pasting up he must trim each strip, as described, and sort the stories by size and subject. For diagraming he must only sort them and mark the number of the page on which each major story, poem, or book review is to be diagramed.

The diagram or dummy completed, he awaits the page proofs. When they arrive the diagram or dummy accompanies them. Now he must make sure that the printer has followed the plan. It is necessary at this time to account for miscalculations, to supply missing subheads, and reread all the type to catch any errors made in shifting it from galley to page form. The proofreader's marks are used on page proofs just as they are on galley slips.

Again proofs change hands until the pages appear errorless. Errorless pages do not exist, as any editor knows, but in so far as his eyesight and patience have enabled him to do so, he has sought for every broken letter, every misspelled word, every transposed line and mistaken identification.

Radio copyreading

Radio copy is edited for reading aloud rather than for silent reading. A printer is not expected to transmute it into metal, as with newspaper and magazine material. The diacritical marks are made by the newscaster himself, to help him read accurately and properly. Radio copy, therefore, cannot be used if it is pocked with pencil marks of the type so familiar on manuscript edited for print.

Such markings on material for the typesetting machines, if not excessive, are acceptable in an editorial office but not in a radio station. Few standard copyreading marks are used for the air. Misspelled words are corrected by printing the correct ones above them, in capitals. The bridge line over dead matter is used as in printed material copyreading, as is the curved connecting line. "More," the usual paragraph mark, and the comma are inserted the same way in both media. But the "x" is not used for a period, and the extra long dash is achieved by using a long dash, a circle, and another long dash, particularly between separate items. Dashes are popular in radio copy, for they are more conspicuous than commas and can do the same work, whereas they are unpopular in journalism for the eye, inasmuch as they make for looseness in writing.

According to the newscaster's personal eccentricities, copy is marked for enunciation with highly individualized lines or strokes.

Churchmen who prepare radio copy for others to use have a simpler task than the religious journalist who edits for print. The headings, if any, are simple news headlines. Type specifications can be ignored.

Appendices

APPENDIX I

A Press Chairman's Manual

The Church Board of Education of the First Methodist Church of Evanston, Illinois, at a meeting held June 9, 1941, ordered this Manual prepared in hope that it would be helpful to the Press Chairmen of the organizations, committees, and divisions of the church. Set forth below are answers to perennial questions about the particular news procedure at that church, as well as general information about the assembling and preparation of news releases. The version reproduced here is that of the second revision, issued in 1950.

I. FIRST CHURCH PRESS PLAN

WHAT IS THE PLAN?

The distinctive feature of the news plan at First Church is that *all* news copy, pictures, memoranda, requests for attention, et cetera are sent or brought to the church office, which makes *all* contacts with the newspapers, press associations, and radio station.

WHAT DOES IT INCLUDE?

It includes only the preparation of news copy and pictures for use in the public press and in *The First Church Review* and the bulletin.

It does *not* include paid advertisements, which may be handled directly with the advertising departments of the newspapers.

It does *not* include preparation of posters, leaflets, or other publicity media.

WHAT ARE SOME OF THE REASONS FOR THIS PLAN?

1. It makes for impartiality in treatment of the newspapers.
2. It helps avoid confusion, inasmuch as editors are obliged to deal with only one rather than with twelve or fifteen press representatives of the church.
3. It is welcomed by editorial offices, inasmuch as most newspapers and radio stations are understaffed and cannot ferret out all this news themselves.
4. It helps avoid duplication.
5. It helps assure presentation of professionally acceptable copy to press and radio.
6. It puts the standing and influence of the church behind each organization's news, so that *all* receive the same consideration from press and radio.
7. It helps assure constant and complete coverage, inasmuch as the church office can act as a sort of city desk and, in emergencies, remind Press Chairmen when material is due.
8. It enables the office to be special help to the Press Chairman who is new at the job, assuring his organization the same treatment by press and radio as that accorded an organization represented by an "old hand at the game."
9. It helps to avoid disproportionate emphasis, inasmuch as the news of all organizations is presented at the same time and well ahead of deadlines.
10. It enables the church office to provide continuity from year to year, making it unnecessary for an organization to re-establish contact with the press with each change of Press Chairman.

HOW LONG HAS THE PLAN BEEN IN OPERATION?

It was developed in 1928 by a professional journalist, who as a volunteer carried on the work assumed four or five years later by the church office.

HAS IT PROVED EFFECTIVE?

It has brought the church as a whole thorough and favorable publicity. It has the support and co-operation of editors. Sociological studies have marked it as unique and successful, and it has been commented upon in national magazines and in books on church administration.

The question frequently is asked: Even though the church and its organizations as a whole benefit by this plan, couldn't an organization get more space if it made direct contact with the newspapers? The answer is "Yes." By sending *exclusive* stories to a publication it is possible to get more space in that publication. But this means that other organizations and the general services of the church are at a disadvantage in that paper, which naturally is limited as to the space it can give to any one church. It also means that the organization which issues the exclusive story is at a disadvantage in all the other publications in which its material might appear. And it must be said, finally, that such action puts the whole plan, with all its advantages, in jeopardy. Complete co-operation is essential to the operation of this plan, which is a practical application of a Christian principle.

II. *HOW THE PLAN WORKS*
GETTING THE NEWS
Said Kipling,

> I keep six honest serving-men;
> They taught me all I knew.
> Their names are What and Why and When
> And How and Where and Who.

This famous jingle sets forth the fundamental information to be included in a news story. (The "How" is seldom used except in reports of events that have taken place.) WHAT will take place? WHERE will it happen? WHEN will it happen? WHO will be concerned? WHY will it happen? Answers to all these five questions appear in the beginning of a news story, as for example:

(Who) Dr. Jonathan Merrick, librarian at Western Reserve university, (what) will speak on "Libraries and Democracy" (why) before the August meeting of the Junior Guild (when) at 12:30 p.m. Tuesday, Aug. 16, (where) in Great Hall of the First Methodist church of Evanston.

Here are some tips for effective news-getting:
1. Establish regular contacts not only with the head of the organization but also with committee chairmen. See or telephone them regularly.
2. Attend meetings of the organization whenever possible.
3. Take careful and complete notes on any news item the meeting brings forth.
4. Check back with the president or committee chairman to make sure that the data are accurate.
5. Procure from speakers their full names, their subjects, and their titles, as well as other biographical material.
6. If an event is a combination business meeting, program, and

social event, be sure that all units are completely covered in the news story.

7. Think of all the activities of the organization and see to it that each is properly publicized.

8. Check over the list of possible news events from time to time to be sure they are covered, as, for example: Elections, social events, meetings, special events (not routine or recurring), out-of-season committee appointments (replacing resigned members, etc.) tours and trips, money-making events, campaigns.

9. Watch for the hidden news, often the best.

10. Know the organization thoroughly—its history, aims, programs, projects, and policies.

WRITING THE STORIES
Mechanics

On page 310 of this book is a sample piece of copy. It will make for accuracy, uniformity, neatness and legibility if all copy turned in approximates this form.

1. Copy should be typewritten, if at all possible. If the Press Chairman does not have a typewriter, he may arrange to use one in the church office. If he does not type nor have access to typing service, he may turn in one copy legibly written in longhand for typing in multiple at the church office.

2. Copy should be double-spaced, *never single-spaced.* It should be written on one side of the sheet only. There should be an inch margin on all sides, except that on the first sheet there should be three inches of space at the top for headlines and changes.

3. Headlines should *not* be written, and the space at the top of the first page should be left blank. The editor of the publication using the material will supply the headline in accordance with the paper's style requirements.

4. All pages should be numbered.

5. It is a good idea to read the story after it is typed and to make corrections, as necessary, on all copies before they are sent to the church office.

6. The office supplies thin paper and carbon for the use of Press Chairmen. Ordinarily, with these supplies, it is not possible to make 10 copies at once. Under these circumstances, it is advisable to make two sets of five copies each. (See SENDING THE STORIES TO THE CHURCH OFFICE, p. 307, to determine the number of copies to make. Add one for the Press Chairman's own file.)

7. Fold the copy as little as possible. Submit it flat, if feasible, so that it can be folded with other stories without extra creasing.

Composition

General Structure

1. Newspapers and radio news broadcasts are prepared so that readers and listeners can tell quickly, by reading the headline or hearing the opening paragraphs of a story, what the news is. News articles, therefore, should follow the principle of putting the summary first, with elaboration to follow. Unlike narration, the news story presents its climax first. It begins with the most important incident. An election story should say at once who was elected. A speech story should say at the outset who is going to speak or on what he is going to speak. Inasmuch as time and place are routine in most instances, they should not be emphasized.

2. The newspaper and radio are impersonal and factual in their news presentations. All articles should be written in third person. It is well to avoid such phrases as "Please call the church office for reservations by Monday." Say, instead, "Reservations are being taken at the church office until Monday." "Our," "we," "they," and "us" and all similar first and second personal pronouns should be omitted. Adjectives and compliments also should be omitted scrupulously, as should opinion, bias, and editorialisms. Opinion may be introduced only by way of direct quotation from a source that is clearly indicated.

3. Cardinal rules of news writing are indicated in the words Accuracy, Brevity, Clarity and Completeness. In particular, it is well to write concisely and sparingly. In the sentence, "The color of the booth was red," there are too many words. It should read, "The booth was red." It is well to avoid cliches, bromides, and platitudes.
Use of yearbooks, telephone directories, city directories, dictionaries and other reference works makes for accuracy. "Get the names and initials right!" is trite but important.
Cross out and rewrite words that are to be changed—do not write through them.
A special point for First Church Press Chairmen: Be sure that the name of the organization and of the church appear in the first paragraph of each story.

4. It is well to use brief paragraphs of not more than six typewritten lines each.

5. If in doubt about how to prepare a story, look at any large newspaper, consult copies of stories formerly submitted, or see the clipping book at the church office.

Style

Good English usage is observed, with some modifications developed for journalistic purposes.

1. Abbreviations.
   Hours are written: 7 p.m. or 2:30 p.m. (Note that unnecessary zeros are omitted.)
   Months of the year are abbreviated only when accompanied by the day of the month, as: Jan. 15, 1958. (Note the "th" is omitted after 15.)
   All thoroughfare words such as "road," "avenue," "boulevard," "street," are abbreviated when used in an exact address, as: 2400 Sheridan rd., 1900 Orrington ave., 333 Ridge blvd., 500 Church st.
   Given names are not abbreviated. Therefore, avoid "Wm.", "Thos.", "Jno.", "Chas.", et cetera.

2. Capitalization.
   Do not capitalize auxiliary nouns when at end of a name, as: "church" in First Methodist church, "university" in Northwestern university, "committee" in Finance committee, "department" in Junior department, "guild" in Junior guild. In Woman's Society of Christian Service, "society" is capitalized because it is not at the end of the name.
   Do not capitalize titles when they follow the name. Example of correct usage: Harris Franklin Rall, professor of systematic theology.
   Do not capitalize titles in lists of officers. Example: Mrs. Arthur E. Swanson, president.

3. Punctuation.
   Separate the parts of a date by commas, as: Monday, Jan. 31, 1953, is a future date.
   Use a period with all abbreviations except government agencies, as: Y.M.C.A.

4. Titles.
   Use "Mr." only with the last name alone, as: Mr. Green. When full name is used, omit "Mr.", as: Harold E. Green.
   Use "Mrs." before the name of a married woman, whether last name only or full name is used.
   Use "Miss" in the same way for an unmarried woman.
   Avoid group titles, such as "Misses," "Messrs.", and "Mesdames." When referring to a minister, use "The Rev." Never omit "the." Thus: The Rev. Albert T. Carmer. When first name and initials are not used: The Rev. Mr. Carmer.

A general rule about titles is always to abbreviate them before the full name and to spell them out before the last name alone, as: Prof. John J. Jones, and Professor Jones. Exceptions are "Dr." and "The Rev."

5. Figures.

All single figure numbers are spelled out, as one, nine, four. All figures beginning with 10 are written in digits, as 15, 49, 23, except even amounts like five hundred or one thousand.

If a sentence begins with a number, spell the number out.

SENDING THE STORIES TO THE CHURCH OFFICE

Regular Coverage

Multiple copies of finished stories should be sent to the church office in accordance with the following schedule for use in the papers and on the radio stations indicated·

Thursday, by noon. *Ten* copies of stories on events occurring in the seven-day period beginning the next Thursday, for distribution to

Evanston *Mail*	Chicago *Sun-Times*
Evanston *Review*	Chicago *Tribune*
First Church Review	Chicago *Herald-American*
Daily Northwestern	Radio Station WEAW
The Christian Advocate	Radio Station WNMP
Chicago *Daily News*	

Monday, anytime. (Up to noon Tuesday, if absolutely necessary.) *One* copy of stories occurring in the seven-day period beginning the following Saturday for use in

First Church Review (If desired, this copy will be substituted for one sent in the preceding Thursday)

Special Coverage

In addition to this regular coverage, the office is glad to send especially prepared stories to The Myers Publications (on the North Side of Chicago) and the Hollister papers—Wilmette *Life,* Winnetka *Talk,* Glencoe *News*—and the Highland Park *Press* (on the North Shore). These stories should stress some local angle in each case, such as the names of persons in the particular community who are active in some project or event.

Inasmuch as stories intended for the *First Church Review* may be written in a somewhat more familiar vein, an enterprising Press Chairman may wish to write a special story for our own publication.

If a special project requiring news coverage over a period of weeks is planned by an organization, the church office is glad to work out with the Press Chairman a schedule of special stories and pictures.

Occasionally a local paper requests a Press Chairman, through the church office, to cover a meeting, attending it and writing a report for publication after it occurs.

Corrections

Press Chairmen who discover serious errors in their material after sending it in are asked to make corrections in written form, if possible, but by all means to telephone to the church office if time is short. If the entire story must be changed and there is time, it is well to retype it and bring the necessary number of copies to the office, which will substitute them immediately for the earlier version even though the earlier story already has been sent out.

PICTURES

Pictures (glossy prints) mats and cuts may be supplied to the office by the Press Chairman, or, if possible, the office will make arrangements for press photographers to take news pictures. In either case, advance arrangements should be made with the church office.

SUNDAY BULLETIN

News space in the Sunday morning bulletin is so limited that special copy need not be supplied. The church office picks up from news stories such information as can be used.

III. WHEN IS IT NEWS AND WHEN PUBLICITY?

The first time an event is announced it is news; thereafter the same set of facts becomes publicity to the newspaper, magazine, radio station, or the public.

All Press Chairmen, then, have an important function to perform in planning their stories so that the news ingredient is present in each. A newspaper is not likely to be indifferent to news, but it may be unwilling repeatedly to give space to the same information.

To avoid this, Press Chairmen should notice the various means of injecting news value in a story. A primary rule is not to tell the whole story in the first announcement, although what *is* told should be complete. For example, Christmas Tree Lane, annual project of the Woman's Society, has multiple phases:

1. The main facts (Answers to the five "W's").
2. Names of committee members.
3. Plans and accomplishments of those committees.
4. Description of the physical form of the bazaar.
5. Its relation to previous bazaars. How many, changes in name,

purpose, character, size, scope.
6. Personalities at the head.
7. Progress of plans.
8. Sidelights—financial merit, wideness of support, etc.
9. Change in original plans.

If the Press Chairman were to cover every one of these points in detail in the first story, the news value would be minimized. It is not desirable from any point of view to say everything the first time.

This principle applies to all stories where more than one on the same event is needed. An advance story on a speech, for example, has numerous aspects, each of which should be stressed in a different way by being placed first:

1. Name, identity, personality, experience, record of speaker.
2. His or her subject and the reason for its choice.
3. Other events at the meeting—election, appointments of committees, reports, other business.
4. Expected attendance if anything unusual.
5. Return of a long absent former officer or attendance by other persons of local interest.
6. Changes in original plans—postponement, new speaker, etc.
7. Novelty of meeting place, special plans for refreshments, etc.

At all times, however, each story should give the basic facts (Who? What? When? Where? Why?) The name and identity of the speaker can be given in each story, but there might be a separate story on his background—education, authorship, official connections, and so on.

IV. FOR FURTHER STUDY

The information given above is necessarily brief. A Press Chairman who desires more help may get it by consulting the following books. Those bearing an asterisk may be borrowed from the church office. Most of the others are available at Evanston Public Library and Deering Library. (The titles are not reproduced in this appendix because they may be found in the reading list appearing with this book.)

V. A SAMPLE STORY

How copy should look when sent to the church office:

Mrs. Jane J. Doe, counsellor to women

at Northwestern university, will address the Service guild of the First

Methodist church of Evanston at 2 p.m.

Wednesday, Oct. 25, in Glenna hall.

Her subject will be ''Some of the

Problems of Today's College Youth.''

She will be introduced by Mrs. Mary

R. Roe, guild program chairman.

The guild board will meet at 10:30

a.m. in Glenna hall under Mrs. Alfred

X. Coe's direction. Chapel at 12:15

will be led by Mrs. H. A. Poe.

APPENDIX II
A Public Relations Plan in Outline

The outline of the conference program of public relations referred to in Chapter II is reproduced here to show the philosophy and scope of the work of the Wisconsin Methodist group which designed it.

A PROGRAM OF PUBLIC RELATIONS FOR THE WISCONSIN AREA

Adopted by the Area Pastor's School, Appleton

Mindful that the best publicity for any church grows out of the Christian character and practice of those who compose it, and is measured by the service rendered in the community and in the world, this Pastor's School, in proposing a program of Public Relations for the Wisconsin Area, would give this fact primary emphasis. It is for the purpose of supplementing this premise that the following suggestions are made.

THE LOCAL CHURCH IN ITS APPROACH TO THE PUBLIC

1. The commendation of the church to the public by the loyalty of its members as indicated by
   - *a*) their own regular attendance and participation
   - *b*) their spirit of democracy and hospitality
   - *c*) their enthusiastic and appreciative conversation with reference to the leadership and program
   - *d*) their organization for friendly visitation at times other than the Every-Member Canvass

2. The making of the church plant attractive and worthy to be called the "House of God" by
   - *a*) immaculate housekeeping, within and without
   - *b*) keeping it in first-class repair, including painting, decorating and landscaping
   - *c*) seeing that the church is properly and adequately identified; that if a changeable letter board is used the letters are fresh, legible, and, if possible, illuminated; that the sign is never out of date; that when needed wayside and directional signs be posted
   - *d*) providing proper inside bulletin boards and literature racks for the display of promotion and educational announcements
   - *e*) providing and using a guest or visitor's book and following up information thus obtained

3. The adequate use of tasteful mimeographed and printed matter
   - *a*) insistence in church calendars, announcements and circular letters on the highest standard of workmanship consistent with economy
   - *b*) the use where practicable of the partly printed forms for the printing and mimeographing of church calendars which describe Methodist agencies and activities
   - *c*) the publication of parish papers, where practicable, to be circulated under second-class mailing privileges
   - *d*) the more careful distribution and fuller use of free printed material from our boards and agencies

4. The education of the constituency in the knowledge of Methodism and the Ecumenical Church by

   increasing the number of readers of religious periodicals, particularly our official weekly, *The Christian Advocate,* and such specialized periodicals as the *World Outlook, Methodist*

Men, Methodist Woman, Concern, Highroad, and our religious education periodicals

5. The maximum use of the local press
   a) by encouraging each pastor and/or lay leader to read a book on journalism or church publicity
   b) by establishing friendly and co-operative personal relations with the news-handling personnel of the local newspaper
   c) by recognizing the local press as an ally in community betterment and by demonstrating toward it an appreciative, understanding and grateful attitude
   d) by making use, where available, of such journalistic talent as may be available within the church constituency

6. The development of acquaintanceship, understanding, and co-operation with the local and near-by radio stations
   a) by personal calls on the management
   b) by letters of appreciation for time given to local and network religious programs
   c) if opportunity is given for the use of radio time to study textbooks on script writing, production, and techniques
   d) to make the best possible use of such time as is made available both for the immediate profit of listeners and as a reciprocal obligation to the station
   e) to encourage church members to commend religious radio programs of quality and to write for copies of manuscripts offered, that station and network managers may see the extent and interest of such audiences

WISCONSIN AREA PUBLIC RELATIONS PLAN

It is recommended that:

1. Each district superintendent of the Wisconsin Area appoint a district public relations chairman whose duties would include
   a) the encouragement of local pastors and churches in carrying out the previously listed and similar objectives
   b) service, where desired by the district superintendent, as district correspondent for the *Christian Advocate,* and such other papers as may be desired
   c) the preparation and distribution of news releases to secular papers of the district
   d) working in co-operation with the conference public relations chairman

2. The resident bishop and the conference cabinet involved name for each annual conference a conference public relations chairman, who with the district public relations chairmen, and such others as the bishop and the cabinet may designate, will compose the Conference Public Relations Committee.

   a) It should be the duty of the conference public relations chairman, aided by this committee, to handle relations with the press and radio stations during sessions of the annual conference and, for the furtherance of conference and general Methodist interests, at other times throughout the year.

   b) It should be the responsibility of the conference public relations chairman to see that the duties of the district public relations chairmen are carried out.

   c) Meetings of an area-wide nature should be reported by the conference public relations chairman in whose conference the meeting is held unless otherwise agreed upon.

3. The conference and district public relations chairmen shall work in co-operation with the Commission of Public Information (Methodist Information) both in supplying and distributing news.

4. It is recommended that the library of every newspaper of the area be supplied with a current copy of the Journal of the annual conference, accompanied by suitable letter of transmittal from the conference or district public relations chairmen.

5. It is recommended that the responsibility for the extension of courtesies and expression of appreciation in the name of the church to individuals, organizations, and agencies should rest with the conference and/or district public relations chairmen when not otherwise provided for.

6. It is recommended that this program, with such additions or deletions as may be desired, be presented to the next session of the annual conference for consideration, and should a program be adopted the conference make adequate financial provision for its operation.

7. It is recommended that in the interim whatever portions of this program which can be in operation without conference action are to be regarded as now being in effect.

APPENDIX III

Style Sheet*

(Note: This style sheet originally was prepared by Dr. Laurence R. Campbell, dean of the School of Journalism, Florida State University, for a book on news reporting and writing on which he collaborated with the author of this volume. A few changes have been made to adapt it to religious journalistic and publicity use: the editorial note and two pages of wire service call letters and special instructions for preparation of wire copy have been omitted. The author wishes to extend special thanks to Dr. Campbell and the Houghton Mifflin Company for their co-operation in permitting the use of this material.)

LOCAL COPY PREPARATION

Paper

1. Use unruled paper that is about 8½ by 11 in size.
2. Do not fasten sheets. Proper numbering and slugging make that unnecessary.

Spacing

3. Write on one side of the sheet only.
4. Double-space all copy.
5. Indent five spaces to begin paragraphs.
6. Leave from three inches to one-half a page blank at the top of the *first* sheet.
7. Leave one inch blank at top of all other sheets.
8. Leave one inch margins on all other sides of all pages.
9. Put each story on a separate sheet, except personals or other materials that are to be run under one headline. Some papers paste together all takes on a story.

Form

10. Typewrite all copy.
11. Put the story slug in the upper left-hand corner of each sheet.
12. Put your last name on the first sheet, under the slug. The last name is sufficient unless some other staff member has it.
13. Put the page number after the slug word.
14. Keep to a uniform length for each line. Write 10 words to the line if your typewriter has pica type; 12 if it has elite.

---

* Reproduced from *Newsmen at Work,* by Laurence R. Campbell and Roland E. Wolseley (Boston: Houghton Mifflin Company, 1949) pp. 529-542.

15. Do not split a sentence or paragraph between pages. In other words, end each page with the end of a paragraph; start each page with a new paragraph.
16. Do not write perpendicularly in the margins.
17. Keep paragraphs within three to five typewritten lines.
18. Avoid erasures and overwritings of typing. Carefully x-out the erroneous material and type the correct wording beside it.
19. If a story does not end on a sheet, write *more* at bottom of the page.
20. End a story with the symbol #.
21. Read your copy before turning it in, to be sure it is correct. But as soon as possible learn to produce clean, correct copy which requires little hand or other revision. If you make long-hand changes in your copy be sure to print all names and to mark the letters m, n, o, w, a, and u so that they are clearly understood. Overscore the m, n, and a, and underscore the u, o, and w.

WIRE COPY PREPARATION

Under this title are style suggestions for use in preparing mail stories for papers at a distance from the point of origin of the news and in preparing copy for wire transmission.

Datelines

Datelined stories should begin with the name of the city or town of origin of the news in all caps, followed by the state name, abbreviated. Follow the table of abbreviations in the style sheet.

State names need *not* be used if:

1. The sending point is in the newspaper's circulation area or is familiar to readers in the locality.
2. The sending point is Boston, Chicago, Cleveland, Denver, Detroit, Los Angeles, New York, Philadelphia, Pittsburgh, San Francisco, St. Louis, or Washington.

Datelined stories should begin with the name of the city *and* be followed by the name of the country or province, abbreviated according to the list in the style sheet.

Examples:

MOHAWK, N. Y., Nov. 16–(AP)–Thirteen children walked into Mayor Lynn Corman's office here today all set to . . . .

REIMS, France, Sept. 12–(UP)–In this historic city today five visiting American congressmen . . . .

ABBREVIATIONS

A. *General Rules:*
1. Use common abbreviations as stipulated here primarily to speed the reading.
2. Avoid uncommon or technical abbreviations, using them only with the approval of the desk.

B. *Abbreviate:*
1. *Academic titles:* When they precede the name—Prof. Warren C. Price, Dr. Earl English, acting Dean Simon Bozarris.
2. *Alumni: By classes*—G. Edward Clark, '38; Gail Tully, BA '45.
3. *Ampersand:* In corporate names in which it commonly is used —Dun & Bradstreet.
4. *Apartments:* In addresses—Shadrach Shemerdiak, Apt. S, 77 S. Second st.
5. *Bible references:* I. Sam. xii: 16-22; Rev. vii: 12.
6. *Big Man on Campus:* In college papers—BMOC.
7. *Big Woman on Campus:* In college papers—BWOC.
8. *Business firms:* If commonly accepted; e.g., NBC for National Broadcasting company; MGM for Metro Goldwyn Mayer; TWA for Transcontinental Western Airlines; C.B. & Q. for Chicago, Burlington and Quincy Railroad; Inc. and Ltd. after corporate firms, but not co., corp., bros.
9. *College degrees:* A.B.; Ph.D.; M.A.; LL.D.
10. *Common abbreviations:* Only when essential—A.D.; AWOL; B.C.; c.o.d.; e.g.; et al; f.o.b.; h.p.; i.e.; IOU—not I O U; I.Q.; k.o. and t.k.o.; m.p.h.; SOS—not S O S; TNT—not T N T; viz.
11. *Ecclesiastical titles:* When they precede the name—Rev. for Reverend and Msgr. for Monsignor, but no others—The Rev. Ernest Fremont Tittle; Msgr. Thaddeus Cavassa; The Rt. Rev. Stuart Knox; but Father O'Halloran. Always use *The* with Rev. and Rt. Rev.
12. *Government agencies:* When commonly used—FBI, ICC, RFC, ROTC, SEC, TVA
13. *Junior:* Philip Ward Burton Jr.; Philip Ward Burton Sr.
14. *Legislation:* Bills, laws, resolutions, etc., to indicate origin—A for assembly, S for Senate—as 144-S; sections of laws or statutes thus: Sec. 1732.
15. *Markets:* In financial section only—barrel, barrels (bbl, bbls); bushel, bushels (bu); cent, cents (c); horsepower (hp); hundredweight (cwt); kilowatt hours (kwh); pound, pounds (lb, lbs); pint (pt); quart (qt); gallon (gal).
16. *Military titles:* When they precede the name, all except chaplain—Pvt. for private of rank; Pfc. for private first class; Cpl. for corporal; Sgt. for sergeant; Sgt. Maj. for sergeant major;

Lt. for lieutenant; Capt. for captain; Maj. for major; Col. for colonel; Brig. Gen. for brigadier general.

17. *Military units:* WAC, but Wac Leslie Van Guelpen.

18. *Months:* In dates and datelines if month has more than five letters—Jan. for January; Feb. for February; Aug. for August; Sept. for September; Oct. for October; Nov. for November; Dec. for December.

19. *Mount:* In proper names—Mt. Vernon, Mt. Rainier (Fort is not abbreviated).

20. *Nations:* Only in U.S.A. or U.S. and U.S.S.R.

21. *Number:* When used with specific figures—No. 13; Nos. 13 and 14; also Vol. 1, Vols. 1 and 2; Fig. 3, Figs. 3 and 4.

22. *Naval titles:* When they precede the name, all except chaplain—Ens. for ensign; Lieut. for lieutenant; Lieut. Com. for lieutenant commander; Adm. for admiral; Wave.

23. *Organizations:* When commonly used—AAUW, BPOE, DAR, GAR, GOP, IOOF, P-TA, YMCA, YWCA, WCTU, but C. of C.

24. *Official titles:* When they precede the name—Gov. for governor of a state, but not for governor of federal reserve bank; Lieut. Gov. for lieutenant governor; Rep. for Representative; Sen. for senator; Ald. for alderman; Supt. for superintendent; but no others.

25. *Points of the campass:* When used with names of street—1419 E. Genesee st.; 1201 16th st., N.W.

26. *Political Parties:* Sen. Wayne Morse (R. Ore.)

27. *Province of Canada:* These only—Alta, for Alberta; B.C. for British Columbia; Man. for Manitoba; Ont. for Ontario; Que. for Quebec; Sask. for Saskatchewan; also N.S. for Nova Scotia; N.S.W. for New South Wales.

28. *Radio stations:* WFBL, KUGN.

29. *Religious titles:* See ecclesiastical titles.

30. *Saint:* St. Paul, Minn.; St. John, the Apostle; Sault Ste. Marie, but San Jose, Santa Clara.

31. *Sports:* For typographical style, see chapter on sports in book from which this appendix is reproduced.

32. *Streets:* st. for street; ave. for avenue; hts. for heights; sq. for square; blvd. for boulevard; pky. for parkway; ter. for terrace; rd. for road; but way, lane, alley.

33. *States* (U.S.): Excepting Idaho, Iowa, Ohio, and Utah; also C.Z. for Canal Zone; D.C. for District of Columbia; P.I. for Philippine Islands; P.R. for Puerto Rico; T.H. for Territory of Hawaii; but spell out Alaska. Standard abbreviations:

Ala.	Ark.	Colo.
Ariz.	Calif.	Conn.

Del.	Miss.	Pa.
Fla.	Mo.	R.I.
Ga.	Mont.	S.C.
Ill.	Nebr.	S.D.
Ind.	Nev.	Tenn.
Kans.	N.H.	Tex,
Ky.	N.J.	Vt.
La.	N.M.	Va.
Me.	N.Y.	Wash.
Md.	N.C.	Wis.
Mass.	N.D.	W.Va.
Mich.	Okla.	Wyo.
Minn.	Ore.	

34. *States* (Mexico): Chih. for Chihuahua; Sin. for Sinaloa; Son. for Sonora.

35. *Student identification:* John Smith, LA '50.

36. *Time of day:* 7 a.m. today, but not 7 o'clock this morning; 8:30 p.m. today, but not 8:30 o'clock this evening; 8 p. m. (EST); omit 12 Midnight and 12 Noon.

37. *Titles:* Mr. and Mrs.; avoid use of Mmes., Messrs; see also academic, ecclesiastical, military, naval, and official titles.

38. *Years:* When referring to college classes—'26 graduate, BA '50, also 1851-61.

39. *United States of America:* When used after military or naval titles or as part of official title, name of vessel, or readily recognized government agency—Lieut. John Brown, U.S.N.; U.S.S. Montana; U.S. marine corps.

40. *U.S.S.R.:* May be used for Russia.

41. *United Nations:* UN; also its important agencies if commonly known—UNESCO.

C. *Do not abbreviate:*

1. *Business firms:* Co., Corp., or Bros. unless commonly used in title.

2. *Cents:* Except in financial section, 45 cents, not $.45, 45 cts., or 45c.

3. *Christian names:* Except in corporate titles, spell out Chas., Wm., Geo.

4. *Christmas:* Xmas is to be used neither in stories nor headlines.

5. *College courses:* Mathematics, not math; political science, not poli sci.

6. *Countries:* Except U.S.A. or U.S. and U.S.S.R.

7. *Fort:* Fort Collins, Fort Ticonderoga.

8. *Measurements:* Spell out, unless otherwise indicated.
9. *Per cent:* 45 per cent, not 45% or 45 percent; don't use per centum.
10. *Point:* West Point.
11. *Port:* Port Said, Port Townsend.

CAPITALIZATION

A. *General Rules:*

1. Use capital letters sparingly, following down style unless otherwise indicated.
2. Titles in lists of persons holding positions are published with names preceding positions—Frank Booth, president; David Ormiston, vice president; William Bancroft, secretary; Kenneth Ehrman, treasurer.
3. Long titles seldom are used before the name, but they may be used with U.S. cabinet positions—Secretary of State Acheson.
4. Acting, ex-, and former are not capitalized when used with titles—former President Herbert C. Hoover, ex-Governor Harold Stassen; acting Dean Rudyard Rutherford.

B. *Capitalize thus:*

1. *Aircraft:* Flying Fortresses, B-29.
2. *Animals:* Proper names of pets, farm animals, racing horses, etc.—Rover, Phar Lap, Dobbin.
3. *Article:* When abbreviated—Art. 1; also Chap. 1; Sec. 1, Fig. 1, Vol. 1.
4. *Associations:* Only when they precede the rest of the name or are within the name—Association of Commerce, National Council of Teachers of English, but Merchants association, National Safety council.
5. *Astronomy:* Planets except the earth, but sun, moon, milky way.
6. *Athletic teams:* Wildcats, Red Sox, Golden Bears.
7. *Automobiles:* Ford, Packard; but use only when essential to news stories.
8. *Books:* "Exploring Journalism," "Newsmen at Work." (But in book publishing usage—*Exploring Journalism.*)
9. *Breeds:* Distinguished parts of names: cats—Maltese, Manx, Siamese; dogs—Boston bull, great Dane, Scotch Collie; cattle—Holstein, Shorthorn, Jersey; hogs—Chester White, Poland China; poultry—White Leghorns, Rhode Island Reds.
10. *Buildings:* Distinguishing part when it precedes the name—

Chimes building; Paramount theater—not theatre; Union station; Hall of Fine Arts; Archbold stadium; White House, Quirinal, Vatican, Yates Castle, Blue room, Executive mansion, but post office, city hall, county building, state house.

11. *Characters:* In books, plays, operas, comic strips, radio programs, etc.—Hamlet, Dagwood, the Great Gildersleeve.

12. *Chemical compounds:* N_2O; but hydrogen, oxygen.

13. *Churches:* Also cathedrals, tabernacles—Wesley chapel, Calvin Presbyterian church, St. Peter's cathedral, Bahai temple, but Church of the Transfiguration.

14. *Chinese names:* With last names first—Chiang Kai-shek, Sun Yat-sen.

15. *Cities:* When city is part of name, except New York city—Salt Lake City, Marion City, Kansas City.

16. *Common nouns:* When commonly used as adjectives—french pastry, french fried potatoes, arabic numerals, bessemer steel, india rubber, morocco leather, panama hat, paris green, prussic acid, roman type, scotch whiskey, but English language, Russian history.

17. *Colleges:* College of Business Administration, but San Jose State college.

18. *Corporations:* John Smith company or John Smith corporation.

19. *Days:* Sunday, Thursday, Ash Wednesday, Good Friday.

20. *Debates:* Resolved: That the U.S. Senate be abolished.

21. *Degrees:* When abbreviated—A.B., M.S., Ph.D., but bachelor of arts, master of science, doctor of philosophy.

22. *Deity:* God, Holy Spirit, Jesus Christ, and personal pronouns —but not adjectives referring to deity, not deities of pagan religions.

23. *Denominations:* Methodist, Catholic, Mormon, but infidel, atheist, unbeliever, agnostic.

24. *District:* Second congressional district, but 10th district.

25. *Documents:* Constitution, Declaration of Independence, Bill of Rights, Magna Charta, Social Security act, Atlantic Charter, Monroe Doctrine, New York State constitution.

26. *Educational institutions:* Syracuse university, but University of California, Menlo junior college; Marysville union high school.

27. *Epithets:* Alexander the Great

28. *First words:* In sentences, direct quotations, and lines of poetry.

29. *Flags:* Stars and Stripes, Tricolor, Stars and Bars, Old Glory.

30. *Flowers:* See plants.

31. *Geographic regions:* Occident, Orient, Far East, New World,

Loop, East side, trans-Atlantic, Barbary coast, Pacific slope, Deep South.

32. *Holidays:* Fourth of July (not July 4th), Christmas (not Xmas), but dollar day, old home week.

33. *Lectures:* "One World Now," "A Look at a Book."

34. *Magazines:* Time, Quill, Editor & Publisher.

35. *Magazine articles:* "Women Editors—Why?"

36. *Nationalities:* Scottish, Chinese, Mexican.

37. *Newspapers:* the Stanford Daily, the Denver Post.

38. *Nicknames:* Persons—Ramon (Silent) Ramirez; pets—Slick Chick; clubs—Cardinals; teams—Bill Orange; states—Evergreen state; East side, Salt city, Hoosier, GI, Old Hickory, Manassa Mauler.

39. *Organizations:* Distinguishing words only unless others precede them—Boy Scouts, American Legion, Community Chest, Camp Fire Girls, Epworth league, Sunday school, Child Welfare association, Liberals club.

40. *Paintings:* "Mona Lisa," "Spring in Big Bend."

41. *Personification:* Of colleges, cities, states, etc.—Old Sol, Mother Nature.

42. *Pets:* Pretty Face, the cat; Coco, the dog.

43. *Plants:* Horticultural varieties—apples—Delicious, Baldwins; pears—Bartletts; roses—American beauties; Reid Yellow Dent corn; Valencia oranges.

44. *Plays:* "The Iceman Cometh," "Front Page," "The Taming of the Shrew" (But in book publishing usage, *The Taming of the Shrew.*)

45. *Political organizations:* Republicans, Democrats, Democratic party, Socialists, Communists—when actual party affiliation is indicated.

46. *Press Associations:* Associated Press, United Press, International News Service.

47. *Proper names:* Of persons, places, things, as indicated herein.

48. *Publications:* Newspapers—the Denver Post; magazines—*The Ladies' Home Journal;* books—"*Effective News Reporting.*"

49. *Pullman:* Wenatchee.

50. *Races:* Negroes, but the black race; use only when essential to news and never disparagingly.

51. *Radio stations:* WAGE; or station KNBC.

52. *Regions:* central New York, northern California, southern France, Holy Land, Back bay, Nob hill, the South; see also geographic regions.

53. *Schools:* School of Speech; Quincy high school.

54. *Sermons:* "Gild on Guilty Men."

55. *Ships:* USS Texas, Old Ironsides, the Queen Mary.
56. *Statuary:* Rodin's "Thinker."
57. *Streets:* S. Scher st.; First st.; 10th ave.; Taliaferro blvd.; Hutchins lane; but the Street personifying the financial district; Unter den Linden; Rue de la Paix, No. 10 Downing Street.
58. *Titles:* When they precede names—Principal Pedro Osuna, but Arthur Butzbach, principal; Wac Jane Chose, Wave Ruth Beck.
59. *Trade names:* Names of brands—Birdseye frozen foods, Old Golds, Milky Way; avoid use in news stories.
60. *Union:* To refer to the United States; also Republic to refer to the United States, but national government, federal government.
61. *Unions:* American Federation of Labor; Congress of Industrial Organizations.
62. *United Nations:* UN.
63. *Wards:* First ward, 10th ward.
64. *Wars:* Franco-Prussian war, World War I, World War II.

C. *Do not capitalize:*

1. *Adjectives* derived from proper nouns: arabic numerals, bessemer steel, bordeaux mixture, french fried potatoes, french pastry, graham flour, india rubber, plaster of paris, paris green, manila rope, morocco leather, panama hat, prussic acid, roman type, scotch whiskey; but German language, Roman history.
2. *Armed forces:* army, air forces, coast guard, navy, signal corps, state police, Canadian mounted, U.S. army, U.S. navy.
3. *Campus terms:* alma mater, alumnus, fraternity, faculty, graduate.
4. *Classes:* freshman, sophomore, junior, senior.
5. *Compound terms:* all-American, anti-Christian, mid-Victorian, trans-Siberian, ex-Governor Baldwin, Senator-elect Ives.
6. *Degrees:* When spelled out—bachelor of arts.
7. *Departments:* of university—department of editorial practice; of government—department of state.
8. *Educational institutions:* When used indefinitely.
9. *Government bodies:* city council, board of supervisors, assembly, congress, senate, house of representatives, supreme court, cabinet, weather bureau, British parliament, student body.
10. *Historic periods:* Christian era, dark ages, colonial period, golden age, 20th century, industrial revolution, renaissance, reformation, paleozoic age, pliocene age.

11. *Medical terms:* arterio-sclerosis, bright's disease.
12. *Points of the compass:* east, west, but S. Wanzer st.
13. *Prefixes:* de, d', la, von.
14. *Religious terms:* heaven, hell, scripture, gospels, biblical, angelic, devil.
15. *Scientific terms:* classes, order, families, genera of plants, animals, insects.
16. *Seasons:* spring, winter.
17. *Titles:* When they are preceded by person's name.

FIGURES

A. *General Rules:*

1. Use figures for numbers—ordinal or cardinal—of 10 or more unless otherwise indicated.
2. Omit ciphers except to line up tabular matter. In time 6 a.m., not 6:00 a.m.; in money—$4, not $4.00; in per cent— 5 per cent, not 5.0 or 0.5; and in all instances in which ciphers add nothing to clarity.
3. Maintain consistency in use of figures thus: 5 out of 12, not five out of 12; 19,000 to 20,000, not 19 to 20,000.

B. *Use figures for:*

1. *Addresses:* 822 Maryland ave., 203 Yates Castle; 1776 Independence building, Apt. 13.
2. *Ages:* John Smith, 81 (not aged 81), the 9-year-old boy has been an orphan since he was 6 years old; it is his third year in Boulder.
3. *Aircraft:* B-29.
4. *Anniversary:* Ninth anniversary; 50th anniversary.
5. *Armament of vessel:* 16-inch guns; 3-inch pieces; 10-inch mortars.
6. *Automobile licenses:* Without commas—1 222 333.
7. *Auxiliary adjectives:* 10-pound; 8-inch; 9-foot; 7-year-old; 45-caliber.
8. *Betting odds:* 2 to 1; a 3-1 favorite.
9. *Bible references:* I. Sam. xii: 16-22; Rev. vii: 12.
10. *Cardinal numbers:* Beginning with 10 and up unless otherwise indicated.
11. *Caliber:* .45-caliber (not calibre).
12. *Conventions:* Ninth Annual, 10th Annual.
13. *Dates:* Oct. 14, March 9, not March 9th.
14. *Days of the month:* Cardinal—not ordinal—numbers are used— Jan. 31, not Jan. 31st; March 11, not March 11th.

15. *Dimensions:* 5 feet 10 inches, not 5 ft. 10 in. or 5'10"; 25 by 32 by 13, not 25 x 32 x 13.
16. *Election results:* ayes, 13, noes, 3; by vote of 42 to 8; Smith, 43; Smythe, 42.
17. *Fire companies:* hook and ladder company 6.
18. *Fractions:* Spell out when denominators are nine or less— one-third, but 4/11, except in markets.
19. *Highways:* highway 42.
20. *Historical periods:* Use ordinal numbers—fifth century, 10th century.
21. *House numbers:* 30 Tait ave.
22. *Hours of the day:* 7:30 p.m. today or 7:30 this evening; 10 p.m. Thursday, not 10 p.m. last evening or 10 p.m. last night; 9 a.m.—not 9:00 a.m.; avoid use of o'clock.
23. *Latitude, longitude:* 37 47 28 N.; 122 1 44 W.
24. *Military units:* 5th regiment, 7th army.
25. *Money:* 40 cents, not $.40 or 40 cts; $5, not $5.00, $16 million, not $16,000,000; English money: £2 9s 2d; 9 shillings 4 pence; six-pence—not 6 pence or 6-pence; for exceptions, see markets.
26. *Oil leases:* Sec. 18, 16-24.
27. *Per cent:* 9 per cent, not 9% or 9 percent or 9.0 or 0.9; for exceptions, see markets.
28. *Political subdivisions:* 10th ward, but fifth Congressional district.
29. *Prices:* See money.
30. *Recipes:* 2 cups of sugar.
31. *Roman numerals:* To designate a king, pope, Bible reference, but not chapters, sections, volumes, figures or tables.
32. *Serial numbers:* dog license 434, motorman 1492, not motorman no. 1492.
33. *Scores:* Oregon 28, Ohio 7; Northwestern 27-21.
34. *Stops:* stop 8.
35. *Street numbers:* 555 W. Main st.; 83½ W. Catalina ave.
36. *Telephone numbers:* 3-9360; University 4554.
37. *Temperature:* 5 degrees above zero.
38. *Time:* See hours of the day.
39. *Wave lengths:* 780 k.c. for kilocycles; 12.45 m.c. for megacycles.

C. *Do not use figures for:*
    1. *Cardinal numbers:* Up to 10 unless otherwise indicated.
    2. *Expressions:* a committee of one-hundred; ninety-nine out of a hundred; half a billion; one man in a thousand.

3. *Numbers together:* twelve 10-inch boards.
4. *Ordinal numbers:* Up to 10th unless otherwise indicated.
5. *Sentence beginnings:* Supply initial word or spell out figures.

IDENTIFICATION

A. *General rules:*
1. Accurate identification of all names in the news is imperative.
2. Accurate identification of the source of news likewise is imperative, for example, in telephone calls.
3. Avoid any identification that is defamatory.

B. *Identify names in the news thus:*
1. *Academic title:* Dean M. Lyle Spencer of the School of Journalism; Prof. Kenneth Bartlett, dean of University college; Dr. Herman C. Beyle, professor of political science; always use correct academic rank.
2. *Achievement:* Dr. Frank Luther Mott, Pulitzer prize winner, spoke . . .
3. *Address:* Dr. Robert W. Turnbull, 420 Willkie st.; Roger Craig Benton of 1860 Lincoln st.; Melancthon Morgenthau, R. I., Hammonton; Joseph Mordaunt, RFD 3.
4. *Age:* Ezra B. Sedgewick, 91, pooh-poohs progress; 4-year-old Malcolm.
5. *Alumni status:* Wilma Avery, '46 graduate; Faye Farnham, LA '46.
6. *Description:* Bent with age, Mordecai Mallory grimaced.
7. *First names:* Christian name of person as he used it—usually first name and initials—except for president of United States, governor of the state, and persons so widely known that such identification is superfluous—President Truman, Governor Dewey, Premier Stalin.
8. *Fraternity membership:* Chetworth Chutney, Sigma Nu.
9. *Nationality:* Mrs. Robert Ruthven, Australian war bride; but never use derogatory terms.
10. *News past:* Laertes Lagomarsino, who swam the English channel in 1933.
11. *Nicknames:* in general news stories only when needed for accurate identification—Nigel (Spike) Nell; in sports stories—Buzzbomb Billings.
12. *Occasion:* Hanley Corning, who will speak at OPA reunion.
13. *Occupation:* Bianchini Capitelli, high school teacher.
14. *Race:* Only when essential and then never in a derogatory sense.

15. *Reputation:* Mrs. Mason Perry, who for 17 years has advocated smoke control; but beware of references which impair reputation.
16. *Relationship:* Miss Charla Clark, daughter of Mr. and Mrs. George J. Clark.
17. *Sex:* A woman known as Theda Thackeray.
18. *Sorority:* Susan Brown, Chi Omega Phi.
19. *Student position:* Arthur Smith, editor.
20. *Student status:* Joyce Wood, LA '47.
21. *Titles:* See also academic, ecclesiastical, military, naval, official titles.

C. *Do not identify names in the news:*
1. *Criminal record:* Refer to a person as a criminal only after he has been so designated by a court decision and then only when his record is of immediate significance in the news.
2. *Diseases:* Avoid statements that a person is suffering from a loathsome or pestilential disease, e.g. . . . leprosy, syphilis, hydrophobia, or insanity.
3. *Moral turpitude:* Avoid imputations of immoral or infamous conduct.
4. *Occupation:* Avoid disparagement of a person in his job, trade, office, business, or profession.
5. *Public ostracism:* Avoid statements exposing persons to public scorn, pity, contempt, hatred, ridicule, scorn, or obloquy.
6. *Radical discrimination:* Avoid needless references to race, particularly those which are derogatory.

PUNCTUATION
Apostrophes

A. *General rule:*
1. Use apostrophe where a letter or letters are omitted.

B. *Use apostrophe in:*
1. *Common possessives:* Bird and Merwin's "Newspaper and Society."
2. *Contractions:* Don't, '95, 'tis, won't.
3. *Figures:* early '70s.
4. *Plurals of numbers and letters:* five 2's, three R's.
5. *Possessives:* Except with pronouns, Burn's poems, the Joneses' dog.

C. *Do not use apostrophes in:*
1. *Contractions:* phone, varsity.
2. *Firm names:* Unless used by firm.
3. *Possessive pronouns:* yours, his.

Colon

A. *General rule:*
1. Use colon sparingly.

B. *Use colons for:*
1. *Bible references:* Gen. 1:10.
2. *Explanations* (or enumerations when used as appositives): His favorite heroes were South Americans: Miranda, Bolivar, and San Martin.
3. *Quotations:* When long or formally announced—The governor spoke as follows: "If we want one world now, we must disarm now . . ."
4. *Resolutions:* "Resolved: That we condemn isolationism as . . ."
5. *Subtitles:* American Journalism: A History of Newspapers in the United States Through 250 years 1690 to 1940.
6. *Time:* The Denver Zephyr left at 4:14 p.m.; the car made the first lap in 0:6:13⅗.

C. *Do not use colons for:*
1. *Time:* In flat hours— 10 a.m., not 10:00 a.m.

Comma

A. *General rule:*
1. Use commas only when essential to clarity.

B. *Use commas with:*
1. *Adjectives:* Time style is curt, concise, complete.
2. *Addresses:* 706 Sanchez st., San Francisco.
3. *Adverbs:* He wrote briefly, yet brilliantly.
4. *Appositives:* Leland D. Case, editor of The Rotarian, said . . .
5. *Complex sentences:* To separate dependent and independent clauses, when the former precedes the latter.
6. *Co-ordinate clauses:* To separate them when linked by an, or, but, for, nor.
7. *Direct quotations:* "If atomic bombs are here to stay, men are not," he asserted.
8. *Directive expressions:* To enclose them—"California, however,

cannot accept . . ."; "Freedom of the press, of course, is the first freedom . . ."; "Liars, we discover, use statistics too . . ."
9. *Election summaries:* "Brown, 30; Browne, 28."
10. *Main clauses:* See co-ordinate clauses.
11. *Misleading combinations:* "Inside, the editor heard the tele-type."
12. *Non-restrictive modifiers:* "Senator Ampersand, who favored a low tariff, denied . . ."
13. *Parallel clauses, phrases:* "If war comes, if bloodshed mounts, if chaos overwhelms, we must blame ourselves . . ."; "With a clear head, with firm hands, with a courageous heart, he faced the intruder."
14. *Parenthetical elements:* See addresses, appositives, directive expressions.
15. *Participal phrases:* "Trouncing his opponent, he won his title . . ."
16. *Series:* "Positions of the wrist in fencing are termed prime, seconde, tierce, carte, and quinte."

C. *Do not use commas with:*
1. *Addresses:* Before of—"Kenneth Knight of Sebastapol."
2. *Junior:* "Truman Hannegan Jr."

Dash
A. *General rule:*
1. Use dash sparingly, for often its use indicates loose construction of sentences or ignorance of punctuation rules.

B. *Use dash with:*
1. *Datelines:* See wire copy preparation.
2. *Emphatic pause:* "I went to cover an obit and I brought back—a front-page scoop!"
3. *Parenthetical words:* "The comics—uncomic as usual—dealt with violent death, torrid romance, and business intrigue."
4. *Testimony:* "Q.—Did you see Chase slug Mill? A.—No."
5. *Unfinished sentences:* "As he expired, he gasped, "All I want is—"

C. *Do not use dashes:*
1. *Commas:* When a comma will do just as well, avoid the dash.

Hyphens
A. *General rule:*
1. Use hyphens as little as possible; that is, only when specifically indicated.

B. *Use hyphens with:*
1. *Adjectives:* widely-known, 9-year-old.
2. *Compound dates:* 1946-50.
3. *Compound words:* With these prefixes or suffixes—brother-, by-, cross-, -elect, extra-, father-in-, great-, half-, mother-, open-, public-, quarter-, -rate, self-, sister-.
4. *Compound words:* with prefixes to proper names—un-American, pro-German, anti-Russian.
5. *Figures:* one-fifth, twenty-seven, eighty-eighth.
6. *Measurements:* If used as adjectives—6-foot ladder.

C. *Do not use hyphens with:*
1. *Compound words:* commonly written as one word, or as two words without the hyphen.
2. *Titles:* vice president, editor in chief, attorney general, but captain-elect.

Interrogation Point

A. *General rule:*
1. Use interrogation point only when questions are asked.

B. *Use interrogation point with:*
1. *Questions:* Actual or rhetorical.

C. *Do not use interrogation points with:*
1. *Exclamation point:* to express amazement or doubt—!?!

Parentheses

A. *General rule:*
1. Use parentheses and brackets seldom.

B. *Use parentheses with:*
1. *Newspapers:* To indicate location—Marysville (Calif.) Appeal-Democrat.

C. *Do not use parentheses with:*
1. *Commas:* Use commas instead if meaning is just as clear.

Periods

A. *General rule:*
1. Observe standard practice unless otherwise indicated herein.

B. *Use periods with:*
1. *Abbreviations:* See abbreviations.

2. *Decimals:* 231.14.
3. *Declarative sentences:* To end sentence.
4. *Imperative sentences:* To end sentence.
5. *Money:* $5.10.
6. *Omission of quoted matter:* Use three periods—"Chaos or communism . . . will submerge the individual."

C. *Do not use periods with:*
   1. *Abbreviations:* See abbreviations.
   2. *Nicknames:* Butch. Billings.
   3. *Per cent:* 45 per cent, not .45 per cent.

Quotation Marks

A. *General rule:*
   1. Use punctuation marks within double quotation marks, but outside single quotation marks.
   2. Use quotation marks at the beginning of each paragraph of an extended statement, but at the end of only the last paragraph.
   3. Use quotation marks at the end of every quotation.

B. *Use quotation marks with:*
   1. *Articles:* In magazines—"One World Now."
   2. *Books:* Except the Bible, Koran, Talmud—"News Gathering and News Writing."
      (In book publishing usage, book titles are put in italics without quotes.)
   3. *Coined words:* If not generally recognized—He was a member of the "Renobility."
   4. *Direct quotations:* "Where the press is in fetters, so are the souls of men."
   5. *Irony:* His "limousine," I found, was really a jeep.
   6. *Lectures:* "Radio Advertising—Bane or Boon?"
   7. *Motion picture films:* "The Road to Bikini."
   8. *Paintings:* "Mona Lisa."
   9. *Poetry:* If quoted—the first line of each stanza.
   10. *Radio Programs:* "Inflammation, Please."
   11. *Speeches* (and sermons): "Golden Rule or Rule of Gold?"
   12. *Statuary:* "The Thinker."

C. *Do not use quotation marks with:*
   1. *Characters:* In books, plays, movies, radio programs.
   2. *Copy:* When set in narrower measure or smaller type.

3. *Magazines:* Coronet, Successful Farming.
4. *Names:* Of pets, pullmans, ships, etc.
5. *Newspapers:* The Denver Post.
6. *Nicknames:* Manassa Mauler.
7. *Slang:* bobby-soxer.
8. *Teams:* B team.
9. *Testimony:* Q—Who was the newspaperman I saw you with?
   A.—That was no reporter; it was Kilroy.

Semicolon

A. *General rule:*
   1. Use semicolons sparingly.

B. *Semicolons with:*
   1. *Addresses:* In series—Francis Holland, San Francisco; Jane
      Yingling, Albuquerque; William Ehling, Cheyenne.
   2. *Clarity:* In sentences in which it is needed for clarity.
   3. *Co-ordinate clauses:* If not connected with and, but, for, nor,
      or, neither.

APPENDIX IV

Press and Radio Glossary*

(Note: Like the material in Appendix III, this vocabulary of journalism was compiled by Dean Laurence R. Campbell of the Florida
State University School of Journalism. With the publisher of the book
in which it originally appeared, Dean Campbell has granted special
permission for its reprinting here. This list includes newspaper, magazine, and radio journalism terms but does not enter the areas of
business operations in journalism.)

ABC: American Broadcasting Company.
Across the Board: A radio news program presented the same time
   each day for five days a week.
Ad lib: Composing as one speaks; that is, without a prepared script.
Add: New copy to be added to a story already written for a printed
   news medium.
Alive: Type or copy still available for use.
ANG: American Newspaper Guild.
A.N.P.A.: American Newspaper Publishers Association.

---

* Reproduced from *Newsmen at Work,* by Laurence R. Campbell and
Roland E. Wolseley (Boston: Houghton Mifflin Company, 1949) pp.
525-28.

A.M.: Morning newspaper.

Angle: A particular viewpoint, aspect, or emphasis played up by the newsman.

A.S.N.E.: American Society of Newspaper Editors.

A.P.: Associated Press.

Assignment: A newsman's task.

Assignment Book: The editor's record of newsmen's tasks.

Back-timing: Timing a newscast's last two or three stories so the newscaster will get off the air on time.

Beat: The regular stops made by a newsman, an exclusive story.

Blotter: Police department record of arrests.

Boil: Reduce the copy.

Bulletin: Late news printed before the lead of the story to which it is related; also the first brief announcement on the air of an important news event.

Bulletin or *Dateline Program:* Written in bulletin style, this is a news program each story of which opens with the name of the town or city from which the news is reported.

Bulletin Interruption: The act of breaking into a regular program to present an important news bulletin.

Bureau: Headquarters or newspaper or press association for centralizing and co-ordinating news coverage.

By-line: Line containing name of newsman who wrote the news story —usually between the headline and the lead.

Call Letters: Letters identifying radio station as assigned by FCC.

Canned Copy: Syndicate and publicity copy.

Catch Line: Word or words used on copy to index it.

CBS: Columbia Broadcasting System.

C.G.O.: "Can go over"; copy to be held or used at another time.

Check: Verify.

City Desk: City editor's desk sometimes shared with assistants.

City Room: Newsroom in which city and local—and often all—news is handled.

Clean Copy: News copy requiring little revision.

Clip: Cutting from any publication.

Clip Sheet: Syndicate or publicity matter in sheet form, to make clipping easy.

Close: Announcement with which program closes.

Column: Row of type extending the length of the page vertically.

Commentary: Program of news with comment.

Continuity Writer: Radio writer who writes copy other than news.

Copy: Written material.

Copy Desk: Where copy is read, revised, headlined.
Copyreader: Staff member who reads, corrects, revises, and head-lines news copy.
Correspondent: Out-of-town newsman.
Cover: To be responsible for getting and writing a specified news story.
Crusade: Journalistic campaign—usually for reform—often involving co-ordination of specialized reporting and editorial writing.
Cub: A beginning newsman.
Cue: A signal—either in words or by sign.

Datebook: Records of dates and notes for future assignments.
Dateline: Line indicating date of news medium's publication; also information at beginning of story indicating where and when it originated.
Day Side: Daytime staff of newspaper.
Dead: Copy or type that no longer has any use.
Deadline: Specified time when news copy is due.
Desk: The copy desk or city desk.
Desk Editor: Editor responsible for giving newsmen's assignments.
Dirty Copy: News copy containing many errors and faults.
District: An area covered by a newsman, usually larger than a beat.
Dope: Information about the news, often the news behind the news.
Dope Story: An interpretative news story.
Dupes: Carbon copies of news stories or manuscripts.

Edition: Copies printed during one press run.
Editorialize: To inject opinion as news in a news story.
End Mark: Symbol indicating end of copy.

Facsimile: Photoelectric reproduction of news medium and its distri-bution by means of radio.
Fake: Fabrication of news copy.
Feature (verb): To stress, emphasize, or play up certain details.
Feature (noun): The news feature, including the human-interest story, is written as a feature rather than a straight news story; that is, with less formal treatment.
File: To send a story by wire or cable.
Filler: Copy, usually not very timely, set in type in advance.
Flash: A short message reporting some important news.
Follow: A story with new details; that is, often related to one in a previous edition.
Follow-up: Same as follow.
Folo: Same as follow or follow-up.

Fotog: Cameraman or press photographer.

Future: Record of coming event.

Futures Book: Book in which coming events are noted for possible coverage.

F.Y.I.: For your information.

Galley Proof: A proof of the galley of type.

Ghost Writer: One who writes under another's name and is employed to do so.

Glossy: Photographic print with shiny finish, preferable for reproduction in halftones.

Grapevine: Source of rumor.

Guideline (newspaper): Part of headline written on news copy to relate the two when type is set.

Guideline (radio): One-word identification of news story.

Handout: Publicity material.

Head of the Desk: Staff member in charge of news or copy desk.

H.F.R.: Hold for release.

Hold: Do not release until so ordered.

Human Interest: News with emotional appeal.

I.N.S.: International News Service.

Interview (noun): A news story obtained by talking with the person featured.

Interview (verb): Talking with a person to get news.

Intro: Wire service term for opening portion of story.

Jumping Cue: Act of starting a program before it is scheduled to start.

Kill: To remove material from copy or to destroy type.

Late Watch: Small staff to handle late copy or produce late editions.

Lead: Opening paragraph or two of news story, not necessarily just one sentence.

Lead All: Summary lead correlating related stories or parts of a single story.

Leg Man: Newsman who gathers news to relay it to the rewrite man.

Libel: Defamation in written copy whether to be read or heard.

Library: Sometimes called the morgue, this is the reference department in a news medium's headquarters.

Local: Copy originating in the news medium's territory.

Localize: To emphasize the community's interest.

Local Room: Room or section of newsroom in which local copy is handled.

Log: The assignment book.

Magazine: Bound publication issued regularly and containing general editorial matter.

Markets: Section of newspaper devoted to market news.

MBS: Mutual Broadcasting System.

Media: Publications, usually those with advertising.

Mill: Typewriter.

Monitoring: Listening to a radio program.

More: Written at the bottom of a page of news to indicate more copy to come.

Morgue: Reference library.

Must: Executive order indicating that copy must be printed.

NBC: National Broadcasting Company.

N.E.A.: National Editorial Association.

News Analyst or Commentator: One who reports, analyzes, and comments on news—editorial writer or columnist of the air.

Newscast: Radio program of straight news.

Newscaster: One who presents newscast—and sometimes writes it.

News Editor: Radio newsman who rewrites, edits, and supervises news programs.

Newshawk: Synonym for newsman.

Newshen: Woman newsman or news-woman.

Newsman: Man or woman who gets and writes news for press and radio.

Newsroom: Room or section of radio station or publication office in which news is handled.

News Sleuths: Synonym for newsman.

Night Side: Staff that works at night.

Nose for News: Ability to get news.

N.P.R.: Night press rates.

Obit: Obituary.

Optional Copy: Extra news stories available if the newscaster or announcer needs more.

Pad: To lengthen story.

Personal: Short news item about persons.

Pick-up: Copy-desk instructions that standing matter may be used.

Pics: Pictures.

P.M.: Afternoon newspaper.

Policy: News medium's attitude on any subject.

Pony Service: Summary of press association news obtained over telephone.

Precede: Additional news often set ahead of the lead.

Press Agent: Person who obtains publicity and deals with news media.

Printer: Teletype machine.

Q. and A.: Questions and answers, as used at trials, etc.

Query: Summary of news wired to paper by newsman or free-lancer.

Release: Usually news copy sent in advance to be held for publication at designated time.

Reading Cold: Reading a program or news story without benefit of rehearsal.

Reporter: Synonym for newsman.

Rewrite: To rewrite a news story.

Rewrite man: Newsman who rewrites copy and takes stories over the telephone.

Rim: Outer edge of copy desk.

Run: Newsman's beat.

Running Story: Continuing story lasting a number of days.

Sacred Cow: Favored material or subjects.

Scoop: A news story exclusive with one news medium.

Sectional Story: Long story coming in sections.

Shorts: Short news stories, usually unimportant.

Slanting: Stressing certain aspects of news to indicate newspaper policy.

Slot: Inlet of copy desk where dealer or chief copyreader sits.

Slug: Word or words identifying news story.

Sob Stuff: Stories with sentimental or emotional appeal.

Special Event: Broadcasting news event on the scene.

Spot News: Immediate news.

Squib: Very short news item.

Straight News: Plain news account.

Stylo: Rules observed in preparing news copy.

Summary Lead: Lead that presents highlights of news.

Suspended Interest: Story in which climax comes at end.

Syndicate: Firm that sells varied kinds of copy to printed media.

Thirty: Written to indicate the end of the news story.

Time Copy: Copy available for use any time.

U.P.: United Press.

APPENDIX V

A Booklist for the Church Journalist

Books printed on journalism, radio, printing, television, publicity, and other aspects of communications number several thousands in the United States alone. The list that follows, therefore, is a small selection of some that may prove to be of greatest usefulness to the churchman who wishes to make elementary use of the media. For a fuller list, with annotations, consult the author's *The Journalist's Bookshelf* (Chicago: Quill and Scroll Foundation, 1951) and the annual supplements to it.

ADVERTISING

Ashley, W. B. (ed.). *Church Advertising.* Philadelphia: Lippincott, 1917.

Brewster, Arthur Judson; Palmer, Herbert Hall; and Ingraham, Robert G. *Introduction to Advertising.* New York: McGraw-Hill, 1947.

Case, Francis H. *Advertising the Church.* New York: Abingdon, 1925.

——————————————. *Handbook of Church Advertising.* New York: Abingdon, 1921.

Hepner, Harry. *Effective Advertising.* New York: McGraw-Hill, 1948.

Stelzle, Charles. *Principles of Successful Church Advertising.* New York: Revell, 1908.

BIOGRAPHY

Grose, Howard B. *George Edwin Horr.* New York: privately printed, 1928.

Hughes, Dorothea Price. *The Life of Hugh Price Hughes* (3rd ed.). New York: Armstrong, 1904.

Mains, George Preston. *James Monroe Buckley.* Cincinnati: Methodist Book Concern, 1917.

Stevens, W. Bertrand. *Editor's Quest.* New York: Morehouse-Gorham, 1940.

Tucker, Irwin St. John. *Out of the Hell Box.* New York: Morehouse-Gorham, 1945.

EDITORIAL WRITING

Waldrop, A. Gayle. *Editor and Editorial Writer.* New York: Rinehart, 1948.

GENERAL BOOKS ON JOURNALISM AND RADIO

Barnhart, Thomas F. *Weekly Newspaper Writing and Editing*. New York: Dryden Press, 1949.

Mott, George Fox, and Associated Authors. *New Survey of Journalism* (3rd ed.). New York: Barnes & Noble, 1950.

Wolseley, Roland E., and Campbell, Laurence R. *Exploring Journalism* (2nd ed.). New York: Prentice-Hall, 1949.

HISTORY

Barrett, J. Pressley. (ed.). *The Centennial of Religious Journalism* (2nd ed.). Dayton, Ohio: Christian Publishing Association, 1908.

Baumgartner, Appollinaris W. *Catholic Journalism*. New York: Columbia University Press, 1931.

Brewer, Clifton H. *History of Religious Education in the Episcopal Church to 1835*. New Haven, Connecticut: Yale University Press, 1924.

Burroughs, P. E. *Fifty Fruitful Years*. Nashville, Tennessee: Broadman Press, 1941. (Southern Baptist.)

Foik, Paul J. *Pioneer Catholic Journalism*. New York: United States Catholic Historical Society, 1930.

Gottheil, Richard, and Popper, William. "Periodicals." *The Jewish Encyclopedia*, IX. New York: Funk & Wagnalls, 1905.

Morehouse, Clifford P. *Origins of the Episcopal Church Press from Colonial Days to 1840*. New Brunswick, New Jersey: Paterson, 1942. See also *Historical Quarterly* (September, 1942).

Mott, Frant Luther. *A History of American Magazines*. Cambridge: Harvard, 1938.

_____. "Periodicals and Press." *The Universal Jewish Encyclopedia*, VIII. New York: The Universal Jewish Encyclopedia, Inc., 1939.

MAGAZINE WRITING

Bird, George L. *Article Writing and Marketing*. New York: Rinehart, 1948.

Brennecke, Ernest Jr., and Clark, Donald L. *Magazine Article Writing* (Revised ed.). New York: Macmillan, 1942.

NEWS REPORTING

Campbell, Laurence R., and Wolseley, Roland E. *Newsmen at Work*. Boston: Houghton-Mifflin, 1949.

MacDougall, Curtis D. *Interpretative Reporting* (3rd ed.). New York: Macmillan, 1948.

Warren, Carl. *Modern News Reporting* (2nd ed.). New York: Harper & Brothers, 1934.

NEWSPAPER EDITING

Bastian, George C., and Case, Leland D. *Editing the Day's News* (3rd ed.). New York: Macmillan, 1943.

PICTURE JOURNALISM

Vitray, Laura; Mills, John Jr.; Ellard, Roscoe B. *Pictorial Journalism.* New York: McGraw-Hill, 1939.

PROPAGANDA

Bernays, Edward L. *Crystallizing Public Opinion.* New York: Boni & Liveright, 1923.

Doob, Leonard W. *Propaganda.* New York: Holt, 1935.

PUBLIC RELATIONS

Baker, Helen Cody, and Routzahn, Mary Swain. *How to Interpret Social Welfare.* New York: Russell Sage Foundation, 1947.

Griswold, Glenn, and Griswold, Denny. (ed.). *Your Public Relations.* New York: Funk & Wagnalls, 1948.

Harlow, Rex F., and Black, Marvin M. *Practical Public Relations.* New York: Harper & Brothers, 1947.

Harral, Stewart. *Public Relations for Churches.* New York: Abingdon-Cokesbury, 1945.

Squire, Irving, and Wilson, Kirtland A. *Informing Your Public.* New York: Association Press, 1924.

Stuber, Stanley. *Public Relations Manual for Churches.* New York: Doubleday, 1951.

PUBLICITY

Brodie, W. Austin. *Keeping Your Church in the News.* New York: Revell, 1942.

——————————————. *Keeping Your Church Informed.* New York: Revell, 1944.

Fortson, John L. *How to Make Friends for Your Church.* New York: Association Press, 1943.

Gilbert, Ralph V. *The Church and Printer's Ink.* New York: Revell, 1925.

Harral, Stewart. *Patterns of Publicity Copy.* Norman, Oklahoma: University of Oklahoma Press, 1950.

Henry, Carl F. H. *Successful Church Publicity.* Grand Rapids: Zondervan, 1943.

Leach, William H. *Church Publicity.* Nashville: Cokesbury, 1929.
Pleuthner, Willard A. *Building Up Your Congregation.* Chicago: Wilcox & Follett, 1950.
Underwood, Kenneth. *Our Story and How to Tell It.* New York: Home Missions Council of North America, 1943.

RADIO AND TELEVISION IN GENERAL

Abbot, Waldo. *Handbook of Radio Broadcasting.* New York: McGraw-Hill, 1941.
Waller, Judith C. *Radio: The Fifth Estate.* Boston: Houghton-Mifflin, 1946.

RADIO AND TELEVISION TECHNIQUES

Allan, Doug. *How to Write for Television.* New York: Dutton, 1946.
Brooks, William F. *Radio News Writing.* New York: McGraw-Hill, 1948.
Campbell, Laurence R.; Heath, Harry E., Jr.; and Johnson, Ray V. *A Guide to Radio-TV Writing.* Ames, Iowa: Iowa State College Press, 1950.
Carlile, John S. *The Production and Direction of Radio Programs.* New York: Prentice-Hall, 1939.
Charnley, Mitchell V. *News by Radio.* New York: Macmillan, 1948.
Crews, Albert R. *Professional Radio Writing.* Boston: Houghton-Mifflin, 1946.
Mosse, Baskett. *Radio News Handbook.* Evanston, Illinois: Medill School of Journalism, Northwestern University, 1947.
Warren, Carl. *Radio News Writing and Editing.* New York: Harper & Brothers, 1947.

RELIGIOUS RADIO

Loveless, Wendell P. *Manual of Gospel Broadcasting.* Chicago: Moody Press, 1946.
Parker, Everett C.; Inman, Elinor; and Snyder, Ross. *Religious Radio.* New York: Harper & Brothers, 1948.
Walker, E. Jerry. *Religious Broadcasting.* Washington: National Association of Broadcasters, 1945. (Pamphlet.)

REFERENCE BOOKS

Directory of Newspapers and Periodicals. Philadelphia: N. W. Ayer & Sons, issued annually.
Kane, James F. (ed.). *Catholic Press Directory.* New York: Catholic Press Association, 1950.
Religious Press Directory. New York: Wagner, 1943.

STYLE

A *Manual of Style* (11th ed.). Chicago: University of Chicago Press, 1950.

Skillin, Marjorie E., and Gay, Robert M. *Words into Type*. New York: Appleton-Century-Crofts, 1948.

Zook, Ellrose D. *Manual of Style*. Scottdale, Pennsylvania: Herald Press, 1948.

TYPOGRAPHY AND PRINTING

Barnhart, Thomas F. *Weekly Newspaper Makeup and Typography*. Minneapolis: University of Minnesota Press, 1949.

Melcher, Daniel, and Larrick, Nancy. *Printing and Promotion Handbook*. New York: McGraw-Hill, 1949.

Sutton, Albert A. *Design and Makeup of the Newspaper*. New York: Prentice-Hall, 1948.

MISCELLANEOUS

Abrams, Ray H. *Organized Religion in the United States*. Philadelphia: American Academy of Political and Social Science, 1948.

Flesch, Rudolf. *The Art of Plain Talk*. New York: Harper & Brothers, 1946. See also the same author's *The Art of Readable Writing*. New York: Harper & Brothers, 1949.

Harral, Stewart. *Successful Letters for Churches*. New York: Abingdon-Cokesbury, 1946.

Lynch, Frederick. *The One Great Society*. New York: Revell, 1918.

Norton, William B. *Church and Newspaper*. New York: Macmillan, 1930.

Ure, Ruth. *The Highway of Print*. New York: Friendship Press, 1946.

Vittoria, Theodore J., (ed.). *The Catholic Voice*. New York: Society of St. Paul, 1949.

Index

Type used in this book
Body, 11 on 13 and 9 on 10 Caledonia, 8 on 8 Textype
Display, Radiant and Vogue